No Love Here
A Priest's Journey

By Martin Gordon

*I dedicate this book to my wife Louise and our children,
Katherine, Victoria and Martin, who have supported me
in the good times and the bad.*

When I first began to put down on paper the events of my life, there was no thought in my mind of it being published. I saw it as being a therapeutic process whereby, I would empty myself of much frustration and anger that had built up over the years. But as the writing proceeded, and a few tears were shed, it occurred to me that some people just might like to read my story.

"The life of man is the true romance, which when it is valiantly conducted, will yield the imagination a higher joy than any fiction".
Ralph Waldo Emerson.

The problem I faced was one common to all writers of autobiography: what to put in and what to leave out. On the advice of a distinguished professor of English at Queen's University, Belfast, I have omitted certain material that she considered would bore the average reader because of its repetitiveness; even though these incidents on my journey were of immense importance to me.

I think, for example of the German printer who claimed that he had not been paid by the distributors on my behalf, yet sent me a bottle of expensive champagne for Christmas.

John Steinbeck, in his novel, Cannery Row, summed up my life's experience.

"The things we admire in men, kindness, generosity, openness, honesty, understanding and feeling are the concomitant of failure in our system. And those traits that we detest, sharpness, greed, acquisitiveness, meanness, egotism and self-interest are the traits of success. And while men admire the quality of the first they love the produce of the second".

But my manuscript would have remained just that had I not joined the Freemasons and eventually met graphic designer Graham Clarke. It has been he who has taken the project in hand and brought it to the day when the pages I had worked on for so many years, off and on, have become a published book.

Martin Gordon, Cork, Ireland. 21st. June, 2011.

In the Beginning

If Tom Gordon had not fled the family farm in 1923, his political opponents in the recent civil war would have murdered him. Instead, helped by the local priest of Easkey, he sailed from the port of Sligo to Glasgow on the first available cattle boat. Tom Gordon was my father.

The Glasgow that welcomed Tom, when he stepped ashore at the Broomielaw, after the ship had unloaded its cargo at Merkland's Wharf, a few miles down river, covered an area of 60 square miles and had a population close to 1 million people and a history stretching back to the early 12th century.

My father would not have been aware of any of this as he sat on the tramcar taking him to Govan Cross, in which district his half-brother Mike lived with his wife. But he probably would have had some inkling of the deep resentment many Glasgow Protestants held against the Irish. They preferred their fellow Presbyterians from Ulster, not only for their religion but because many of them would have learned some sort of trade. The result was that the Irish Catholics were kept at the very bottom of the social and economic ladder. Their living conditions were in many instances, less than human; generating further prejudice against those unfortunate people.

Just 100 years earlier, Govan was a tranquil place, a small fishing village, whose inhabitants engaged in salmon fishing. In those earlier years the district was dotted with prosperous farms which gave their names to many of the area's streets: Langland's Road; Broomloan Road; and gentlemen's residences, which are retained by their names: Linthouse, Fairfield and Shieldhall.

It was to Helen Street, however, that my father made his way to surprise Mike Gordon with his unexpected arrival. A knock on his door at that early hour, as he and his wife were preparing to go to work, would have been an unusual occurrence for the couple. One can but imagine the surprise Mike experienced upon opening his front door to find Tom standing there. Once indoors, there would have been time only for the briefest of explanations for the younger man's sudden appearance, before Mike and his wife left for their work: a fuller account would have to wait until evening. In the meantime, my father would have ample time to recover from his arduous journey, and later in the day to explore the streets of Govan.

Tom's father had married again after the suicide of his first wife due to *"Post Partum Depression"*: a medical condition little known in those times. Mike was one of the children of that marriage, and the only one to settle in Scotland; the other two children went to America.

Having heard the story of my father's sudden flight on more than one occasion from my aunt Sarah Ellen, his sister, I can set down almost verbatim, what he would have told Mike Gordon and his wife, as they ate their evening meal.

The civil war in Ireland was almost ended in 1923, when my father, who had been a soldier in the Free State army, returned to the family farm in Easkey, County Sligo. Like in all civil wars both sides had committed terrible atrocities. Eventually, the anti-Democratic party led by Eamonn de Valera had been forced to surrender. But the end of hostilities did not dispel the bitterness and hatred that remained in the hearts and minds of the defeated for many years to come: and indeed up to the present day.

On an April evening of that year, 1923, the Gordon family had completed their chores for the day: the hens and other fowl were locked up for the night; the cattle fed and a bag of turf placed inside the back door. As they settled their chairs around the fireside, a loud knock sounded on the front door. Conscious of the dangerous times they lived in, Martin Gordon, the father, beckoned to Tom, to go into the bedroom behind the fireplace. Meanwhile Tom's sister, Sarah Ellen, picked up the heavy, iron tongs from the hearth. At a signal from her father she went to the front door and very slowly drew back the bolt and cautiously opened the door. In the light from the kitchen paraffin lamp she saw two men, one of whom asked: 'Is your brother inside?' 'Who are you and what you do you want with him?' 'It doesn't matter who we are,' the other man said. With that, Sarah Ellen brandished the tongs in their faces and told them to be about their business and if they didn't she would split their skulls open. Whereupon, the man who had spoken last reached into his overcoat pocket, only for his companion to lay a restraining hand on his arm. 'Tell your brother we will get him.' 'Be off with you,' Sarah Ellen shouted, before slamming shut the door and ramming home the bolt. The big question was, and still remains up to this day: who were the two men?

Within a week of his arrival in Glasgow, my father was working alongside Mike on a building site. On his first pay day, he would have held in his hands more money than he ever had possessed in his life. The money more than likely helped him to overcome feelings of homesickness that he must have been experiencing. He was to continue in this line of work for the next five years until he met and married Elizabeth Hackson in 1928. She was the youngest of five children, whose father worked in Fairfield's shipyard on the Govan Road. Three sons and another daughter made up the rest of the family. The Hacksons were a nominally Protestant family. How the Catholic man and Irish, and the Protestant woman met I have no idea. One explanation might be that Elizabeth Hackson went as one of a group to St. Anthony's League Hall in Hamilton Street, on the occasion of a dance or a concert and there met her future husband.

That there must have been intense opposition to the marriage, not to mention my mother's conversion can be taken for granted; especially from her brother Jimmy who would have been to the forefront of any resistance to the union: he was an Orangeman and a Freemason. The bride's father would have been quite relaxed about the proceedings, as he had served in the Army in France and as a result had met many Catholics and been impressed by the bravery of their chaplains; especially a Jesuit priest from Dublin, Father Willie Doyle, who was killed while attempting to rescue a wounded soldier from *"No-Man's-Land"*.

The newlyweds set up home at 5 Harmony Row, directly opposite St. Anthony's church and school. A Pawnbroker's was situated on the first 'landing.' Living there meant that my father had but a couple of minutes walk along the Govan Road to Fairfield's shipyard, where he now worked alongside his father-in-law. His departure in the morning regulated by the quarter-to-the-hour horn and finally the eight o'clock horn.

Shipbuilding was begun in Govan in 1839 by McArthur and Alexander, just to the east of Water Row; two other yards were founded in the same area. Harland and Wolff, the Belfast shipbuilder which was to be forever linked with the Titanic, took over all 3 yards in 1912. This amalgamation brought with it and influx of mainly Protestant workers from Belfast. Once settled in Govan they adopted the local Rangers football club as their own; attracted to it by its colours of red, white and blue. The presence of these men, with their hatred of Catholics and the Catholic Church, generated a bitterness that exists down to the present day, and is seen at its most violent whenever Rangers play Celtic, the team that most Catholics and those of Irish descent support.

When my father entered Fairfield's shipyard, he was joining a company steeped in shipbuilding history; one of the original owners, William Pearce had initiated the coveted *"Blue Ribbon"* for the fastest crossing between Britain and New York. Two of Fairfield's own ships were to win the award: the Unbrea and the Etrusia. But the most interesting vessel that the shipyard built was the steam yacht Livadia for the Czar of Russia. It was described as a *"Water Palace"* fitted out with a rose garden, illuminated fountains and wine racks for 10,000 bottles of wine: a ship never seen on the Clyde before or since. Livadia survived storms in the Bay of Biscay and arrived in Sebastopol, only to find that the Czar had been assassinated.

The Tenement 'hoose' in which my parents began their married life consisted of two rooms a scullery and an indoor toilet. Not every family was fortunate enough to possess their own toilet. In most cases three families shared the single facility that was situated on the landing, one flight down from their doors. It was reckoned that almost 75% of Glasgow families lived in such accommodation. The architecture of the Glasgow tenements, with their shared 'close'- an entrance passage leading to the upper floors and through to the back court - was a concrete expression of community.

Families who lived up 'oor close' made a little community founded on strict rules for cleaning the stairs and using the wash house, and by a sense of mutual responsibility for the children. It would have been almost impossible for a murder, as that of little James Bolger, to have taken place; some adult would have ensured the poor little lad's safety. A strong community feeling existed as a response to the harsh economic conditions under which families lived. It was into that world *"I"* came on 15 April, 1931.

A Citizen of No Mean City

"I was born in the shadow of a Fairfield's Crane,
And a blast of a freighter's horn,
Was the very first sound that reached my ears,
On the morning I was born".

The Shipyard Apprentice by Archie Fisher.

It was not an auspicious time to be born, as a serious economic depression was beginning on Clydeside. Eventually, large-scale unemployment was to cause thousands of workers to lose their jobs. Fortunately I was not aware of any of this when my parents carried me across to St. Anthony's to have me baptised Martin James: the names of my maternal and paternal grandfathers. The lovely Margaret Gordon, my father's niece, was my godmother. Just over a year later I acquired a sister, Betty.

When I reached the age of two years my parents became deeply concerned at my inability to walk properly. They made the decision to take me to Carfin Grotto situated near Glasgow, in the hope that I might be cured of my disability.

Carfin, a mining village in Lanarkshire, and a mile from the town of Motherwell, was populated mainly by Irish and Lithuanian miners and their families. The name Carfin in Gaelic means 'beautiful residence.'

In 1920 a small group of parishioners from the local church made a pilgrimage to the shrine of Lourdes in France, and upon their return decided to build a replica of the famous shrine in their own parish. Volunteers began work on the project in October 1920 and in 1922, 2000 people gathered for the shrine's official opening. But it was not until the following year that the Grotto came to the attention of the general public, when Father Taylor, the parish priest, placed a small statue of a recently Beatified young, French nun in the grounds of the shrine. Crowds began to flock to Carfin in ever-increasing numbers. To accommodate the growing influx of pilgrims, Father Taylor decided to purchase five acres of adjacent land. And when many miners were laid off work during a lengthy, industrial dispute, nearly 200 of them from Carfin and nearby districts began work on developing the newly acquired property and erecting shrines. By the time of my visit in 1933, pilgrimages from Ireland and many parts of Great Britain were visiting the Grotto.

Of more contemporary interest in the shrine is the Glass Chapel, which has been relocated there from the site of the Glasgow Garden Festival. It was to be known as Our Lady Star of the Sea. However, during its reconstruction, an aircraft fell out of the sky and onto the Scottish town of Lockerbie. It was decided therefore to change the name of the Chapel to that of the stricken aircraft, *"The Maid of the Seas"*.

Plaques bearing the names of the 256 victims of the disaster are mounted on pillars inside the church.

I have no memory of my visit to Carfin, but family tradition has it that soon afterwards I began to walk more normally, and went on to become a useful footballer in Ireland and London.

My parents must have been concerned when a third child was born to them in 1935. Unemployment was growing at an alarming rate, and it was only a matter of time before my father would have been forced to join the long queue of the unemployed at the 'Buroo' - the unemployment office in nearby McKechnie Street. A lifeline had been thrown to some in the shipyards when, in 1933, the government of the day decided that work would recommence on ship 534 - the future Queen Mary - in John Brown's yard. Their decision, in the memorable words of the member of Parliament, David Kirkwood, *"sentenced Clydebank to life"*. But upriver from Clydebank, the future looked bleak for the workers in the Govan shipyards.

Two events happened in our family in 1936: I acquired another sister and our father went on the 'Buroo.' The worst aspect of this situation was that eventually the family had to call 'On the parish,' as it was then called. This dreaded and humiliating step would arise when a man had not enough stamps on his unemployment card, because of long-term unemployment he had run out of benefit. In such circumstances the unfortunate man had no alternative but to call 'On the parish.'

For children this meant having to wear the dreaded 'parish clothes.' I can still recall all these years later, the feel of their rough texture against my skin and knowing that other children would be aware of our poverty. Actress Molly Weir in her book, *"Shoes Were For Sunday"*, provides us with an excellent description of the 'parish clothes.'

"Parish clothes were made from scratchy, wooden material with a built-in itch quality, which made them agony to wear. The genius who invented the dull, grey, porridge colour should have had a medal for successful depression of the human spirit. These clothes were instantly recognisable by their ugliness and harsh usability, and anyone unfortunate enough to have to wear them avoided the rest of us in the playground".

In their poverty one method a family had of purchasing essentials, especially clothes, was to use their *"Ménage"*, a classical word probably derived from the French. *"Ménage"* was a form of credit whereby the borrower paid a small weekly sum, usually a shilling to the *"Ménage men..."* When a person's *"Ménage"* book showed a prearranged sum, they then could go to the warehouse and choose goods to that value. It was an expensive way to shop because of the high built-in interest rate on the loan, but if one was poor there was no alternative. If a client defaulted on their regular payments, then the *"Ménage man"* would appear on one's doorstep to issue a warning. It usually worked.

By now I was practically living full-time in my grandfather's home at 22 Langland's Road, known locally as James's Place. Two of my uncles were still living there and, I am certain, spoiled me. The flat was on the top landing and was a great deal brighter than my own home in Harmony Row. Its one drawback, however, was the lack of an indoor toilet. Instead, the three families on the landing had to share the one toilet. There was a hole in one of the door's wooden panels that I always make certain to stuff with a wad of newspaper, before using the lavatory. With a large window there was always plenty of ventilation in the spacious room. In addition, the three families kept the place spotlessly clean, taking it in turns to wash and disinfect the room on a weekly basis.

Granddad's immediate neighbours were an elderly married couple, Mr. & Mrs. Wilson, who were from a rural part of Scotland, and as a consequence had a very broad Scottish accent that made them difficult to understand at times.

Their apartment was a 'single end' - so-called because it consisted of just one room that served as bedroom, living room and kitchen. The bed was recessed into the wall to afford more space for general living requirements. Single ends were usually occupied by newlyweds as a starting place after their marriage, and more often than not situated within a short walk of the bride's family home.

Before moving on, a description in more detail of what the interior of a tenement flat was like will be of interest. The kitchen in a single end was the only room, as already described. But in apartments like my grandfather's there were usually two rooms and a scullery; two beds were recessed into the walls of the kitchen, a table and chairs and a black range which was meticulously polished weekly until it shone. Another recessed bed was in the front room.

Fixed to the ceiling above the table was the 'Pulley,' a sort of clothes horse suspended by ropes and pulleys. Washing to be dried or freshly ironed clothes to be aired were dropped over the pulley's slats and then hauled up tight to the ceiling, where the warm air from the range circulated. It was quite a common occurrence for wet clothes to drip onto one's food while one was eating.

Although the range was used frequently for cooking, especially in winter, at which time of the year that fire blazed continuously, an apartment with a scullery usually had a gas cooker for use during the summer months. In the lobby stood the big coal bunker large enough to hold at least three bags of coal. More likely than not a large chest of drawers was also in the lobby; and if the family were fortunate enough to have an indoor toilet that also was in the lobby.

The second room had one recessed bed, as already mentioned; a wardrobe and sometimes a dressing table completed the furnishings; a large window looked out onto the street and made this particular room bright and cheerful, as well as providing a grandstand view of the teeming life in the street below. Great emphasis was placed on keeping the apartment spotlessly clean. The same also applied to the landings and the stairs. A strict rota system for cleaning them prevailed in each close. Scrubbing the landings and the stairs entailed the woman having a brush and a cloth - perhaps an old undershirt or an old towel - a bucket of soapy water and sometimes another one of clean water for rinsing. The woman required something to kneel on, as the stone stairs were very hard and very cold. Frequently a pipe clay design was made down the side of the stairs as a final flourish. The last task of maintaining one's close, was the polishing of the brass ornaments on each door, most of which had a name plate, a handle and a letterbox. Very often a large brass door-bell added to the decoration.

Mondays and Saturdays mornings were the busiest days of the week, when the wives went to the nearest pawnshop with their husband's best - and only - suit, in order to raise enough money to see them through to the next payday. Then on Saturday morning they returned to redeem their 'pledge' before their man came home at lunchtime. Whether my own mother was a client of the Pawnbroker I cannot say: but as the family increased in size it would not surprise me if she were.

One thing I missed from living in Harmony Row was the ability to stand at the bedroom window and look down into the classrooms of St. Anthony's school opposite. I watched the young children playing with plasticine and using coloured crayons to draw their pictures, and I longed for the day to arrive when I would join them.

It was a joyful occasion therefore, when on a sunny August morning of 1936, my mother led me by the hand through the gate of the school to join dozens of other children. Most of them stood quietly clutching their mother's hand. A few were already shedding some tears, not sharing my enthusiasm for the great adventure we were about to embark on. Then at the loud clanging of a bell, a couple of smiling teachers appeared from somewhere and began rounding up their charges: a signal for the more timid amongst us to cling desperately to their mothers. I walked nonchalantly towards the inner school yard. But just before I disappeared from my mother's view, I turned around and gave her a wave. Some of the women I noticed were rubbing at their eyes.

St. Anthony's school had three buildings in its grounds. The main one had a balcony off which where a row of classrooms. The remaining two buildings were situated in the school's main playground. One of these was where I and my fellow pupils were to begin our academic careers. The windows of our classroom faced on to the Govan Road. Through them we could hear tramcars rattling past on their way to and from Renfrew. The girl's toilets were situated in a small playground behind the main building. The Priest's house backed onto this area, and a door from its garden allowed them easy access to the church's sacristy, whose door opened on to the main playground.

The young priests played an important and highly visible role in the lives of their parishioners. One met them, naturally, in the church, on the streets and more intimately, when they paid regular visits to their parishioners homes.

My memory recalls that there were four young curates and a more elderly parish priest. The priests were between 25 and 40 years of age and were all Irish. They were mostly good looking with a ready smile and a cheerful word. It was not uncommon for them to join the older boys in a game of football in the school playground. On one occasion one of them kicked the football in the direction of a classroom window, shattering it into fragments. When one of us asked 'What will we tell the Janitor, Father?' The Culprit replied: 'Just tell him Father Burns broke it.'

My own favourite was Father Conlon, who had a gold-filled tooth to match his gold-rimmed spectacles. Whenever he came into our classroom we would demand of him that he perform one of his sleight-of-hand tricks. I don't recall him ever refusing. His colleagues I remember during my years in the parish were: John Battel, James Hogan, Bart Burns, Joe Sweeney and Tim Healy. The parish priest was the very Rev John Devine, who came to the parish in 1928 and died in 1944.

In October of that year 1936 another sister came into my life. She was given the name Annie, after her mother's sister Annie, who worked in the paint department of Stephen's shipyard.

By the start of 1938, I had become better acquainted with the boys who played in the 'back courts.' Soon I was accepted as a member of their *"chain gang"* as Granddad called us... We were only one of groups of boys who swarmed all over the back courts of the island formed by Langland's Road and Helen and Burleigh St.

The back court of each tenement was separated from its neighbours by a four foot wall into which iron railings were firmly embedded. In the middle of the back court stood the communal washhouse and 'midden:' a large, covered area where families deposited all their domestic rubbish.

Within the washhouse were two large sinks and a wringer or mangle to squeeze the water out of the washing before it was hung out to dry in the back court on a rope stretched across and attached to an iron hook and then raised up with a long, wooden pole. If it were raining, the wash had to be brought upstairs and hung on the 'pulley' and even on the back of chairs placed around the fire. Again, like the system operating for the cleaning of the stairs, a rota system operated in the use of the washhouse, with one housewife passing the key on to the next woman whose turn it was to use the facility. On a cold winter's night the washhouse was a magnet for us children, who liked nothing better than to enter its hot, steamy atmosphere and stand in front of the blazing fire that glowed at the bottom of the big boiler, into which all the family washing had been dumped. In summer the washhouse served another purpose when it became a place in which the children had all the days dirt washed away; most of it accumulated by frenzied activity in the back courts or in the nearby Elder Park.

The park, a short walk down the Langland's Road, was an oasis amongst the tenements and tarmacadam of Govan. It was a gift of Isabella Elder, widow of John Elder who founded Fairfield shipyard. She purchased the 36 acres in 1883 and turned them into a public park for the benefit of the people of Govan. The land was formerly the Fairfield farm, and it became known locally as the *"Govan Prairie"*. From the deed of gift the park was to provide the inhabitants of the borough with a healthful recreation by music and amusement.

Amongst the parks more unusual bylaws were those stating: *"No persons shall exercise or break in a horse, ass or mule... wash any clothes in the lake nor place any dry clothes, shake, beat or clean mats, rugs or set of any balloon... read or recite any profane or obscene ballad... expose wounds or deformities inducing the giving of alms"*.

Further gifts from this fine woman included the Elder Park library, opened in 1903 by the philanthropist, Andrew Carnegie. 'I should like to say to the workers of Govan that Mrs. Elder had you chiefly in mind when she claimed she donated funds for this living monument with a soul in it. I trust that this may not be forgotten by you,' where the great man's words to his audience.

The Govan library, as it became known, is the oldest general public library in Glasgow. Further gifts from Mrs. Elder were the Elder Cottage Hospital and her posthumous bequest of the Pearce Institute, situated directly across the street from the statue of Sir William Pearce, known locally as the 'black man' (due to the bronze being discoloured and tarnished by years of exposure to the elements).

A statue of Isabella Elder by McFarlane Shannon sits elegantly in its own garden facing her husband's shipyard. Her husband's statue by Sir J. E. Bohem was erected in 1888 and stands between the Elder Park library and the monument to his wife.

The Pearce Institute, already referred to, was designed by a Sir Rowland Anderson and opened in 1906. It's a combination of Dutch and Scottish Renaissance architecture. Its exterior features are crow-stepped Gables, a tower with a balconied cupola, Oriel windows, a clock and a fully rigged ship's filial. The architect's aim was to make the Institute resemble a large 17th century townhouse.

The Institute's interior contains the Macleod Hall with its magnificent organ, stage and gallery; there is also a billiard room, kitchens and Reading Room - which is now the Lithgow Theatre. Inscribed on the entrance walls are the words:

"This is a house of friendship
This is a house of service for families
For the people of Govan
For the strangers of the world.
Welcome!"

The Pearce Institute still operates to this day, providing a welcome to individuals and community groups who use the restaurant and recreational facilities. The administrative headquarters of the Iona Community was based within the building.

Of all these endowments, it was the Elder Park that my companions and I owed a debt of gratitude to Mrs.Elder. During school holidays in the summer, we spent many happy hours in its open spaces. It was not unknown for a bunch of us hyper-active boys to sit quietly on a summer evening listening to the Govan Borough band, or that of the Co-Operative, play stirring music from an old cast-iron bandstand in the heart of the park. Unless one has fallen into that Elder Park pond, one is not regarded as a true Govanite: an honour I can legitimately claim.

We also used the 'swings' at the bottom of McKechnie Street. It was a great place to be in the quiet of an evening, when the shipyards in the vicinity were silent, the hammers dingdong having ceased for the day and the Clyde was at high tide. It was then that the big ocean-going ships slipped from there berths and headed to the open sea. As these vessels glided past the park, their superstructure towering above us, we ceased our activities to wave to members of the crew leaning on the ships rails, their faces smiling as they returned our greetings. In my imagination I used to visualize these men braving mountainous seas or, if they were lucky, sailing on a glass-like ocean into a golden sunset.

Naturally, all of this frantic activity of ours generated a desire for more than our usual supply of snacks between meals. So when the pangs of hunger could be tolerated no longer, it was customary for a boy to stand in the back court and yell loudly, 'Hey Maw.' It might be necessary for the call to be repeated at least once more before the window opened and the boy's mother appeared 'Whit de ye want?' She would ask crossly. 'I want a piece and jeely,' her hungry son would answer. Like a fledging in its nest, the boy waited patiently, face uplifted in the direction from which his life-saving food would descend, if not from the heavens, then certainly from a second or third story tenement window. Eventually, the mother's head would reappear and a package would come hurtling earthwards into the grasping hands of her son. 'Thanks Ma,' he would cry, as he tore open the paper to reach the thick slices of bread liberally spread with margarine and jam.

Where food was concerned I have no memory of ever having been deprived of good, wholesome meals during childhood years. On weekdays, for example, the breakfast consisted of cereal and fresh hot rolls from one of the bakeries in the street; in winter, the cereal was a large bowl of porridge, the meal for which had been soaked overnight. When I commenced school I always had one of the rolls to enjoy with a small bottle of milk that the education authority thoughtfully provided for the children of Glasgow. At lunch, we sat down to a plate of mince, vegetables, potatoes and doughboys. On a Monday, there would be a bowl of vegetable soup left over from Sunday. A supper of fish and chips or sausage and egg filled our stomachs for what remained of the day. However, it was on Sundays that the real cooking took place.

The day began with an enormous breakfast of bacon, egg, sausages, black pudding and potato scones. Then it was off to the children's 10 o'clock mass in St. Anthony's. Granddad, though not a catholic, always made certain that we went to mass and handed us our coin for the collection.

Our lunch consisted of: Scotch broth, beef, potatoes, vegetables and pudding; the soup having been cooked on Saturday night.

High tea in the evening gave us a selection of scones, cake and sandwiches, providing a perfect culinary end to the day.

A standard piece of cooking equipment found in most kitchens of that period was a big, heavy iron pot, whose main function was to make that nutritional broth flavoured by a chunk of beef. Mention of the pot reminds me that it had another function besides that of making soup; it was also used frequently to make the very popular 'clootie' dumpling. This was a boiled or steamed pudding with raisins and currants in it, wrapped in a muslin cloth. The four corners of the cloth were then tied together, and a wooden spoon slipped under the knots and the whole thing loaded into the boiling water, with a plate at the bottom of the pot.

Teachers at school told us how lucky we were to be fed so well, when babies in Africa were starving, and gave us boxes with pictures of black, unfortunate children on them for us to collect money that would alleviate their hunger.

We satisfied our need for entertainment in the cinema, of which there were initially three: the Lyceum, the Plaza and the Elder - better known as the 'fleapit.' A fourth cinema became one more venue when the Vogue opened down the Langland's rd. However, before the Vogue opened, the number of cinemas was temporally reduced to two when the populace of Govan woke up on 24 October, 1937, to find that a fire had destroyed their beloved Lyceum.

The Lyceum cinema had originally been designed as a music hall. In 1859, the Carol Rosa Opera Company gave the opening performance of Carmen, before an audience of 3000 people, headed by Provost Kingwood and the entire Govan town council. By 1912, the Lyceum had become established as one of Scotland's leading cinemas and variety theatres. In 1923 it became solely a cinema.

No matter how scarce money was, we always found sufficient funds for a weekly visit to one of the cinemas. We cared little for the feature film; what was important was the 'serial' currently being shown, 'the follow-up,' as we called it. Flash Gordon the Lone Ranger and one featuring the USA coastguard, whose name I forget, were our particular favourites. My own personal choice was the Lone Ranger. Who, I asked myself, could not be excited by the opening frames showing the black-clad rider on his magnificent white horse rearing up on its hind legs, while its rider cried out 'Hi Yo, Silver, Away,' before galloping off to the thrilling music of the William Tell overture.

The contrived secret of the follow-up was to have the hero, or in some cases the heroine, in danger of being killed at the end of each episode. This ensured that the audience returned the following week to see the outcome. Did the hero survive the raging flood? Would the blonde-haired woman tied to the rails have her ropes cut in time to save her from the oncoming express train?

The Plaza on Govan Road was the chain gang's favourite cinema because of the ease with which a number of us were able to gain admittance for free. With a door near the stage, which in turn led to a corridor with an emergency exit opening onto the Govan Road, it was a simple matter for one of our members who had paid the admission money, to slip into the passage once the film had begun and let those of us on the street into the darkened cinema.

The children attending the Plaza had their own song:

"We are the boys and girls well-known as, Minors of the ABC
And every Saturday we line up,
To sing the songs we love and shout aloud with glee.
We love to laugh and have a singsong
Just a happy crowd are we
We're all pals together, we're Minors of the ABC".

In addition to our cinema going, we boys found much pleasure in reading the weekly comics: The Rover; The Wizard; The Hotspur and The Beano - one of which sold for 12,000 pounds in March of 2004. I was always able to find time to have a quick glance through the pages of the two comics that came on sale on a Tuesday, before I left for St. Anthony's school. With money a scarce commodity, boys had to make do with purchasing just two of the comics; these they would swap with their friends for the other two.

The name of a funny little man in Germany began to appear regularly in the newsreels and in the newspapers, as we went through the year 1938. There was talk of war.

But all of that was of little concern to me because I had fallen in love.

The object of my affection was Susan Woods who lived directly opposite in Langland's Road. Her home was a floor lower than my grandfathers, which enabled me to look down into the bedroom that she shared with her younger sister, Martha. But no matter how often I stood at that window, I never caught the slightest glimpse of either of them dressing or undressing; to my disappointment. Susan had the loveliest of smiles and was well built for her age. We were also in the same class at St. Anthony's. But despite my best efforts to attract her attention, she showed no interest in me whatever.

One morning, on my way to school, I stopped to look at the window display in the chemists in Burleigh St., a colourful carton caught my attention: 'California Poppy' the words in red proclaimed. With such an exotic name, I reasoned, this object would prove irresistible to Susan, and there and then decided I would buy it for her birthday; once I discovered when that was. Surely then I would win the heart of Susan Woods?

During class that very morning, I wrote a brief note to Susan declaring my undying love for her and promising to give her a gift of California Poppy for her birthday. I watched anxiously as the love letter made his tortuous way from one classmate to another, in the direction of Susan, who sat at the front of the room. To my dismay, the last boy in the chain held up my note and called out 'please sir.' I hung my head in embarrassment while the teacher read my literary effort. 'Martin Gordon, you have spelt California wrongly,' I heard him say, while all around me giggled.

1938 was an exciting year for the people of Glasgow. John Brown's shipyard at last launched the magnificent liner, the Queen Mary, and the Empire Exhibition opened in Bellahouston Park.

Built on 175 acres, the dozens of pavilions and exhibits attracted over 13 million visitors, despite the atrocious weather experienced that summer, making it one of the wettest in over 100 years. Dominating the site was the Thomas Tait Tower. The intention was for this edifice to have remained as a permanent structure once the exhibition had closed. But it had to be dismantled a year later due to the deteriorating relationship between Great Britain and Germany. If war came the tower was considered to be a possible aid to German pilot navigation.

My own personal memory of the exhibition is one of looking in wide-eyed wonder at the sight of the Canadian Mounties in their splendid uniforms, and the imposing presence of the turbaned Indian soldiers.

But before and after the Exhibition, the children of Govan used the Park, on Easter Sunday, to roll their brightly painted Easter eggs down its grassy slopes.

Hogmanay, ushering in 1939, we celebrated in the traditional Scottish manner. But even as a young boy I was puzzled at how this celebration of a new year had come to relegate the Christian feast of Christmas to an non-event in Presbyterian Scotland: a fact accentuated when we listened to the wireless and heard Christmas being celebrated joyfully in England, as indeed it was all over Catholic Europe.

In the days preceding Hogmanay the house had to be cleaned thoroughly. Every nook and cranny was inspected, dusted and polished. Anything brass was worked on until it shone as the sun. Fresh bedclothes went on the beds and the last of the old year's rubbish was deposited in the 'midden.' The two rugs we possessed were taken down to the back court and walloped with the bamboo beater. Pride of place indoors went to the kitchen table. A pristine, white, linen tablecloth covered the table in readiness for the plates of cherry cake, shortbread, black bun and Dundee cake that would adorn it. Later that evening bottles of port, Ginger wine and whisky stood proudly on some other available surface. The temptation for children to savour the delights laid out invitingly in front of us was difficult to resist; but we knew better than to place even a finger on any one of the items on display.

Hogmanay and New Year's Day are no longer celebrated as they were in my boyhood. Christmas is now restored to its rightful position as the Christian event it always should have been in Scotland. The change resulted from the growing number of Catholics who began absenting themselves from work on Christmas Day. Their action led ultimately to the closure of industry for the Christmas holiday, bringing Scotland into line with the rest of mainly Catholic Europe.

As the name of Hitler began to dominate the news on an ever increasing scale, I'd at last gained a brother, when William was born in April of 1939. Shortly afterwards, our parents with their children moved permanently into Granddad's in Langland's Road. There were now four adults and five children living there. The conditions were cramped: but we were all under the one roof as a family. Granddad, William and I shared one of the kitchen's recessed beds; Aunt Annie and my three sisters occupied the other recessed bed, while my parents slept in the front room.

Looking at Adolph Hitler on the cinema screen he was a figure of fun to our eyes. We had whistled and jeered as he ranted and raved during his mass rallies at Nuremberg and Munich. In our innocence, little did we know that he was not to be dismissed lightly, as events were to prove.

Then Prime Minister, Neville Chamberlain, returned from meeting Hitler and waving a piece of paper in his hand, as stepped off the airplane: "Peace in our time", he cried triumphantly. How wrong he was, the nation discovered on the 3rd of September, 1939, when he broadcast that Great Britain was now at war with Germany.

And on the very day war was declared its first casualty was the liner Athenia which had left Glasgow two days previously bound for Montréal. A German submarine torpedoed her 250 miles west of Co.Donegal, in Ireland. The number of persons on board the 18 -year-old vessel was 1418; of whom 311 were American citizens. 128 persons died in the sinking. The sinking of the ship was keenly felt in Govan, because many of the men, including granddad, who worked at Fairfield's had helped to build her.

The first reaction of the chain gang to the outbreak of the war was to form ourselves into a unit of some sort for the defence of Govan; even Rags, Uncle Jimmy's wire-haired terrier was conscripted. Our main task, we decided, was to patrol our side of the Clyde from Govan to Linthouse, on the watch for the tell-tale periscope that would reveal the presence of a German submarine. Why enemy submarines would want to put themselves at risk by venturing so far up river and to what purpose, not to mention the probable lack of sufficient depth of water, never crossed our young minds.

All around us the inescapable signs of war began to appear: Barrage Balloons and guns in Elder Park; sandbags being filled and piled high ready to be placed in position; guns and searchlights on top of the tall Granary building across the Clyde from Fairfield shipyard; the increase in the number of men in uniform to be seen in the streets: yes, we were truly at war.

The shipyards began working at a feverish pace to equip the Royal Navy and the Merchant Navy with the ships that were going to be needed to meet the threat from a better equipped enemy, who had been allowed to prepare its fleet for the eventual outbreak of hostilities.

Because so many men were being conscripted into the armed forces, women were recruited in ever increasing numbers to take their place in the workplace; even my own mother began work in the Govan freight depot. The country was fearful for its future. But then on the 13th of May of that year 1940, Prime Minister Winston Churchill rallied the nation when he spoke in the House of Commons and despite pointing out the hardships that lay ahead, he promised victory in the end.

It must have been around that time when Ration Books were introduced to the population to ensure fair distribution of food. Before the war, the country imported 55 million tons of food a month; once hostilities began, this figure soon dropped to 12 million.

The books came in three colours: Buff for most adults; Green for pregnant women, nursing mothers and children under 5 years of age; Blue for children between 5 and 16 years of age. Each family was required to register with a local supplier from whom the rations would be bought, upon presentation of one's book. For groceries our family registered with the Co-Op in Helen Street; the butcher was the one we always used in Burleigh Street. To give one an idea of the miniscule amounts of food people were expected to survive on, here is a list of the weekly allocation, unless otherwise stated:

Bacon and Ham: 4oz. (100g).
Meat: 1 shilling and 2 pence worth. (6p. in today's money)
Cheese; 2 oz. (50g)
Milk: three pints.
Jam: 1pound every two months.
Eggs: 1 egg a week, if available
Sweets: 12oz. every four weeks...
Tea: 2 oz.

Up until the spring of 1940, the war had been what became known as the 'phoney war.' But in April and May of that year the real war began in earnest when the Germans invaded Norway and Denmark, Holland, Belgium and France. France had not yet capitulated when the Prime Minister, Winston Churchill, stood up in the House of Commons on 4 June 1940 to deliver another one of his great wartime speeches he ended on a defiant note by saying that:

"We shall never surrender."

Despite this rallying call to the nation, when France collapsed and Italy entered the war on the side of Germany, the future looked bleak for Great Britain. Italy's alliance with Germany was the signal for mobs of angry Glaswegians to attack and loot many Italian owned ice-cream shops, including the one opposite the Elder library.

Standing on the corner of Arklet road and Langland's Road, I watched a large crowd break down the shop door and shatter the windows before surging inside. Within seconds, some of them emerged with cartons of cigarettes, boxes of chocolate and tins of wafers, jars of sweets and crates of minerals. Meanwhile the terrible destruction of the shop's interior continued. It ended only when a shout went up from some of the bystanders, 'The *"Polis"* is commin,' and the mob began to flee in all directions carrying their booty with them, as they sought refuge in closes and back courts along Langland's Road and in adjacent streets. Not all were successful. Of those hauled before the courts some were fined one or three guineas, or alternatively 14 to 21 days in prison. Bailey T.A.Kerr later described the attacks on the ice cream shops as; *"a dastardly outrage and as being particularly un-Scottish"*. Within days, notices began appearing in many Italian-owned shops proclaiming: 'We are British Citizens.'; too late, of course, to save many of them from the wanton destruction of the previous two days.

Meanwhile life in the tenements continued in much the same manner as before: men and women married, children were born and people died. Because of the deep feeling of community 'Close' living generated, funerals and weddings became happenings of sadness or joy for everyone in a particular 'Close' and in the street as a whole. When someone died for example, neighbours of the bereaved would visit every house in the street taking up a collection for the bereaved family. A portion of the money collected would be spent on a large wreath and to pay for the funeral. On the day of the burial itself, crowds lined the pavements to pay their respects to the deceased neighbour or fellow worker, who like themselves, had probably lived in the street for most, if not all of their life.

For us boys, weddings or christenings were of greater interest because they generated cash for usually empty pockets. In the case of weddings, the custom was for the groom to open the window of the limousine taking him to church, and as the vehicle edged slowly away from the pavement, he would scatter a fistful of coins amongst the children who had gathered there in anticipation of this happening. A frightful, good-natured scramble developed as the combatants struggled to collect as many coins as possible. One's haul would then be spent in the nearest sweet or ice cream shop.

One of the sweet shops we frequented was the Govan road branch of Birrel's, opposite the Lyceum cinema, whose window display and interior were a constant source of attraction for children. I recall on one occasion when a group of us were in the shop, the lovely lady behind the counter had to go into the back for something, she said to us that if anything was stolen she would have to pay for it. By the time she returned, one of my companions had pocketed a few bars of chocolate.

Christenings were also another source of income for us. If one were lucky enough to be the first child of the opposite sex to the infant going to be baptised, one of the adults from the christening party would present a neatly-wrapped package to the lucky boy or girl. Inside would be two biscuits and a silver coin, usually a half crown: a small fortune to children of our age. But christenings and weddings became fewer in number as the war intensified and more and more men left Govan for the armed services, leaving their womenfolk behind bereft of male companionship, at least for a while.

Young as we were, we all realised that the war that was being written about in the newspapers would soon touch our lives more directly and in a more deadly fashion. We had only to look around us to see that Govan must be on the Luftwaffe's list of targets. The shipyards, the docks, Harland and Wolff's Clyde Foundry, known locally as the 'glasshouse' because its seven acre site was completely covered by glass and the huge Co-Operative plant at Shieldhall were all prime bombing targets. An interesting fact about the Shieldhall factory was the number of diverse trades that were carried on under its roof, and that it manufactured the boots for the Glasgow police force.

In anticipation of the bombs that were surely destined to fall on us, our fathers decided that the Shiloh Hall adjacent to number 22 Langland's Road would be 'our' place of refuge during an air raid. It had sturdy pillars, which, it was hoped, would support the roof in the event of the tenement above receiving a direct hit: thankfully their theory was never put to the test.

Then on the 18th. of June of that year, 1940, when the future looked bleak for Great Britain; with Europe lost, the Nation stood alone against the might of the Nazi war machine, Winston Churchill once again stood up in the House of Commons to deliver what is now regarded as one of the most inspirational speeches in history:

In hundreds of years to come, mankind will proclaim:
"This was their finest hour."

It is not surprising then that Ed Morrow, the renowned American journalist in war-time London said of Churchill:

"He mobilized the English language and sent it into battle".

On 19 July 1940, the air-raid sirens wail went for the first time of the war. 43 bombs fell on Glasgow that night, but there were no casualties. Another raid followed on the 18th of September, when bombs hit George Square, but missed all the main buildings. But one bomb hit HMS Sussex which was berthed at Yorkhill Quay, across the water from Govan: it was being prepared for Murmansk convoy duty and was having last minute repairs done in the engine room. A few deck plates had been removed to allow access, and a bomb dropped right through that hole and travelled though the lower and platform decks before exploding in the engine room near oil fuel tanks. Four members of the crew were killed, and 12 others died later of their wounds. The lower deck at that point was destroyed, fire and bilge pumps were put out of action, the fuel tanks caught fire and flames were soon spreading fore and aft. But the worst part was the fact that all the magazines were full of ammunition, torpedoes, shells and depth charges, as well as torpedoes in the tubes on the upper deck; if the fire reached these magazines a large part of Glasgow would have been threatened with death and destruction.

The crew that was on board that night started to fight the fire, but due to the lack of the fire and bilge pumps, as well as the black smoke from the oil fuel, they were struggling to contain the flames. However, the fire brigades arrived and the navy lads were glad to have some help. The firefighters took over and soon had pumps going and water being sprayed just where it was required on the fire.

Quite a few of the navy men were sent to the Western infirmary with severe burns; and it was then noticed that the torpedoes in the tubes were getting very hot and would probably explode with the heat. It was then that the fire chief called for the Govan vehicular ferry to be used as a fireboat, with fire engines being put on board. She arrived about 5:30 a.m. on the 19th, and soon had 16 powerful water jets playing on the Sussex. It was not until the next day that the fire was brought under control, and the ship was sunk alongside the quay wall, so that she was flooded to finally extinguish the blaze and prevent any ammunition from exploding.

Uncle Jimmy was amongst many men who went down to the riverside to witness the action; they assisted members of the crew ashore who had dived into the Clyde and had made it safely to the Govan side. My uncle bought two of these sailors home with him. And while they dried themselves in front of the fire, his wife Lottie prepared tea and sandwiches for them. Just how nervous they were after their experience, we discovered, when they threw themselves to the floor upon hearing the kettle whistle, as it came to the boil. Of course not all the bombers returned safely to Germany. I actually saw one hurtling to its doom above the rooftops of Govan, heading in the direction of Shieldhall. I later learned that it crashed into part of the Co-Operative factory. None of the crew survived. But the strangest part of this story was that the bombing of the Sussex and it being destroyed in the heart of Glasgow was kept secret till long after the war had ended. The blast from the explosion on the Sussex blew in our kitchen window, despite it being protected with sticky brown paper to prevent such an eventuality happening.

Despite the dangerous times we lived in life in the tenements went on as near to normal as was possible. Mothers still had to care for their children and husbands had not yet got accustomed to their wives working outside the home. Fortunately, some form of help was available for the hard pressed women in the form of the 'steamie.' In this building they were able to wash and dry all the family clothes in the space of two hours. Such was the demand for the 'steamie' that I had to rise from my bed at 6.30 in the morning of each week, to book washing machines.

It was a hothouse atmosphere within the building, where the women laboured amongst the boilers, mangles and dryers. The dryers were the big attraction, especially in the winter time .Once the mangle had squeezed the water from the clothes, they were then draped over the dryers rails before the trolley like apparatus was pushed into the drying chamber and the door clanged shut.

I often entered the building to help collect the family washing and wheel it home in an old pram. It was not unusual to see a woman sitting in a corner, partly shrouded in steam, breastfeeding her baby. I recall observing the young wife who lived in the single-end on the landing below us nursing her infant in this manner. She smiled at me as I tried to pretend I had not seen her breasts. I was to witness her on another occasion doing the same thing, a she sat in the shelter of the small park across the road from the 'steamie.'

Attached to the 'steamie' was the bath and swimming pool complex. In the former, one could have a bath for the princely sum of four pence. This payment also included a towel of rough material. A sum of nine pence gave one a towel of softer material and a better tiled cubicle. There was always great demand for the baths during the winter, and especially on Fridays and Saturdays. Generally a woman was in charge, and one could often hear her cry out, 'Hurry on, there's mair than youse wantin in the night,' as the queue downstairs grew longer and impatient. The baths were noisy, with friends calling to one another and vocalists trying to out sing their neighbours. But the loudest noise of all was reserved for the moment when someone turned on the cold shower as the finale to their weekly ablutions. Every person in Govan it seemed made certain they got to the baths in the days preceding Hogmanay, heralding in the year 1941.

During that night, men and women surged up and down the stairs each man carrying his own whisky or beer with which to 'first foot' all the homes he would enter over the next four or five hours. This bacchanalian celebration led to some fights and sexual incidents. I saw one neighbour of ours groping his sister-in-law on our landing, something he would never have attempted at any other time of the year.

It was in that year I experimented with sex: my companion was red-haired Farquhar Gray, who lived opposite in a Burleigh street 'close.' How we came to find ourselves alone in the graveyard of the Old Govan Parish Church, I can't recall. But alone we were.

Before Farquhar and I sat down under a tombstone, I noticed that some of them had skull and cross bones displayed on them; with my vivid imagination I deduced that they were the graves of pirates. However it is only in recent months I discovered that skull and cross bones are associated with Freemasonry.

Without any conversation between us, she pulled down her knickers and I fumbled to expose my penis. But my limp little member remained disinterested as I continued to press it between Farquhar's legs. Surely a boy and girl so young had not been influenced by the loose morals of the war years? Given the relatively innocent times we lived in compared with today, how were so many boys of my age so sexually aware? Nudity on the screen was unheard off, and there were no 'girlie magazines' lying around. Yet despite these facts there was an obvious awareness of sex amongst boys and girls of my age. But the nearest most of us got to sexual pleasure was when we played at nurses and wounded soldiers, with the landing of the 'close' serving as the casualty ward. The touch of the nurse's hand on one's fevered brow, or better still, to have a girl you had long admired probe for a bullet in the area of one's groin was sheer ecstasy. Was it any wonder that our nurses were kept busy with a steady flow of casualties from the battlefield, and that some of us somehow just kept on getting wounded.

In later years, we would graduate to the more intimate and sexually exciting indoor games of 'post-man's knock' and 'subway.' Both of these pursuits involved much kissing and touching of one's partner in the darkness of the lobby and even sometimes in the kitchen itself, with the light still on. Needless to say there was little to touch on a 12 or 13-year-old girl. But sometimes if one were lucky, there would be a couple of older girls at the party whose bodies were more satisfying to the touch. With those in their late teens and early 20s, most of their courting or 'winching' in the local vocabulary, was done in the cinema or on the landings of the 'close.' It was quite a common occurrence to come upon a couple in a passionate embrace, as they said goodnight to each other.

Speaking of which reminds me that granddad had a strict rule that his daughter Annie had to be indoors by 10p.m., at which time he locked the door. I recall a number of occasions when he refused her admittance because she was late, and she had to go and find somewhere else to sleep.

My classroom at St.Anthony's was not immune to the sexual precociousness of my classmates. The object of their attention was a girl who sat directly behind me, and whose features I can still recall to this day. She was plump, wore glasses and was continuously sexually molested by the boys around her, on every occasion that the teacher left the classroom. I often wondered how no person outside the classroom failed to hear the girl's loud squeals, as her assailants groped her between her legs or fondled her ample breasts.

The back courts of Govan took on a bare look in 1941, when the railings topping the dividing walls between them were removed to help the war effort. Other railings to disappear were the ones protecting the small gardens in front of the tenements on the Langland's rd., opposite the Elder Park. I recall some of my companions rubbing the palms of their hands on both sides of the wire mesh that replaced the railings, and them saying how it felt like a woman's fanny. When I tried it, I had no way of telling if they were correct or not. All I could sense was a warm, pleasant sensation.

It was around this time that I was hospitalised for a couple of days, as the result of an accident at school. I had left the classroom one misty, dark morning to visit the toilet in the playground. Going down the marble stairs I slipped on the damp steps and tumbled head over heels to the bottom. When I failed to return to my classroom after a long absence, the teacher sent one of my classmates to search for me.

When I recovered consciousness, I found myself stretched out on a small bed in the janitor's room with the headmaster, the doctor and the janitor, Mr. Fitzgerald, all looking down anxiously at me. They encouraged me to sit up and handed me a cup of warm milk. The doctor decided that I ought to be taken to the Children's Hospital at Yorkhill for x-rays and detained overnight for observation. The two days I stayed there would have been most enjoyable, were it not for the presence of a younger boy who kept on whining for his mammy.

I returned home cleared of any serious injury and was granted a further two days absence from school to convalesce. But after a few weeks back at St.Anthony's, I decided that schooling was unnecessary for my needs and began to play truant. During that time I was a fugitive from education, I hid on the stairways of numerous 'closes' and, money permitting, spent a number of afternoons in the cinema. I tried to give the impression of normality by leaving for school and returning home punctually each day. And when in a cinema, I left on time no matter how exciting the film.

My freedom was brought to an abrupt end when one lunchtime I entered the house to find the truant officer waiting to question me as to why St. Anthony's had not been enjoying my presence in the past two weeks. 'Just wait till your father comes home the night,' my mother warned me. What my father did to me that evening is still a painful memory.

Funnily enough, school began to be a pleasure once I realised that in less than two years time, I would be moving on to secondary school: provided I passed the qualifying exam. And as my academic record showed at the time, that was very unlikely. Even Mr.Gallagher, one of the teachers, concurred with my assessment, when he told me one morning, when I was washing the cup and saucers in the teacher's staff room, that, 'You'll never pass your Qualifying.' At the time I thought it a very unkind thing for a teacher to tell a pupil. But on reflection, perhaps he was deliberately spurring me on to greater effort.

As the conflict progressed and families were bereft of their men folk, many women took up with servicemen who were lonely and far from home. For example in our own 'close' I had noticed a growing number of men in uniform entering a woman's house on the second landing: the husband was in the RAF, leaving his wife to care for their two children. In my innocence, I presumed that all of these visitors were friends of the woman's husband and were simply visiting her for a cup of tea and a chat. Two years later I was to witness the husband in his Air Force uniform walk across the back court towards Burleigh St., carrying the youngest child in his arms, with the other child walking by his side. Some of the women in the tenement opposite were visibly crying as they watched this sad scene from their windows. It was only then I realised that there had to be some connection between the women's tears, the man in removing his children from their mother, and her visitors.

My own mother was still working handling boxes of foodstuffs, like spam and powdered eggs, new items on our menu and imported from the USA. One afternoon, after I had just got home from school, I heard a loud knock at the door. Two tall men stood outside, easily recognisable as detectives. They identified themselves and entered the house to begin searching of cupboards, wardrobe and a chest of drawers. They also looked under the beds and in the coal bunker. Neither men spoke as they worked. Failing to find whatever they were looking for, the two of them left with a curt 'thanks son.' It was only when mother came home from work that evening that I learned the reason for our visitors. It appeared that a lot of pilfering had been taking place in the goods yard. As a consequence, houses of everyone working there had been searched that afternoon. They arrested some of my mother's colleagues for possession of stolen goods.

On the night of March 13, 1941, a 'bomber's moon' illuminated Clydeside in its white light. My father and a neighbour stood at the landing window smoking their pipes. I was leaning on the banister outside our front door. The drone of an aircraft caught my attention. 'That's a German,' my father said. 'It's too bright for any raid,' the neighbour replied. 'That's a heavy load it's carrying, my father continued; just listen to its engines.' Immediately the sirens sounded all over Clydeside. Within minutes the stairs were full of families making their way to the Shilo Hall. But granddad refused to leave the house. 'I'm no going to run away from any Germans,' he said defiantly. Well he would, having fought them on the battlefield during the Great War.

Govan escaped the worst of the bombing that night but not Clydebank, where 2,000 people were killed and thousands injured as 236 tons of explosives and 1650 incendiary bombs fell on the borough. The obvious targets for the Luftwaffe were the big shipyards and the huge Singer factory. After two nights of savage bombing, only seven houses were left undamaged, and of the population of 55,000, all but 2000 had to leave the area and live where they could find accommodation. Although the official casualty figures were high it was widely accepted that they had been sanitised for obvious reasons. One member of the Home Guard, who had been on duty in Clydebank during the air raids, greeted the casualty figures with the remark: 'In which street?' The number of fatalities would have been much higher had it not been for the decoy fires, given the codename, Starfish,' that were prepared in the vicinity of large cities and likely targets. These decoys were lit whenever an air raid commenced so as to induce the follow-up force of planes to unload their bombs at a distance from the real targets. Such a system was in operation in the hills above Clydebank; and in the raid a great many of the bombs fell harmlessly on those decoy sites.

The worst single casualty of those raids was that experienced at Yarrow's shipyard, where two bombs and a land mine fell on an air-raid shelter in which workers were taking cover. 47 were killed. Govan, in contrast, escaped almost unscathed, despite its high concentration of targets. A land mine hit a tenement at Linthouse wiping out the entire Egan family as they made their way down stairs to a shelter. The obvious target was Stephen's shipyard nearby. Another land mine fell on Moore Park, the home of our local junior football team, Saint Anthony's. My father, a staunch supporter and I believe a committee member, walked up Helen Street the next day to inspect the damage. Most of the corrugated iron fencing had been flattened; but the pavilion remained intact. But where the land mine had fallen in the penalty area nearest the road, there was now a huge crater, at the bottom of which lay the club's heavy roller. Intriguingly, the goalposts adjacent to the crater were still standing; but those at the Ibrox end of the ground had been uprooted and were nowhere to be seen. The bomber was clearly aiming for Harland & Wolff's Foundry, barely 100 yards away across Helen Street.

A feature of those times was the way in which whole families gathered around their wireless sets at Nine o'clock at night to listen to the B.B.C. news in order to find out how the war was progressing. But before Alvar Liddell began to speak, the opening bars of Beethoven's Fifth Symphony came over the air waves. The notes corresponded to the Morse code sign for the letter 'V.' What we didn't realize at the time was that thousands of people in Nazi -occupied Europe were listening clandestinely to the broadcasts. Later on in the war, coded messages directed at the many Resistance Groups all over Europe, but especially in France, became the norm after the news ended.

1942 was to become our family's *"Annus Horribilis"* when my mother died from a botched illegal abortion. It was a time of war, and she already had five young children. In addition there were the overcrowded living conditions prevailing at the time. But what is most terrible about the event is the memory I still have to this day of my admitting the two *"Angels of Death"* into the house. How was I to know that they were about to murder my mother and her unborn baby? After a few minutes conversing with mother in the bedroom, one of the women emerged and handed me a slip of paper and told me to take it to a chemist close to Ibrox Stadium, the home of Rangers Football club.

As I walked up Govan Road past the Plaza cinema, I thought it strange to be going so far when there was a chemist in Burleigh Street that we used all the time. Shortly after returning home with a tiny packet given to me by the chemist, the same woman walked past me carrying the chamber pot used by my parents. In it there was a small, white object like a skinned rabbit. The woman went downstairs to the toilet. When she returned I noticed that the chamber pot was empty.

Two days later, ambulance men carried my mother out of the house. I stood at the banister looking down on her pale, upturned face. She smiled up at me just before disappearing from my view. She died on 13 February. A neighbour, Janet Boyd, was in the same ward and heard her cry out 'William, William,' the name of her youngest child, seconds before she died.

When I looked at the lifeless figure lying in the coffin placed on trestles in the bedroom, the only emotion I felt was one of disbelief. This could not be the cheerful, lively person I had known the past 11 years; what I was looking at now, so cold to the touch and wax-like was an imposter. My real mother would soon appear and expose this thing for the fraud that it was, I reasoned, before going through to the kitchen and Asking Aunt Annie if I could go to the pictures. She explained to me that this was not the correct thing to do when my mother lay in her coffin in the other room. Then she burst into tears.

Rather than stay indoors where there was nothing but whisperings and gloom and tears, I went over to St. Anthony's Chapel. In its cool, dark interior I prayed for my mother, and asked God to send her back to me. The statues – Saint Anthony and the Little Flower stared silently at me, Saint Joseph was probably there as well. The young French nun was a particular favourite of mine; after all had she not promised before dying at the age of 24 that she would spend her Heaven doing good upon earth? The sanctuary lamp's red light flickered comfortingly to let me know that Jesus was in the Tabernacle watching over me and listening to my every word. Blessing myself fervently with holy water, I left the chapel and returned home to find a number of relatives had gathered to discuss the funeral arrangements.

It was a cold, bright day when mother left us for the journey to Barhead cemetery. Father Burns from St. Anthony's was present to carry out the Catholic ritual. The one memory I have of the events of that day is of my aunt screaming, 'don't take her away,' as the pallbearers lifted the coffin and moved towards the door, while relatives meanwhile struggled to restrain her from preventing her sister's body leaving the house. I felt deeply embarrassed at the scene of excessive emotion, as I looked on cruelly detached from the events around me. When the room emptied, I moved over to the window.

Neighbours from all the surrounding 'closes,' and beyond, stood in their hundreds, along with some workmates of my father and friends from St. Anthony's football club. There was movement amongst the onlookers as the coffin emerged from the 'close' and was placed carefully in the hearse. Many of the women in the crowd began to weep as the hearse moved slowly away from the pavement. I remained at the window until the cortege disappeared beyond the chapel house, and the last of the bystanders had dispersed a couple of female relatives had joined me and now tried to comfort me. But it was they who needed consoling, to judge by their tear stained faces. When my father and granddad and the other members of the family returned, the women who had stayed behind fed them with steak and kidney pie, and there was a wee dram as well to dispel the chill of the February day.

Three days later I opened the door to two tall men, who identified themselves as detectives. They asked if they could come in for a minute. We stood in the lobby. 'My mother is dead I complained.' We know son, one of the men said. I looked blankly at them both. 'Did any strange women visit your mother a few days ago?' the other detective asked. I recalled Uncle Jimmy's injunction not to say anything about my mother's death, if asked. 'I don't know I was at school; they might have come then.' The men looked at each other. 'Well then, did you hear if your mammy had any visitors?' I shook my head. Well if you do hear anything, son, be sure and contact us.'

It was only when I was much older than I learned the facts of my mother's death, and the significant part that her sister had played in encouraging her to have the abortion. 'You have five weans already and ye canny have another,' Annie had warned her weeping sister. Ever since, I have regretted my silence when questioned by the police. Though I would have been unable to reveal the identities of the two women, I could at least have given them the address of the chemist.

Given my personal experience of backstreet abortion and its deadly consequences, one would expect me to be in favour of Liberal M.P. David Steele's abortion Bill of 1967; whose aim it was to prevent such a death as my mothers. The power to terminate the life of an unborn child would henceforth be placed in the hand hands of doctors. But on the contrary, I am vehemently opposed to legalized abortion. Abortion is murder of the innocent. It is a crime against humanity. Since 1967, when the abortion law came into effect in Great Britain, close on 6 million unborn children have been murdered in their mother's womb. Surely this Frankenstein scenario was not what the Member of Parliament had in mind in proposing his bill? Abortion today is now a worldwide phenomenon being used often as a contraceptive. It is mostly sought by women who find themselves pregnant as a result of an affair with a married man. Indeed abortion law has become so trivialised that it is on record that an English woman sought an abortion because the pregnancy would interfere with her holiday plans.

Our society today goes to great lengths to hide the unpalatable truth about abortion. Coded language is used to camouflage what terrible things are done to the unborn child in the name of women's 'right to choose;' or 'I have the right over my own body.' Ladies, it is not your own body, but that of a defenceless human being that you are killing.

"From the moment that the foetus is fertilised its life begins which is neither that of the Father or of the mother. It is rather the life of the new human being with its own growth. It would never be made human if it were not human already", so wrote Pope John Paul 2 in his majestic encyclical letter, *"Evangelium Vitae"*.

Mother's death brought to the surface the deep hatred her brother, Jimmy, had for my father. Within a week of the funeral, I had to rush in between them when I found the two men pummelling each other in the kitchen. No doubt Jimmy was blaming father for his sister's death and using it to vent his hatred against all things Irish and Catholic. Ironically his stepdaughter was even then taking instructions in the Catholic faith, while serving in the Army.

Annie, who had been engaged at the time of her sister's death, broke off the engagement to look after us children. She was very caring but at times could be very angry, as when,on one occasion, she knocked me to the lobby floor and stamped on my head.

The war, meanwhile, continued to dominate our lives, with food rationing continuing to increase in severity. Radio programmes like ITMA, (It's That Man Again) Worker's Playtime and Henry Hall's Guest Night tried to provide some relief from the hardships the population endured each day. Back court concerts, which had been running for over a year, increased in their frequency during the summer of 1942; apart from providing entertainment they also raised money for the war effort. The concerts were joyful occasions in which all the locals were given the opportunity to display their vocal and instrumental talents in front of their neighbours. There was no age limit. So impressed was Lord Provost Dallas with the quality and variety of entertainment on display, that he suggested the concerts should move indoors when the summer was over. But nothing came of the idea.

Feeling safer now that the threat from German bombers appeared to be over, we children began to wander farther than the confines of Govan. One of our favourite excursions was to take the tram to Renfrew and then wander through the Bluebell woods. It was there that dozens of balloon-like objects lay scattered on the ground amongst the trees. On another such expedition, a group of us noticed the recumbent figures a man and a woman in the grass some way ahead of us. We hesitated, and then saw the couple rise to their feet and begin adjusting their clothing.

For the return journey we took the ferry across the Clyde and boarded another tramcar to carry us as far as Partick. Once there, it was a short walk to get the ferry back to Govan.

In mentioning the tramcar I am reminded of what an important feature of Glasgow life they were. The first tram took to the streets on 19 August 1872, along a route between St. George's Cross and Eglinton toll: Further routes were gradually added to a total of 40 miles. By 1914 the length of tramway lines had increased to almost 100 miles. And then an astonishing three million passengers used the tramcars annually. These Glasgow trams were unique in having different colours on the panels around the top deck for the different routes, (red, blue, yellow, green and white) so that intending passengers could easily identify them from a distance.

Glasgow's tramcars lasted until 1962, when on the evening of 4th of September, a memorable and moving procession of old and new tramcars made their last journey through the streets of the city. Many of the thousands of onlookers were in tears. And I must confess that even as I write these lines I too am close to tears, so much where these noble vehicles part of my boyhood.

However, it was a tramcar that was to take the life of one of the younger boys from the next back court to ours. Around eight of us had been standing on the Govan Road gazing at the mouth watering display of chocolate and sweets in the window of the ice cream shop next to the Brechin public house: directly opposite were the gardens and graveyard of the Old Govan church.

Tired of looking at the window's contents, all of the group, save the young boy and I, crossed the road into the gardens. Once the boy realised that the group had gone he suddenly turned and raced onto the road and under a tramcar. There was nothing the driver could have done to save the little lad. His mangled body lay exposed for a few seconds, until the driver of a passing lorry came forward and threw a sack over the wee lads severed legs. What made the accident all the more harrowing was the fact that the boy's father himself was a driver in Glasgow transport. A huge crowd turned out for the funeral, amongst whom were dozens of the father's colleagues in their uniforms; adding a greater poignancy to the occasion.

The following year, 1943, the Allied air forces began bombing German cities with ever increasing ferocity. But I had a personal battle of my own to fight: I just had to pass the Qualifying examination; if only to spite that Mr. Gallagher. His psychology worked - if psychology it was. I passed, and was duly informed that I would enter St. Gerard's Senior Secondary school, Southcroft Street, Govan. This meant that I had no need to use public transport, as the school was a six minutes walk past the Govan Cross and the Plaza cinema.

Cllr. P. J. Dolan officially opened St. Gerard's on 20 December 1937; a year later, there were 680 pupils in the school. I began my career there on 6 August 1943. An Army Leader Force of 40 pupils was formed in October of the same year. The school's motto was *"SursumCorda"* - Lift Up Your Heart.

I spent two happy years there, under the headship of Mr. William Moore and a dedicated staff of teachers. Amongst them was Colm Brogan, whose brother was on the B.B.C. Brains Trust.

He left teaching around 1946, to begin a new career in journalism and writing such books as: *"Our New Masters"*, 1947; *"Patriots? My Foot"*, 1949 and *"The Nature of Education"*, 1962. Evelyn Waugh in a letter to Nancy Mitford declared that in his opinion Colm was superior to his better known brother.

My favourites amongst the teachers were Mr. Stewart, who taught English, and Miss McPherson, the teacher of music. Mr. Stewart was a handsome man with dark wavy hair. When dressed in the uniform of an officer of the Army Leader Force he had the appearance of a film star: what effect he had on the attractive, young women teachers can only be guessed at. He did his best during my time at the school to get me to pronounce the letter 'r' correctly. For example in the word 'Drummond,' as in 'Bulldog Drummond,' I would pronounce it as a 'w,' to the delight of my classmates. Mr. Smith did his best, and with saintly patience, to teach me mathematics. He was also in charge of the school's football teams. So it was not unusual to see a couple of footballs, a pump and his own football boots lying in a corner to the right of his desk. The most hated teacher in the school was a science teacher to whom we gave the nickname, 'density.' This appellation arose from the frequency with which he had us pupils define 'density.' But the worst and most frightening thing about him was the brute's aptitude for inflicting physical punishment on his pupils. To be struck 8 to 12 times on the palms of one's hands with the leather strap was not uncommon. I personally suffered stinging blows, because I had failed a science test.

Miss McPherson, on the other hand, was a tall, lovely, elegant lady in the best Scottish tradition, and one who clearly loved the music she was trying to impart to us. Amongst the songs I recall where 'Bobby Shafto' and another one about the sinking of the Spanish Armada.

Being a Catholic school, religion permeated the school ethos. Prayers were said before classes began, for example. And on the first Friday of each month, the entire school walked to St. Saviour's Church for Benediction. On the way we had to pass a Protestant school whose pupils spat out at us from behind railings. We ignored these attacks accepting them as part of the religious bigotry Catholics had to endure in Glasgow.

It was around this time that I got the job of delivering the Sunday newspapers for Miss Carmichael whose shop in Burleigh Street must have been one of the smallest in Glasgow: four people would have filled it. Burleigh Street was named after Bennett Burleigh - famous war correspondent of The Times and prospective Liberal MP for Govan (1885).

The owner, in keeping with her premises, was small and dressed severely in dark clothes, even at the height of summer. Despite her forbidding appearance, she was always kind and considerate, as long as I did my job. She paid me four shillings for the Sunday morning's work. Reporting promptly at eight o'clock, I first helped Mrs. Carmichael sort out the papers to be delivered; then before leaving to begin my paper round, she gave me a mug of sweet tea and a thickly buttered roll. When I had finished the deliveries I collected my wage and went home to have breakfast, prior to attending the 12 o'clock Mass in Saint Anthony's.

A second job increased my weekly income by another two shillings, when a local bakery employed me to wheel a barrow load of its products down the Govan road to another of its branches at Linthouse. And to this day I can still get the aroma of the fruitcakes and treacle scones rising from under the canvas cover shielding them from dust and flies. With the money I was now earning, I was able to buy pair of socks for myself, and on an occasional Saturday morning take the subway to Saint Enoch's Square and in John Lewis purchase such records as Harry James playing the Flight of the Bumblebee or the latest Bing Crosby singing 'Dear Old Donegal.'

My father, who by now was working on building sites, also increased his earning capacity when he became an agent for the Irish Hospital Sweepstake - a lottery set up in 1930 to raise money for the Irish hospitals. Selling these tickets in Scotland, as in the rest of the United Kingdom was illegal: a fact my father made me fully aware of as he handed me books of tickets to take to various clients in Govan and across the Clyde.

The sweepstake was set up in 1930 by Dublin man Joseph McCracken, a former member of the IRA and Sinn Fein minister in the first Irish government; Richard Duggan, a Dublin bookmaker; and Spencer Freeman, a former British army officer. All three became hugely wealthy as a result of the lottery's success, because, while it raised money for Irish hospitals, it was run as a private for-profit company.

Prizes reached £350,000 - about 30 million in today's money. The winners were decided by the outcome of several horse races, including the Epsom Derby and the Grand National. It is estimated that the sweepstake raised 133 million Irish pounds (€169 million) for the Irish health service between 1930 and 1987. Some 247 million Irish pounds was handed out in prize-money.

On the morning of the 6th. of June, 1944, the B.B.C. newsreader told us that Allied Forces had invaded France, with landings on four Normandy beaches. Fierce fighting was occurring, as the invading troops fought to establish a beachhead, and the German defenders used every man and weapon at their disposal in an effort to throw their enemies back into the sea. By the end of August 1944, France had been liberated. But the cost of the Normandy battles had been high: over 250,000 allied causalities was the price paid for that freedom.

Soon, the German prisoners of war were flowing back to Britain; some of them being temporarily held at Ibrox Stadium; guarding them were Polish soldiers. A number of us went along to the stadium to inspect the enemy. They were a sorry sight, I recall, sullen and dishevelled. They bore little resemblance to the seemingly invincible Wehrmacht who had bulldozed their way across Europe during the past years of conflict.

Eventually on the seventh of May 1945, Germany surrendered unconditionally. Naturally, there was great rejoicing on the streets, much hugging and kissing of anyone in uniform by women to thank them for their bravery in the war. A photograph in one of the Glasgow newspapers showed the son of one of our neighbours boarding a troopship heading for Europe. But the sailing was postponed indefinitely, and the young man returned to Govan to join in the celebrations. Street parties were organised, and bunting was erected at individual 'closes' welcoming home Archie, Tom or Hughie But some 'closes' had no one to welcome home.

But one man who did return was Mr. Brown, who lived across the back court from us in the flat above Uncle Jimmy. He had been a prisoner of the Japanese and came home in time for Christmas. Sadly, he was committed to Hawkhead Asylum three weeks later.

With hostilities at an end in Europe, the government announced that people could now travel to Ireland or Eire, as it was then known. Immediately my father and Aunt Annie began making plans to travel there during the Glasgow Fair holidays in July. But then Daddy decided that he would wait until September and that his sister-in-law would take me to Enniscrone, County Sligo, where his sister, Sarah Ellen, was married to a farmer. As soon as Burns and Laird Steamship Company announced that it would resume sailings to Ireland, queues began forming to obtain the much prized boarding ticket, without which one would not be able to travel.

Such was the demand for these small pieces of cardboard, that it was necessary for families to operate a shift system amongst themselves to ensure their place in the ever-lengthening queues. My father and I took it in turns to stand or sit in the long line of people that stretched up to 100 yards or more from the Burns and Laird offices. It was quite common for people to queue overnight.

Eventually, I was the one who approached the desk at the shipping lines counter and was handed two boarding passes for the sailing to Derry on 11th. July. When the eventual day of departure arrived Annie and I stepped into the taxi that was to take us to the Broomielaw.

What we didn't realise, as we climbed the gangway, was that the vessel we were boarding had that morning unloaded a cargo of Irish cattle at Merkland's Wharf. It then had its stalls dismantled and the decks hosed down in preparation for its human cargo. I could still smell the cattle as we found ourselves a corner below deck that was to be our home until we reached Derry, the following morning.

The ship was packed. At Govan, we saw granddad and father waving to us. Although I was a little sad at leaving them, the thought uppermost in my mind was the realisation that, by the same time tomorrow, I would be in Bay View house and in a strange, new country.

"Of the greatest moments we think in human life, is the deporting upon a distant journey into unknown lands".
Sir Richard Burton.

Ireland Of The Welcomes

As the Sligo to Ballina bus bumped and growled its way towards Enniscrone, the nausea that had afflicted me since disembarking in Derry had almost gone. In its place there was a growing excitement as I contemplated meeting my father's sister: we had already met, but then I was only three years of age at the time.

Daddy had told me to watch out for the Seafield hotel as the bus approached Easkey; because the family farm was just 100 yards beyond it, and his brother Willie and his wife would be at the gate to give us a wave. But I must have fallen asleep and never saw the welcoming party.

When I next looked out from the bus, the rooftops of Enniscrone on the shores of Killala Bay, its waters sparkling in the bright evening sunshine were now visible. Beyond the town I just had time to see the tops of some sand dunes and miles beyond them a round tower, before the bus went almost freewheeling down into the resort's main street.

On our way through town I saw a small, stone-built church, and opposite, the ruins of what was clearly an ancient abbey; perched on a hill beyond it:, the crumbling remains of a castle. The bus pulled up outside Hopkins Pub. I allowed Aunt Annie and the other passengers to get off before making my way to the door. As I hesitated on the top step, a small woman of a red complexion and a short, straight hair approached: 'Martin,' she asked? I smiled and stepped down to greet my father's sister. 'You are heartily welcome,' she said, extending a hand, two fingers of which I noticed were severely bent. 'We'll go over to Mary Rafter's shop, 'she told us, 'and wait for the Hackney car to take as down-home.'

Within the premises dark interior, the first thing I noticed was an aroma the like of which I had never experienced before. When my eyes became accustomed to the faint light, I saw some bread neatly stacked on shelves; trays of rashers, black puddings and sausages; jars of sweets and boxes of chocolates, tins of biscuits and an assortment of fruitcakes. Hanging from the wooden ceiling were sides of ham and items of horse tackle. The other part of the shop served as a bar. 'The car is here,' Aunt Nellie, called from the doorway.

During the Ford car's slow drive along the Cliff road I saw for the first time the breathtaking grandeur of the Enniscrone strand.

'Fully four miles long,' our driver, said. The beach was divided in two by a small river, the section beyond the division being by far the longer. That part of the sand underneath the cliff was crowded with children doing the things that come natural to them in that environment. Farther on we passed the stone built pier where a number of small fishing boats were drawn up on the slipway, and an old derelict with the name, the *"Nancy Lee"* still visible, lay drunkenly against the pier wall. A small house stood at the top of the slipway, in its extensive but overgrown grounds stood the grass-covered remains of what must have been a substantial group of buildings. 'That is the old Coastguard Station. It was burned down in the time of the *"troubles",* ' my father's sister remarked, as we drove past. I determined to learn more about the 'troubles 'and the burning of the Coastguard Station.

An attractive looking house, with the name Buena Vista painted on stone pillars at the entrance to a short slope leading to the long, slated building, was the first building that I thought might have been my aunt's. But the car drove past, while the driver discussed the number of visitors on holiday in Enniscrone. 'Here we are then,' Aunt Nellie announced. I looked at the house outside of which the car had pulled up. It wasn't quite what I expected. After all, hadn't she put her address as Bay View House? It certainly had a fine view of the Bay; there was no question of that. But Bay View House it certainly was not. Instead I was looking at the traditional Irish country dwelling with a thatched roof whose whitewashed walls reflected the strong sunlight, hundreds of which I had seen already on the bus journey from Derry. 'Hope you enjoy your holiday,' the driver said, as he removed our suit cases from the car's boot.

A frail looking man wearing spectacles peered at us from the door of the cottage. I followed my two aunts along a short, concrete path. 'This is Tom's sister-in-law and his son, Martin,' Aunt Nellie told her husband, who viewed us through glasses that were as thick as the bottom of jam jars. After shaking hands with Aunt Annie, he turned to me and said 'you are very welcome, 'gasuir,' extending a thin hand towards me.

Inside the house, I was shocked at how dark it was, with only one small window allowing any daylight to lessen the darkness. This ceiling appeared to be made from squares of some sort of turf held in place by cords of strong rope; the fireplace was a large gaping hole about 3 feet wide, its back and sides black with soot. The kitchen's only redeeming feature was the blazing fire in the hearth, despite the warmth of the day. Above the mantelpiece hung pictures of the Sacred Heart of Jesus and the Immaculate Heart of Mary; black rosary beads were draped over a corner of the former.

After a supper of boiled eggs and still warm home-made soda bread, the four of us sat around the fire while Aunt Nellie plied her sister-in-law with questions about the war and Mammy's death. Very soon a combination of tiredness and the heat from the fire brought on a bout of yawning. 'I think you'd better go to bed,' John McGowan suggested, as Aunt Annie and I tried to suppress another huge yawn.

The bedroom that Annie and I occupied was filled with bright, sunlight that came in through windows to the front and back; four double beds and a couple of chairs were the rooms only furnishings. An assortment of cheap religious prints decorated the walls along with three family pictures, including one of my sister Sadie on the day of her first Holy Communion; a couple of statues and a small, black crucifix stood on the mantelpiece.

'You can have any bed you want,' my father's sister told Aunt Annie. I chose the one in the far corner of the room, while Annie chose the one near the fireplace. What were all the beds for, I wondered as I undressed and climbed in between the rough sheets, only to feel the bed moving as if I were still on the ship. I only had time to observe Annie removing her bra and to admire her ample breasts, before falling asleep.

On awakening the following morning, sunlight filled the room, this time entering through the back window which looked out onto a walled garden, and beyond that to a gently sloping field at the top of which was a strange - looking grass mound. The almost total silence was broken only by the sound of the sea lapping on the shore to the front of the house. Refreshed after an unbroken sleep of almost 10 hours, I used the porcelain chamber pot which had been conveniently left next to my bed while I slept. Aunt Annie stirred at the noise and turned round to look at me, just as I finished urinating.

An exploration of the farm after breakfast revealed that it had three fields at the back of the house and two across the road, where, inside a low stone wall, stood outbuildings, which, I discovered later that day, were a hen house and a pigsty.

When I stood on the highest point of the land behind the house, I had a panoramic view of Killala Bay which was calm and blue in the windless morning. To the south a large mountain dominated the skyline, with a range of smaller peaks extending to its left. Far to the North, mountains appeared to rise sheer out of the ocean. From this vantage point I could see most of the houses that comprised the townland of Carrowhubbock South. I counted 10 thatched roofs, three red - tiled cottages, two flat roofed concrete dwellings and two slated houses. I gazed with delight at my new surroundings and took deep breaths of the pure air. A couple of miles across the fields a church poked its spire heavenwards from a protective clump of trees: the few that were to be seen within miles of where I stood. Govan, and all that it represented, seemed to exist only on another planet.

The town of Enniscrone consisted of the Main Street, the Cliff Road, Pier Road and the Burma Road: so called because it was constructed during the Burma campaign of the 1939-45 war. The town's population of 400 doubled each summer by the influx of families from surrounding towns and other parts of Ireland, eager to avail of the excellent bathhouses and, as the late Canon James Greer wrote in his much loved book the *"The Windings of The Moy"*:

"Then as to the strand, all experts who have walked upon it know that there was nothing approaching it in the whole of Ireland. I have seen and admired Brighton and Bournemouth, and they have no strand where they could run a four mile horse race".

The sand dunes, which ran the entire length of the beach, were called locally the 'burrows,' because of the huge rabbit population that lived there. But some years later, the disease myxomatosis was eventually to wipe them out. Within a year I was to learn that rabbits were not the only inhabitants of the 'burrows.'

Later that morning, I was handed a galvanised bucket and asked to fetch water from Mullaney's well. Following directions I had been given, I turned left at the barn, and after a short walk turned left again into the 'boreen' leading to Mullaney's cottage and the spring well to which everyone came for their drinking water. The well itself was nothing more than an uncovered, shallow hole in the ground whose excess water became the stream that flowed through two of John McGowan's fields to the sea.

My first experience of life on a small, west of Ireland farm came a couple of days later, when I accompanied John McGowan to the bog: a journey that took us two hours sitting in the cart pulled by Sam, the ass: our intention was to advance the saving of the turf supply by gathering the sods from the 'footings' and putting them into the much larger 'clamps.' But by the time we reached our destination, heavy rain was already falling from a leaden sky. Along with other men from Carrowhubbock, we sought shelter alongside a stack of turf already built at the roadside in readiness for transporting home. As the downpour continued, I was ordered to take shelter under the ass cart, from where I gazed out at the sodden landscape and revised my romantic notions about Ireland. The men appeared unconcerned as they crouched down, canvas bags over their shoulders, their only protection from the elements, and while away the time with much good humoured banter. I heard one of them advise John: 'Go and see how the 'gasuir' is doing.' Although I knew no Irish, I realised that the word referred to me. 'I am all right, I called out,' startling Sam, the donkey, who had obviously forgotten my presence under the cart to which he was tethered. By two o'clock, and with no sign of the weather clearing, the farmers decided to return home.

'40 days and 40 nights we're going to have,' said John McGowan gloomily as we sat eating huge helpings of bacon, cabbage and potatoes. I looked enquiringly at his wife. 'This is St. Swithin's day, if it rains today, it will rain for forty days and forty nights.' The bad weather was with us for the next two days, much to the delight of the ducks.

In addition to ducks, geese and hens, the other animals on the farm were two cows and their calves, and two one–and-a-half-year-old bullocks, Sam the donkey and Sam the horse. There were also two pigs in the sty; one of which would be sold before Christmas, and its companion killed to provide a diet of bacon for months ahead. I was to discover eventually how difficult it was for my aunt and her husband, along with their neighbours, to subsist on 13 acres of shallow, stony soil; then there was always the inclement weather to contend with. A great help in making ends meet were the pensions of two-and sixpence a week John received because of his partial blindness, and the two shillings a week for his endeavours in the War of Independence.

Since my arrival, the one thing that had continued to puzzle me was the nine double beds in the house. In addition to the four in the room where and Annie and I slept and the one in the single room off the kitchen, there were a further four beds in the room behind the fireplace. An explanation came a week later, when a husband and wife walked into the kitchen and asked if there was any place for them? They're 'canters,' my aunt explained, after she had shown the couple to the room behind the fireplace.

I raced back to the fort field where John was doing some weeding amongst the potato drills to tell him the news. 'Why are they called' canters,' I wanted to know. John stood up and while filling his pipe, began walking to the nearest headland where we sat down with our backs resting against a cock of hay. Satisfied that his pipe was full, John put a match to it and began to suck vigorously. 'Canters,' he told me, were people from County Mayo, other parts of County Sligo and Roscommon who left their farms, small shops and pubs, to come to Enniscrone for at least a week during the summer months. In the not so distant past, they travelled by horse and trap or on a sidecar, hence the name 'canter.' Most of them came for the sole purpose of taking a course of seaweed baths in one of the resorts two bathhouses owned by the Kilcullen family and the Maughan brothers, swearing to their efficacy in alleviating the pain of their arthritis and rheumatism and preventing winter colds. Part of the cure was drinking a glass of whiskey, or in some instances 'poteen,' last thing at night.

Almost all of the farmhouses in Carrowhubbock kept these visitors as a means of augmenting their meagre farm incomes. I suppose it is fair to say that my aunt and her neighbours were the pioneers of Agri-Tourism, long before it became the fashionable thing it is today.

Landladies, like my aunt, usually charged between seven-and-sixpence and 10 shillings a week; for which princely sum they provided their guests with a bed, milk and potatoes and the fire upon which to cook their meals. Most of the food the visitors needed during their stay they brought with them in an assortment of jars and tins, storing them in suitcases pushed under the beds, where also stood the ubiquitous chamber pot. What surprised me during that summer was the fact that despite eight women trying to cook the dinner on one fire simultaneously, I fail to recall any serious outbreak of hostilities between them.

In times past when there was no town of Enniscrone, the visitors, according to Canon James Greer in the, *"The Windings of the Moy"*, used the precincts of Cahill More fort as a place to pitch their tents. This fort is situated at the end of the Carrowhubbock road and is graphically described by the Canon:

"It is one of the largest forts I have met in County Sligo, or in the several parts of Ireland where I have been. Its inner ring is fully an acre. It is surrounded by four rings or mounds which plainly formed part of its fortifications. It is situated over a high cliff facing the Atlantic and is one of the loved haunts of young and old who visit Enniscrone during the bathing season".

It has the usual rooms built of flat stone and without mortar. The entrance that was on the side near the footpath has been closed up for years as being dangerous for cattle and sheep; but 60 or 70 years ago the youth of the locality used to explore the dark, damp rooms and passages, with rush lights, fir lights and candles.

The visitors in those days used to pitch their tents there to enjoy the bathing and drink the waters of the ocean. The mounds of the tents that were erected are still quite plain to see all along the coast from the bath houses in present day Enniscrone to the 'basins.' It is said that in inclement weather, they fixed up these damp rooms of the Fort, where they lit big fires and probably enjoyed their holiday gladly and sociably. Despite the large number and the interest in them, only about 100 of these forts have been scientifically excavated.

Often a son or daughter home from England or America accompanied their parents to Enniscrone, or at least paid them a visit. So not surprisingly, romance often blossomed under the influence of sun, sea and sand, not to mention a night's dancing in the Marine Ballroom. There's many a married couple in the West of Ireland who met in Enniscrone, John said.

'How did you and Aunt Nellie meet?' I asked John

John had taken the pipe from his mouth. 'It was a match.'

What's that?'

'Some people thought that it was time I took a wife, so they hired a *"matchmaker"* to look around for a suitable woman for me,' John said.

What a strange custom, I thought. I wouldn't get married that way. It wasn't like that in the films. 'Do these marriages still take place?'

'Not a lot nowadays; only in some backward places,' John replied.

It was not unusual in such 'arranged' marriages, that after the wedding breakfast, the bride and groom's honeymoon consisted of only a car drive to some place thirty or forty miles away, before returning home to begin their married life together. Very often too, the brides wedding night would have her husband's parents, and on occasions, a brother for company.

'It looks like the weather is on the mend,' John said, glancing up at the sky.

Sure enough, there wasn't a cloud to be seen, and the sun was feeling a bit warmer. Maybe I'll get to swim at the pier before long, I mused.

On the last Friday of July, Aunt Annie began her return journey to Glasgow, reluctantly leaving me behind until my father came in September. During the two weeks we shared the room together; I had got used to seeing her in various forms of nudity and was amazed not only at the size of her thighs - which gave the impression of small tree trunks - but also the immensity of her breasts. I had no idea that breasts could be so big.

The following day, with the weather gloriously sunny and hot, John and I set out once more for the bog. At first the work was enjoyable; its novelty and the freshness of the mountain air hiding for a while the pain in my fingers caused by handling the ragged edges of the turf and my aching back from the continual bending. Sam the donkey wasn't the only one who was glad to head for home at around six o'clock that evening.

As I helped John look after Sam, I could hear a swishing sound coming from the stable that was joined on to the southern gable of the cottage. I looked in and saw Aunt Nellie was churning: something I had already seen her do a few times before. With its walls whitewashed and the stone floor scrubbed clean and disinfected, one would never have suspected that during the preceding winter it had housed the cows and their calves. All it contained now was a table on which stood a large crock containing the cream for churning. And standing in the middle of the floor the churn itself: a wooden affair about three feet high and bound with three copper bands; the third one of which pulled in the staves, much like a corset does to a woman's figure. The wooden lid had a hole in its centre from which protruded a long, wooden handle which was attached to the wooden disc within the churn. When enough cream had accumulated in the crocks, the contents were poured into the churn. My aunt invited me to help finish the churning, showing me how to move the handle up and down with rhythmic motions, until about half an hour later the first signs of butter were discernible. Aunt Nellie left me to continue the final minutes of pounding the cream into butter, while she went to fetch a kettle of boiling water, which she then poured into the churn to wash away any residue of butter on its sides. The final part of the process was simply to lift out the butter and place it on a large plate to wait salting and making up into blocks or decorative rolls, by means of wooden patters. The buttermilk was deliciously cool to drink and was also used for making the appetising soda bread baked in the skillet, with red hot coals underneath and piled on its lid.

There were a number of superstitions attached to churning. The first was that whoever came into the dairy while the work was in process, could not leave until they took a turn at the churning. The second 'pishrog' was that if a man came in and was smoking a pipe he couldn't leave until he extinguished the pipe; otherwise, so it was believed, he would take the butter with him.

With the August bank holiday approaching, we were putting the finishing touches to the bedrooms in the expectation that they would be filled with visitors. From early morning until just before dusk all the windows were opened to enable the air and whatever sunlight managed to enter through the small windows to freshen the mattresses and bedclothes.

I was now sharing the lower bedroom with three elderly men, one of whom was almost bent in two from his years working as a miner in Wales. Because of the amount of stout they had consumed in the pubs, the men had to make frequent use of the chamber pots during the night, thereby wakening me up when they did so. During the day, without any indoor toilet in the house, the 'canters' roamed the fields looking for a solitary spot in which to take care of their bodily functions.

John and my aunt still slept in the small room off the kitchen; but when more visitors came looking for accommodation, she decided it was time for the three of us to move out to the barn. 'Anyway, we're all the same family,' my aunt said.

The barn was a small building that formed the southern side of the yard and had a galvanised roof. The interior was divided into two compartments by a high, wooden partition; the inner room served as a bedroom and a place to eat. Cooking was done on the open hearth. Underneath the window was a single bed for me, and about 6 feet across the room was the double bed for the married couple. Our mattresses were bags filled with straw and laid on any bits of timber found lying around the barn itself or the haggard. The inside walls of the building had been freshly whitewashed before my arrival.

That first night we slept there, I was woken up by noises and whisperings coming from the other bed. The next morning, through half closed eyes, I watched my Aunt slide out of her bed and noticed a dark area between her legs. She asked if I had slept well.

On the first Friday in August, I persuaded Aunt Nellie to let me swim at the pier. Very reluctantly she agreed, but only if she went with me. The pier was crowded when we got there. At its head the springboard was in constant use. The steps at the slipway were where most of the boys and girls of my own age were doing their swimming. It didn't take me long to join a cluster of them on the steps leading down to the water. As I stood there shyly waiting for an opportunity to make my dive, a lovely, fair-haired girl with a laughing face and small, turned-up nose arrived at my side. 'Can you swim?' She wanted to know I nodded my head. The next thing I knew, I was under the water. Coughing and spluttering as I surfaced, I looked up at my assailant. She was smiling down at me as I swam towards the steps intent on getting my own back on her. But as soon as my feet were on the bottom step, I heard her cry out 'by,' and watched in frustration as she dived into the water and swam speedily away to the other side of the basin.

I enjoyed that first dip in the Atlantic. But my thoughts were centred on the girl the remainder of that day. My aunt didn't know who she was, only that one of the other girls was Superintendent Kilroy's daughter from Ballina, in County Mayo.

That evening I walked up to the pier. It had been another hot and sunny day but now the sun was going down like a great ball of fire behind the hills of Mayo across the other side of Killala Bay. The pier was strangely quiet, as was the expansive stretch of sand across the water. I climbed aboard the derelict hulk of the *"Nancy Lee"* and sat down to enjoy the silence and the wonderful view.

'Hello.' The voice startled me. I turned towards the stern to see the blonde head of a small boy appear.

'Hello,' I replied, as the youngster clambered aboard and made his way forward. He looked to be about nine years of age.

'What are you doing?' he wanted to know.

'Just sitting here admiring the view,' I said.

'I am on holiday, I live up there,' the boy said, pointing to the small house at the top of the slipway. I have a brother and a sister; mammy is there too.'

'And what about your daddy?'

'He has to work in the shop. But he does come down on the half-day and on Saturday nights.'

'What shop?' I enquired.

'Lipton's; he is the manager there.'

The boy looked at me with a frown on his face. 'You talk funny. I must go and tell Mammy.' He lowered himself over the side of the boat and ran towards the house, from which he appeared a few seconds later and beckoned me to come up.

An attractive woman in her early 40s, of medium height, slightly plump and wearing glasses, met me at the door; her hair was soft and auburn; but it was her smile behind the glasses that I found most appealing.

'I'm Frank's mother, Mrs. Conboy,' she said, extending a hand. 'Frank said that you were Russian,' she continued, taking care, I noticed, to enunciate every syllable slowly and distinctly.

I hung my head with embarrassment in the knowledge that it was my Glasgow accent that had led the woman's son to come to that conclusion.

'No, I'm from Glasgow.'

Mrs. Conboy turned laughingly to her son: 'Frank, what an imagination you have. What's your name,' she asked. 'James Gordon,' I answered. I had always hated the name, Martin. Now that the opportunity presented itself amongst strangers, I was determined to adopt a new identity for myself.

The hour that I spent with my newly found acquaintances answering their questions about Glasgow and my Aunt, and enjoying the large piece of chocolate cake and a glass of milk Mrs. Conboy handed me, made me very happy indeed.

'Mammy made the cake herself,' her son said proudly.

Before leaving, I learned that the daughter in the family was called Joan, and that she was almost 13 years of age. Mrs. Conboy invited me to visit any time I liked.' It's a pity that Joan is not here, I'm sure she would have liked to have met you, as you are around the same age,' she said.

It was two evenings later before I called again on the Conboys. There was no reply to my knock on the door. Disappointed, I turned to leave when I almost collided with a girl who had come running through the open gate.

'I'm sorry,' she said, starting to blush.

'That's all right,' I replied.

You must be Frank's friend,' she said, giving me a puzzled look.

'Are you Joan?'

Before she could answer, Mrs. Conboy came through the gate carrying a black prayer book and a rosary beads in her hands. 'I see that you have met Joan,' she said.

'I think we've met before, Mrs. Conboy.'

Mother and daughter looked at each other. It was Joan who spoke first, the colour starting to rise on her neck then spreading upwards over her face. 'You were the boy...' she looked away in the direction of the Coastguard Station ruins. 'It was two days ago at the pier,' I explained quickly to Mrs. Conboy. Looking at a mother and daughter it was easy to see where Joan got her smile from. But it was her little upturned nose which I found most appealing.

From that night until the end of the month, Joan Conboy and I became inseparable companions. Most days the two of us swam at least once; in the evenings we divided our time between the house at the pier, the farmhouse or the Town Hall, where we sat through such chilling dramas as *"Gaslight", "Murder in The Red Barn"* by Maria Masten or the lesser dramatic, *"East Lynne"*, based on a successful, mid-Victorian novel; all of which a summer touring Company, The Shannon Players, presented annually at the resort during the month of August.

On the first night that Joan and I attended, I stood to one side to allow my companion to enter the row of seats first: a fact noted by a friend of my aunts and related to her the following day.

It must have been around this time that we heard the news that an American airplane had dropped one bomb on a Japanese city, killing thousands of people; followed a few days later by a repeat performance on another city. But the event was so far away and was not like the war in Europe, which was on our doorstep, so to speak, that the event did not impinge on our daily life in Enniscrone.

One night as Joan and I walked home from the Town Hall, she suddenly stopped and bent down on the pretext of tying her shoelaces. But I noticed the furtive glance she gave in the direction of the people walking ahead of us, and the time that she took until she was satisfied that they had put enough distance between us and them.

When we neared the little road leading down to the pier, I put a hand on Joan's arm. 'Listen,' I whispered. Over in the deep grass of Kilcullen's field a Corncrake was filling the night sky with its distinctive, haunting sound. In the waning light Joan looked at me, smiled and took my hand in hers. I kissed her on the cheek. Then still holding hands, we walked towards the pier where, before parting, we arranged to go picking blackberries the following day.

When I called to collect Joan the next afternoon, I had with me a small bag of potatoes for her mother that I had dug up that morning. That was the occasion when I encountered her father for the first time.

George Conboy had thinning, blond hair and wore gold-rimmed spectacles. In appearance I thought he looked Teutonic because of his colouring and sullen appearance. It was quite apparent where his son, Frank, got his looks from. When George Conboy spoke it was with the faint trace of an English accent.

Because of the plentiful harvest of blackberries that year, it didn't take Joan and I very long to fill the jars. However, instead of taking them immediately home, we sat down alongside the haystack which I had helped to build the previous day. How long we sat there eating our way deeper and deeper into the jars, I can't recall; it was the sound of the Angelus bell that told us it was time to leave. I helped Joan to her feet and holding hands, we left the field to a couple of rabbits that had emerged from a hedgerow.

Through my friendship with Joan and her mother, I got to know the Kilcullen family who operated one of the resorts Seaweed Baths, and who were also one of the largest landowners for miles around. There were two boys and three girls in the family. Mary, the eldest, was about the same age as Joan and I. When the two of us visited the cafe attached to the Bath House, we were always assured of a piece of one of Mrs.Kilcullen's delicious cakes. Occasionally, I helped with the washing-up if the cafe was anyway busy. Of course I had a price to pay for my constant presence at Joan's side. Mary and her brother Edward teased me regularly about our relationship. But I didn't mind. I loved Joan, and that was that.

I had never been happier as the two of us continued to enjoy each day to the full. Inevitably, we had one or two 'lover's quarrels,' as for example, when she refused to dance with me at a children's fancy dress in the Marine ballroom. But we made up that night and went to the Town Hall.

Midway through August, John started bringing home the turf, using the horse and cart to make two trips a day to the bog. I went with him; and although tired I always made certain I met Joan for at least an hour each evening, during the five days it took us to build the stack of turf across the road from the house.

With the holiday season now at its peak and every dwelling in Enniscrone: and Carrowhubbock packed, it was not unusual for me to arrive home after leaving Joan, to find a crowd of young men and women gathered around the doorway, while inside, John McGowan and a couple of other traditional musicians, including neighbour Katie Mullaney on the violin, supplied the music for the energetic couples who swung one another around the kitchen, urged on to greater Endeavour by the shouts of: *"Round the house and mind the dresser"*, from the onlookers crammed into every corner of the kitchen. My Aunt looking on was always terrified that one of the women would lose the grip of her partner as they swirled around and around like Dervishes, to the vigorous playing up the fiddles and melodeon.

On the eve of Joan's departure, we spent the evening together at the farm. There was a dance on, and my aunt urged the two of us to go out on the floor. We declined and instead walked back the fields.

With the harvest Moon high in the clear, night sky, Joan and I stood holding hands at almost the same spot where I had seen my surroundings on that first morning six weeks previously. We could still hear the music from within the house, even though we were two fields away. The sea was sounding on the rocks down by the big fort: another of the signs for good weather. Killala Bay lay calm and bathed in the moonlight; two dogs were holding a conversation in the distance. Neither of us spoke, perhaps due to the sadness we both felt at our impending separation. But I also like to think that we were afraid to break the magic of that moment, fearful that even one word would transport us back into the real world of pain and disappointment. We were content just to be together.

I was a child and she was a child,
In this Kingdom by the Sea;
But we loved it with a love that was more than love
I and my Annabel Lee.
E Allen Poe, Annabel Lee, 1849.

Joan was quieter than usual as I walked her home. There were so many things that I wanted to say to her before we reached the pier, but they remained locked in my heart. We stood briefly at the gate, conscious that our young lives had been touched by something neither of us fully understood. With a promise that I would be on hand the next day to bid her goodbye, I brushed my lips quickly against Joan's and rushed out the gate.

I kept my promise and was there to help load their taxi with suitcases and an assortment of household items that had been brought from their own home. Mrs Conboy told me to be sure to call on them any time I was in Ballina. 'You've got the address, James,' Joan reminded me through the open window of the car. I nodded. 'Bye,' Frank Conboy called out, as the car moved slowly away. I stood and watched it go past Maughan's Bathhouse and begin to climb the hill to the Cliff Road until it disappeared from view. Since I was in no mood to talk to anyone, I walked home along the shore fields. In the windless day, Killala Bay looked black and sullen: almost as if it too knew that the summer had come to an end.

With Joan no longer my constant companion, I began forming friendships with some of the local boys in Carrowhubbock, most of whom were slightly younger than me; with the exception of Peter O'Neill, John McGowan's nephew, who lived with his father and two younger sisters in a house built on a corner site across from the farmhouse. Tim O'Neill supported his family by fishing during the summer, and by harvesting sea rods and picking winkles during the winter. I soon discovered that my Aunt didn't like the family, but took pity on the two young girls because their mother was dead.

In the farmhouse nearest to us lived the Devaney family of old Pat, his son Mike, daughter Delia and her son Paddy. When I asked Aunt Nelly about Paddy's father, she mumbled something about him not being around the place. Mike had bad eyesight and was of limited intelligence.

Amongst these companions of mine Tommy Ford was my favourite. He lived in one of the three Council cottages along with his parents and sister. According to my aunt, the family was very delicate. 'There is disease in them, God between us and all harm,' she said, making the sign of the cross. 'Sure most of his uncles and Aunts have died from it.' Then to emphasise just how serious the matter of their health was, she told me the following story.

"One day, when the family returned to the house over in the 'hollow,' after burying one of their members, they found another one of them dead in bed.' She warned me not to enter the Ford's house too often, and not to eat or drink anything if I did. 'I don't think Tommy will have a long life", she prophesied.

I had helped to build the haystack; had worked at saving the turf and at carting it home. Now I was out in the fields again as the corn ripened and John set about mowing it with his scythe. My task was to bundle the barley and wheat into sheaves and at the end of the day gather them into a 'stook.' It was fascinating to watch John swing the scythe in a wide arc and to hear the swishing sound it made as it cut through the stalks. My aunt loved to work in the fields, but she inevitably attracted harsh words from her husband whenever she stood up to pass some comment on the weather or a neighbour's house or express an interest in the identity of the car going the back road. Above us a skylark hung high up in the sky singing its head off. As I observed it, the glorious melody stopped and the bird plummeted towards the solitary strip of meadow left in the field.

Attending Mass every Sunday and Holy day since I arrived in Ireland, I soon noticed that not every man reaching the church went inside: at least a dozen of them stood outside the main door and the two side doors, removing their caps when the bell sounded at the moment of Consecration. When I asked about these men, my aunt she told me that some of them had been members of the I.R.A., and at some time in their life had been refused absolution in confession; others, she continued, suffer from claustrophobia.

A letter arrived from my father informing us that he would be coming in the second week of September. My initial reaction to this news was one of joy. But then I became saddened at the thought of leaving my new life on the farm; not to mention Joan. That night, not only did I say my prayers more fervently, but I asked for a miracle to enable me to remain where I had found a new dimension to life.

When the fateful day arrived for father to return to Glasgow, I remained behind. Whether it was his sister's persuasion or the efficacy of my prayers didn't matter, the effect was the same. Wait until I tell Joan, I thought excitedly, forgetting for the moment that she was nine miles away in Ballina. I've got to go and see her as soon as possible, I decided.

When it was time to say goodbye to my father, I felt so sad at his going, that I avoided the actual moment of his departure, and instead went into the field behind the house, where I watched him walk up the road past O'Neills. But I couldn't let him leave like that, I thought, and called out 'daddy.' He stopped and looked back in my direction. A smile broke over his face and he lifted his free hand to give me a wave. I continued to watch his lonely figure until he went out of sight beyond *"Buena Vista"*. I began to cry. The tears were not only for myself, they were also for my father; for I knew that he would have given anything to remain in Enniscrone for the rest of his days.

It was around this time that I encountered one Sunday at mass the practice of the priest in reading out the names and the amount each parishioner had contributed to the harvest collection. Starting with the largest figures of five or £10 he slowly descended to the smaller figure of two and sixpence. Those who had given the bigger sums of money - usually the shopkeepers or those working in the civil service or in a profession, Father James O'Connor used the prefix 'Mr.' So we had Mr. Pat and Mr. John Maughan; Mr. Tom Nicholson; Mr. Cowell; Mr. Cawley, Mr. McCarrick and Dr. O'Connor. But once the priest came to the names of the small farmers and poorer people of the town, he dropped the prefix 'Mr.' and instead used Christian names only of these people. Even at my young age, I sensed that this amounted to a form of intimidation and ought to have been banned by the bishops; but they too had been a parish priest themselves at one time, and furthermore belonged to that club, Maynooth, where they all studied prior to their ordination.

As the nights began to lengthen, John began teaching me a simple tune on the violin. Noticing that I seemed to have some little talent for the instrument, Aunt Nellie decided to send me to the convent for more formal training.

The nuns in Enniscrone belonged to the French order of Jesus and Mary which had been founded in the city of Lyon. The nuns specialised in teaching young girls. They were addressed as 'mother,' except those who did most of the manual work around the convent: they had the title 'sister.' According to my Aunt, they were uneducated and came from the poorer families who were unable to provide them with a dowry to take into the convent. Mother Bruno, a sweet, refined lady took me for piano lessons, and Mother Evangelist, with the twinkling eyes and a flirtatious manner, was my violin tutor.

In addition to enrolling me for the musical lessons, the nuns began to teach me catechism. This puzzled me as I had attended two good Catholic schools and, like most of my co-religionists in Glasgow, was closely identified with the Catholic Church. In fact, I probably knew more about my faith than most of the boys in Enniscrone.

Since there was very little work to be done, now that the harvest was in – digging up the potatoes and the threshing of the grain would come later - I decided that now was an opportune time to visit Joan in Ballina.

The town of Ballina straddles the River Moy, a stretch of water known primarily for its excellent salmon fishing. It is a cathedral town where the bishop of the diocese of Killala lives in his 'Palace' overlooking the River and adjacent to St. Muredach's College, named after the local patron saint. The town is also famous in the history of Ireland for the part it played in the invasion by the French in 1798. It was down Bohernasup - in English, *"The Street of the Straw"*, so-called because of the row of thatched cottages that existed there at the time, that General Humbert led his small invasion force into Ballina.

When I stepped off the bus in the town, the first shop I noticed was Lipton's on the opposite corner of the street: it looked just like the company's other branches in Glasgow.

Following my Aunt's directions, I turned round Tyler's corner, and walked until I came to Shamble Street. After passing a large premises called the Gas Company and farther along the street a builders provider and sawmill called Beckett, I emerged at the top of the street to find the river rolling past at high speed on my left, and ahead of me the houses of Morrison Terrace.

The Conboy home was number 23 in a row of thirty six built before the war by the local council and occupied by families whose breadwinners were employed in a variety of jobs, ranging from the police force and a band-leader to the local stationmaster. A tiny, postage stamp-sized garden fronted each house. As I neared Joan's home, I crossed over to the other side of the street and walked past number 23, wishing that someone would look out of the window or open the front door and see me. But even when I retraced my steps no curtain moved and the door remained shut. My journey would have been wasted had not Joan seen me pass by the bottom of the lane leading from the Station Road down to Morrison Terrace, as she and other girls were arriving home from school. I heard my name called out. Then I heard it a second time. 'James!' There was no mistaking that voice. I retraced my steps and looked up the lane to see Joan rushing towards me, not even stopping to pick up her school bag that had fallen on the ground. 'James, you've come at last,' she gasped, holding out a hand for me to take until her two companions reached us. The girls looked at me curiously.

'Have you been with Mammy?' Joan wanted to know.

'No,' I said shyly.

'But you were going away?' I could see the puzzled look in her eyes. 'You would have gone home without seeing me,' she said accusingly.

I felt such a fool standing there tongue-tied in front of her companions who were smiling knowingly at each other. The two girls, I discovered later, were called Heffernan, Philomena (Ena) and Frances, and lived almost opposite the lane way. We were to become close friends and remained so for many years.

Joan put a hand on my arm. 'Come, come home with me,' she ordered.

'Mammy, look who's here,' Joan called out, as soon as we entered the tiny hallway of the Conboy home. She opened a door and motioned me to follow her. Mrs Conboy emerged from the kitchen to greet me.

'Hello, James, you've come to visit us at last,' Mrs. Conboy said, extending a hand.

While Joan's mother went about serving up dinner to her daughter and her two sons, Joan and I reminisced about the holiday, and I answered Frank's questions about work on the farm. While her family ate their meal, Mrs. Conboy and I sat in front of the range and had a cup of tea and ate a portion of sponge cake.

Sitting there in the cosy room opposite that woman, I had for the first time since my mother's death a deep sense of the loss I'd suffered. And as I continued to sit there, I was conscious of the first stirrings of an attachment to Joan's mother. She was the embodiment of the mother I would have selected as my own, had I been given the choice.

All too soon it was time for me to leave. But I would return as soon as possible, I promised myself, as Joan accompanied me to the front gate. She was still standing there when I turned around after I had gone about 20 yards down the street and waved to her. Joan returned my salute by raising her hand.

Small farms like those of my aunt's husband could not afford to feed too many animals for the winter; which is why I went to Ballina again in the month of October to sell the two older bullocks, thus leaving only two cows and their calves to be fed until next spring's grass. We joined up with two neighbours to walk our combined six cattle the nine miles to Ballina, leaving Carrowhubbock at 3 a.m. on a journey that was to take us along the Quay Road which followed the river Moy the whole way into Ballina, and our destination outside St. Muredach's Cathedral. This was the site of the town's Fair that was held in May, June, October and December. In addition to these, a monthly Fair took place in the market square.

The journey to Ballina took place in almost total silence; for apart from the men's muted conversation and the soft sound the cattle's hooves made on the earthen road, only a solitary dog's bark broke the stillness of that October morning. The few houses that we passed along the way were in darkness. Twice the men stopped to rest and smoke their pipes, while the cattle took the opportunity to munch a few mouthfuls of grass from the hedgerows. The River Moy, a field or two away from us slid silently by on its journey into Killala Bay. Turning onto the main Sligo to Ballina Road, the clock of the Cathedral stuck seven o'clock. Ahead of us were other groups of men and animals. As we neared St.Muredach's college, 'jobbers' approached to make offers for the cattle. But neither John nor his neighbours accepted these first bids of the day.

We found a spot for the animals midway between the town's two bridges. Five hours later, with our charges still unsold, it began to cross my mind that we might very well be retracing the morning journey. John had received two bids, but just when I thought that a deal had been done, he held out for another few shillings. At midday, John sent me up town to buy a block of cheese, a packet of ginger snaps, a bottle of double X stout and a bottle of lemonade for our lunch.

As I sat on the wall eating and drinking, I glanced up anxiously at the cathedral clock. At 1p.m., a 'jobber,' who had already tried to buy the cattle, approached once again. As he and John began the long drawn-out ritual of 'striking a bargain' I looked towards the cathedral and whispered a silent prayer that this time John would see sense and balance the difference between himself and the buyer, against walking the cattle all the way back home.

'Hold out your hand then,' the 'jobber' cried. But John displayed a marked reluctance to comply with the man's request. 'Go on John McGowan,' a bystander urged. John continued to show no desire to become involved in these preliminaries, and continued to gaze down at the pavement as if he had lost something.

O God, I thought, surely he's not going to say, 'no' again. A man pushed forward. 'Here, give me your hands,' he said, grabbing hold of one of John's hands and one of the 'jobbers' 'Strike a bargain the two of you,' he ordered. John and his opponent eyed each other warily like boxers in the ring. The 'jobber' took John's hand and turned it palm upwards, then spitting on the palm of his own right hand slapped it hard against John's hand. 'There, now, have we deal?' The faintest of smiles flickered around John mouth as he nodded his head. The man moved in swiftly to mark his purchases.

There was nothing for us to do for the next couple of hours except mind the cattle until it was time to drive them up through the town to the railway station; then return to be paid outside one of the banks and hand over the traditional 'luck money' to the 'jobber:' usually a half crown. Then it was to the 5 o'clock bus home with two crisp £20 notes safely in John's pocket. 'Now, all we have to do is to pick the spuds and then wait for the thresher to arrive,' John told me on the bus. Although very happy that we had sold at the fair, I felt sad that I had not been able to meet Joan and her mother.

Since the income the 'canters' had generated during the summer had stopped, our diet became very basic indeed, consisting mainly of eggs, potatoes, soda bread, cabbage and turnips. Very occasionally we would kill a hen or bought a few rashers for Sunday. The lamb chops that were on the menu almost daily during July, August and into September were now but a distant memory.

The weather turned really wintry the day we commenced digging up the twenty drills of potatoes in the field behind the 'fort.' Every so often, we had to seek shelter along the hedgerow from the squalls and the showers of hailstones sweeping in from the Atlantic. Of course every shower only made the land that much more difficult to walk on, never mind trying to separate the potatoes from the clinging mud. To my aunt and her husband the conditions were no more than they were used to. But for a city boy it was a most trying experience. My hands were caked in mud and almost frozen stiff. Fortunately, over the next few days the weather improved and we finished the potato harvesting in the most pleasant weather we had seen for a couple of weeks.

When finished digging, we buried the Arran Banners, the Kerr's Pinks and Sligo Champions in pits built out in the middle of the field opposite the gable of the Mullaney house, and then covered the crop with straw and plenty of earth.. The field, now bereft of its crops, looked wet and desolate. It was difficult to imagine it as it was that evening when Joan and I sat eating our blackberries.

On Halloween when it was time to go to bed, Aunt Nellie pulled all the chairs back from around the fireplace as was her custom, and then began sweeping the hearth.

'Why as you doing that?' I enquired.

'I wanted to see if there is going to be any footprint in the morning.'

'Footprint?' I exclaimed.

'Yes, on Halloween, if anyone is going to come into the house in the next year there will be the mark of a foot facing inwards; but if anyone is going to leave the footprint will be facing out.'

I must have looked sceptical. 'Last year there was a clear trace of the foot facing inwards, and you arrived, didn't you?' Aunt Nellie told me. Next morning, the hearth bore no trace of any ghostly visitor.

There was just one more major seasonal job to be done before we settled down for the long, winter sleep: the thrashing of the two stacks of corn standing in the haggard. A few days later I heard the sound of a large machine coming from the Scurmore direction The poultry recognised it for what it was and began running frenetically around the yard and haggard. 'It'll take another week before it gets to us,' John said, as we cleaned out the stables.

The Thresher, pulled by the biggest and nosiest tractor I had yet seen, arrived in Carrowhubbock and one night stood in our haggard to await the morning. I don't know how many times I went out that evening just to stand beside the monster. The large, wide belt which, when connected to the thresher, powered that machinery for separating the grain from their stems, was already in position. All we needed now was a fine day for the threshing.

Next morning, all three of us rose early. The weather was ideal for the task ahead: a blue sky and a just the faintest of sea breeze. I went into the haggard to watch the operators of the machine make their final adjustments before the big, pink - coloured wooden contraption burst into life. As it did so, John's neighbours began drifting into the haggard, each one carrying his two-pronged fork. In the Irish language this gathering is called a *"Meiathal"*: a system of co-operative seasonal farm work involving reciprocal exchanges of labour and farm animals. When, for example, John McGowan's neighbours knew that it was his turn to have the thresher, they turned up that morning to lend him a hand. Instead of money their reward would be food and drink, and not a little merriment; added to all of that an assurance of help from John when it was each of their turn to welcome the thresher.

Once there were sufficient workers to do all the jobs around the machine, work started in earnest; but all the time more men were arriving to lend their support. From years of experience, each one knew his allotted place in the team. Two of them were up on top of the machine: one to cut open the bands around the sheaves, the other to feed them into the monster's voracious mouth. But once that thresher had spewed out enough straw to start building the rick, there were no idle hands.

I stood alongside John and watched the first grains of the harvest flow into the bag hung below a metal opening. From time to time, John interrupted the flow with his hand to take a sample of grain which he then placed in his mouth to chew. This test complete, he pronounced himself satisfied with the quality of that year's crop.

It wasn't until two hours later that I began transporting the filled bags round to the barn with the ass and cart, and emptied their contents onto the stone floor of the inner room that during the summer had been our bedroom. Soon it was time to stop for lunch.

The men - all eleven of them - were seated at two tables. Before joining them I gave my aunt a helping hand in serving up the bacon and cabbage and two huge plates of flowery potatoes bursting out of their skins. To wash it all down there was a plentiful supply of stout, cider, lemonade and milk for anyone with a bad stomach. If all that were not enough, mugs of tea and currant scone finished off the meal. Soon after returning to work, and as we reached the last few rows of sheaves in the first stack to be thrashed, our dog, became agitated and began to growl and circle around the stack.

'Get a stick,' John said to me.

As I stood midway between the almost vanished rick and the haggard wall, I heard a shout: 'there's one!' I turned around just in time to see Karl himself through the air and land on a rat, whose squeal sent a shiver down my spine. Meanwhile, a few mice scurried away to the safety of the stone walls.

By four o'clock, the work was completed. Where once stood the two majestic stacks of corn, there was now a big rick of golden straw which would be used for the animals bedding during the winter and for any repairs that John might have to do on the thatch roof.

With the tractor and threshing machine gone next door to Devaneys, the fowl claimed the haggard as their own, as they began a frenzied search for the myriad of grains hidden within the heaps of chaff. The din they created was something fearful as they clawed and pecked away, like a bunch of children having the most wonderful time at a birthday party.

The majority of the men climbed over the low, stone wall separating our farm from our neighbours, the Devaneys. But I noticed the two brothers, Pat and Batty Burke, were not amongst them. Instead, they walked past Devaney's house without so much as looking at it. I made a mental note to ask my aunt about this, as I rushed to join the *"meithal"*.

That Thresher stayed in the townland for almost a whole week, operating every day except on Sunday and the feast of St. Martin, who, tradition has it, was martyred by being crushed in a mill.

Martin was a native of what is today modern Hungary. He is best remembered as the soldier who, on a bitterly cold night, took off his cloak and using his sword sliced the garment in half, giving one half to the beggar who had called out to him for alms. That night, the beggar appeared to Martin in a dream; but as a figure surrounded with shining glory - Christ himself, still wearing the half of Martin's cloak. Our Lord reminded Martin of his words:

"I was naked and you clothed me..."

If you ever visit the French city of Amiens you will see that the sight of his encounter with the beggar is still marked to this day.

The soldier was converted to Christianity and became a priest; eventually being chosen to become the Bishop of Tours. But considering himself unworthy of such an honour, he tried to hide himself amongst a flock of geese. But his presence in their midst made the geese cackle excitedly, thereby revealing the bishop elect's hiding place to the townspeople who had come looking for him. That is why in many parts of Europe to this day his feast is still celebrated with the killing of a goose. In Ireland, however, people make do with a hen, whose blood is then sprinkled on the four corners of the house as a protection against evil.

Fuelled by the abundant supply of grain now available to them, the hens and ducks began producing great quantities of eggs. The turkeys and geese soon looked heavier. Poor things, I thought, you have only another few weeks left in this world.

With whatever money my aunt got from the sale of eggs to the travelling shops that called to the house, she purchased such things as: jam loaves of shop bread, creamery butter; a packet of biscuits - especially fig rolls - St. Bruno tobacco for John and a bar of chocolate for me. I never recall her buying anything for herself, except the occasional spool of the thread or writing paper and envelopes.

In the knowledge that across the road stood a plentiful supply of turf, John was deaf to his wife's pleas to be careful in case he burned the house down. At night the heat was so intense that the 'ramblers' had to sit well back in a semicircle, to escape being scorched by the intense heat from the huge fire that John had arranged for the night.

At one time, nearly every district in rural Ireland had a 'rambling' house, where the locals would gather, on a winter's night. During the course of the evening each visitor would contribute to the evening's entertainment by engaging in political debate or talking about times past or football or boxing. Very occasionally they would play a game of cards.

Amongst the men Martin Carroll was my favourite. He came from that part of the townland given the nickname, *"The Six Counties"*, because it was cut off from the rest of the townland by the length of the back road. Although more than 70 years of age, Martin didn't look a day over 60, and with his cheerful, red countenance, white moustache and fine head of white hair, he could easily have played the part of Santa Claus with the minimum of make-up. A jolly man, he would from time to time during the course of the evening, leap to his feet to give a brief exhibition of step dancing, or taking hold of the broom use it to perform some trick.

Another character was 'Niger' Tighe. Small and dark, he had a high-pitched voice which, when he became excited during the many heated discussions about football or politics, became a squeal; making it almost impossible to understand what he was saying. He was separated from his wife, who lived, along with one of their two sons, with a bachelor brother, while her husband lived with his unmarried sister and the other son.

The third 'Rambler' worth mentioning was James Mullaney, who farmed the land on the town's side of our farm. He was still single and shared the family home with his mother and three sisters, all spinsters. One of them, Alice, had returned from that United States, and with the money she had earned there built a new house at the start of their 'boreen.' She also bought a two story house in the town as an investment, which was currently rented out to Sgt. Blighe of the police. Katie, the youngest of the three women, was a fine traditional musician, who, as earlier mentioned, often teamed up with John for the house dances during the summer.

Although around 60 years of age, James had been keeping company for at least 10 years with Katie Leonard, a Grand Aunt of my friend, Tommy Ford. I myself had seen them on a couple of occasions during the summer, walking down the road with a gap of three or 4 feet between them. When they arrived at Mullaney's 'boreen,' James turned right while Katie just kept on walking.

By nine o'clock every chair in the house was occupied. Aunt Nellie retired to the small room where she wrote to her sisters in America or worked on a patchwork quilt. When she emerged at around 11 o'clock, that was the signal for the visitors to bring the night's 'rambling' to a close. Once satisfied that they had all departed and had gone a sufficient distance from the house, Aunt Nellie would order me to: 'Go out and count the stars;' her way of telling me to urinate before going to bed.

My own contribution to the 'rambling,' was to sit at one corner of the fireplace and read whatever newspaper happened to be in the house; even if it were a week old. The sports pages containing news and reports about boxing were of special interest to the men, whose resulting discussion sometimes became a little heated.

One night I listened intently as the troubles occupied their minds for the best part of an hour. John McGowan and some of the men present had all taken an active part in the struggle for Irish Independence. For all of their work in cutting roads, pulling down telephone lines and burning down the local Coastguard Station, the Irish Government awarded them a pension of a couple of shillings a week and a medal.

The attack on the Coastguard Station was of particular interest to me, as it was in its grounds that Joan had spent her summer holiday in the small house belonging to pilot McKeown.

During the discussion I learned that on the night of August 27 1920, up to a 100 men had surrounded the Station; the garrison oft ten men and one woman put up no resistance, except for one man who fired a few defiant shots. The captives were then moved to the nearby farmhouse belonging to the Tighe family. The Station's store of twenty rifles, twenty revolvers and six thousand rounds of ammunition were removed, along with the furniture and personal effects of the garrison, before the building was set on fire and completely destroyed.

During the civil war that followed the signing of the treaty with Britain, I heard how anti-treaty forces raided the many branches of the National bank and around £50,000 had been stolen. Prior to that 331 post offices had also been raided between 23 March and 22 April 1922. In a recent conversation with the noted authority on the IRA, Tim Pat Coogan, he referred to such raids as 'balaclava banking.'

It was the unanimous opinion of the 'ramblers' that many of those who held the rank of officer pocketed some of the proceeds from those raids, and after a gap of some years were able to set up in a variety of businesses. The name of a local man was mentioned, as well as a number in Ballina, who became shop owners and other types of enterprises. Such conduct on the part of the anti-treaty officers, I learned, was not confined just to Ballina: the towns of Ballyhaunis and Castlebar in County Mayo, and the town of Sligo itself were also included.

From time to time the talk centred on the recent war. I was interested to learn that the men had often seen the flashes of gun fire on the horizon as German submarines attacked British convoys. When a blaze lit up the night sky, the onlookers knew that another ship had been torpedoed. A good deal of timber from the sunken vessels washed up on the shore and on the Enniscrone strand. The farmers used some of it to make gates. On one occasion, a boatload of frightened survivors came in at the pier and its occupants billeted in the local school, until arrangements were made to transfer them to the County Hospital. One interesting fact I learned during those nights was that there were sixteen bachelors and ten spinsters living in our townland of twenty two dwellings.

Apart from the 'ramblers,' John 'Nancy' visited us twice a year. John had no home and roamed the area, walking summer and winter in his bare feet. As a result they were almost black and their skin was like that of a Rhinoceros. He had no regard for paper money or silver coins and would accept only copper ones.

John 'Nancy' was born in the village of Glenree, situated in a picturesque u-shaped valley about three to four miles long and running in a westerly direction from the Ox Mountains. It is situated about 2 miles North West of the village of Bonniconlon. His proper name was John Durcan, but to distinguish him from his immediate namesake also John Durcan, he was called John and Nancy being his mother's Christian name. When his mother died, John paid no heed to his little house and small patch of land and eventually ran away from his home and never returned to it.

When he visited a house, like my aunts, he liked a mug of hot tea and a big slice of soda bread with plenty of butter. And when available, he would enjoy a bottle of porter. One peculiar habit he had if he stayed overnight in a house was that he would not sleep in a bed but preferred to lie on the cement floor in front of the fire.

After I wrote a piece about John Nancy for the Western People Newspaper, a Margaret Ensley Smith, then living in Leeds, sent the following poem to The Western People:

> *"He walked along roads; no one gave him a home*
> *His lovely brown hair, he could never comb;*
> *The sky was his blanket; the ground was his bed,*
> *Sometimes when in Currower he would sleep in a shed.*
> *How on earth did he live just on tea and dry bread?*
> *With no shoes on his feet and his head bare,*
> *He'd bathe them in salt water then bow his dear head*
> *Then my mother would give him his tea and dry bread.*
> *John Nancy was happy he had nothing to fear.*
> *John Nancy has gone now, God give him at home*
> *For as long as I live I'll remember his name.*
> *He would call on an evening as the rosary was said*
> *With his poor feet all blue and oh, how they bled,*
> *With no shoes on his feet and no cap on his head,*
> *John Nancy, God rest you, our farewells are said".*

One of the enjoyable experiences of that first winter was to sit with my aunt in front of the dying fire *"toasting our toes"*, as she described it, until perhaps 2.a.m: John having gone to bed hours ago. It was on one of those nights she told me this story of how her sister-in-law informed her that Tim O'Neill, her husband, had found a *"French Letter"* in his fishing nets. 'But what good was that, sure Tim can't read French,' Aunt Nelly said. There was just enough of a smile around her mouth to indicate that she knew now the purpose of the balloon like item scooped from the sea.

Only when the fire was too low to keep us warm, would we reluctantly get up from our chairs to go to bed. Aunt Nellie's last task of the day was to rake the coals and bury them in the pit of ashes over which the fire was built. The next morning, these embers would be used to bring the fire to life for another day. In this sense the fire in the cottage was eternal. And it was not unknown, I discovered, for a fire to be kept alive in this manner from generation to generation. In addition, if a move was made from the old house to a new one, the fire was brought along with everything else in the house.

David Thomson in his excellent book: *"Nairn in Darkness and Light"* writes:

"I myself having stayed in the houses of the poor in the Highlands and Islands of Scotland, have seen that domestic fire itself was holy. Like the sacred fires kept alight by the Vestal Virgins regions and by the Parsee priests of India, the domestic fire was never allowed to go out. To revive it every morning from the embers of the night before, to keep it alive from the date the house was built, often for hundreds of years. To carry the burning embers to a new house when the old one falls down, still has, even now, a meaning derived from religions older than Christianity".

Lying curled up in my bed I could listen to my aunt reciting an ancient prayer:

"I save the seed of the fire tonight
And so may Christ save me;
On the top of the house let Mary,
In the middle let Bridget be.
Let eight of the mightiest angels
Round the throne of the Trinity,
Protect this house and its people
Till the dawn day shall be".

That supplication finished and satisfied that we were not going to be burned alive in our beds, she began a long list of prayers that culminated in her shaking holy water around the house and over me, especially me, all the while invoking all the saints in heaven to protect us as we slept.

With the threshing out of the way, there was little work to be done until the following spring. For apart from feeding cattle and cleaning out the stables, the only other job that occupied John was repairing the ditches and rebuilding some of the stone walls around the farm.

My own personal task was to visit the potato pits in the field behind the fort. I always brought our dog Karl with me and armed myself with a sturdy stick. If I found traces of rats having succeeded in boring their way through to the crop, John and I would return that evening to set a couple of metal traps on the visible trail of the rodents.

One morning I approached the two pits with more than my usual caution. As I drew near them, Karl ran ahead barking excitedly. It was then that I heard for the first time the defiant squeal of a tapped rat. I stopped. My heart pounded against my chest. Meanwhile, the dog was making tentative lunges at the victim, causing it to squeal even more loudly. I moved a few fearful steps nearer and got my first glimpse of the rat. It was big. 'Karl' I ordered. The dog ceased its barking but continued to stand and growl menacingly within a few feet of its prey. The rat, now aware of my own presence, turned its head to face me; it's small, yellow eyes full of venom. I was afraid. Karol, tired of waiting, made a sudden lunge at the trapped thing. Its attention momentarily diverted, gave me the opportunity to step forward and deliver a couple of heavy blows to its head. The dog came forward to sniff at the corpse lying bruised and bloodied amongst the debris of mud, straw and a few half-eaten potatoes.

At that time of the year, the killing of the pig was a major event. It was then that I learned at first-hand what the expression, *"to squeal like a pig"* meant. A neighbour helped John McGowan hold the animal, while the executioner hired for the job, used a small sledgehammer to stun the pig with a blow to its forehead. I, meanwhile, stood waiting with a basin in my hands, ready to catch the blood when the animal's throat was cut. Even in its stunned condition the pig struggled and squealed to escape its fate. But as its blood flowed red and warm into the basin, all its movements and squeals gradually ceased. A few last tremors ran through its legs. Then it was still.

That evening Aunt Nellie made sausages and puddings, using the animal's intestines as containers for the home - made mixture of blood mixed with oatmeal, onions, lard and seasoning. The intestines were to between eight and ten inches in length and sewn at one end before being a little over three quarters filled with the mixture, and then the other end sewn to complete the task. Some of this she shared with her immediate neighbours, - but not the O'Neill's, - who would reciprocate when it was their turn to kill a pig.

Three weeks before Christmas, we sold the turkeys and geese to Maughan's shop; keeping one of the geese for our own festive dinner. Part of the money from their sale went to reduce our grocery bill with the retailer; the balance was used by Aunt Nellie to buy a pair of warm knickers in the drapery shop.

Near to Christmas, and carrying a dozen eggs, I took the bus to Ballina. On this occasion, I walked up Morrison Terrace without the shyness of my first visit. Mrs. Conboy opened the door. 'Why, James, what a surprise,' she said; 'we were wondering if you would visit us before Christmas. Joan was just asking about you last night. She won't be home for another hour,' she told me as I followed her into kitchen.

'These are for you,' I said, shyly holding out the box of eggs.

Mrs. Conboy was upstairs in the back room when I heard the front door opening, then the living room door was flung wide and Joan stepped into the room. She stopped and stared at me with such a look of surprise that I couldn't help smiling. 'James!' She exclaimed, and it came quickly towards me. I stood up. 'Hello, Joan,' I said softly. She removed a glove and held out her hand. It felt warm and soft as I continued to hold it until the sound of her mother coming down the stairs made us separate.

When it was time for me to leave, Joan accompanied me to the door. 'Have you missed me?' She whispered, as she helped me on with my coat. I looked at the living room door 'yes,' I told her. 'I missed you too,' she said and gave me a quick peck on the cheek. I took her hand in mine and it gave it a gentle squeeze. 'See you on Christmas Eve,' I promised.

That first Christmas in Ireland was a revelation and a delight to me. It all began early on Christmas Eve, when I got on the packed bus for Ballina. The conversation all the way to our destination was animated and cheerful. I thought with a tinge of sadness, of my brother and sisters in Glasgow for whom this day and Christmas Day would be no different from any other day of their week.

The streets of Ballina were thronged with country people and with large numbers of men and women home from England and Scotland, all intent on finishing their shopping prior to crowding into one of the town's many bars, before catching their buses home to destinations around the counties of Sligo and Mayo.

Joan opened the door to me just as I was about to knock. 'I saw you passing by the window,' she said, making no attempt to hide her pleasure at seeing me again so soon. 'Mammy, James is here,' she called over her shoulder. 'I thought you weren't going to come,' she whispered, as she closed the door behind us. The house was sparkling, with every piece of brass and silver gleaming and the furniture and linoleum looking like new. A large cake stood on the dresser waiting to be iced; and I caught a glimpse of a huge turkey lying on the scullery table.

When Mrs. Conboy came in after collecting eggs from the six hens she kept in the turf shed at the bottom of the garden, I handed her the parcel from my hand containing a large soda scone sprinkled with generous amounts of currants and raisins.

Apart from having a cup of tea with Joan and me, Mrs. Conboy went busily about her preparations for Christmas. As I watched her quick movements around the house, while talking with her daughter, I had a sudden longing to be part of that family, to remain there with them instead of returning to Carrowhubbock. When I left two hours later, I carried with me a porter cake: Mrs. Conboy's gift to us.

On the homeward journey the bus was again crowded; in addition, every available space was utilised to accommodate the piles of parcels and boxes accompanying their owners to the thatched cottages which dotted the countryside between Ballina and Skreen. The animated conversations and laughter amongst the passengers was evidence that quite a lot of the men, and indeed some of their wives, had already begun to celebrate the Nativity.

As he collected our fares, the conductor entertained us with snatches of popular carols, ending with *"I'm Dreaming of a White Christmas"*, as the bus came to a halt in Enniscrone.

A few coloured Christmas lights hanging in Mary Rafter's two shop windows and a short string of them over in Hopkin's pub and the Pilot Bar, across the street, were an attempt to bring something of a Christmas spirit to the town. I turned my face into the stiff wind blowing in from the Atlantic, and headed homewards along the Cliff rd.

My aunt and John had just arrived home from their shopping and were emptying two large shopping bags, when I entered the kitchen. The fire was almost extinguished and the dismal light from the solitary paraffin lamp combined to dissipate the happiness I had felt all afternoon. For a brief moment the warmth and relative luxury, not to mention the presence of Joan, made me wish that I were back in 23 Morrison Terrace.

'That's a Christmas box from Mary Rafter,' I heard my aunt say as she held out a box for my inspection. Gifts from Maughan's, from whom John bought all his seed and fertilizers each spring, included a Madeira cake and a bottle of ginger wine. With all of these and a rich fruit cake from Aunt Linda in New York, it was obvious that there would be no shortage of something to eat with one's cup of tea for the next week.

Once John had the fire blazing again and the presents were visible around the kitchen, my temporary depression lifted a little. But I still couldn't dispel the memory of the time spent with Joan and her mother earlier that day, nor the cleanliness and warmth of their home.

After supper, I helped to put lighted candles in each of the three front windows of the house. These, I was told, were to welcome the Holy Family if by any chance they happened to be passing by. When I went out with John to bed down our animals for the night, I could see many pinpricks of light dotting the darkness of the hills of County Mayo across Killala Bay.

In honour of the night that was in it, we gave all the animals an extra helping of fodder. Was it my imagination, or did the animals themselves know what we were about to celebrate? There was just something about all of them as they lay on their straw beds chewing the cud or stood looking inquisitively at us, which gave one the impression that they knew more than we mere mortals did: after all weren't they present on that first Christmas Night?

Of that first Christmas in Ireland, the one thing that stands out in my memory is the simplicity with which the country people celebrated the birth of Christ; with most of the emphasis placed on the religious aspect of the feast.

In the darkness of Christmas morning, I joined up with many of our neighbours as we made our way to the chapel for the first mass of Christmas. The building was almost full by the time we got there. Every available light and the extra candles around the sanctuary illuminated dark corners that had never been seen since the previous Christmas. The choir, trained by Mother Loyola, was singing *"Come to the Manger"*, as I knelt down alongside my aunt near the back of the chapel: John had gone in the 'poor door,' as he called it. Around us were mostly people from the town whom I recognised but whose names I still didn't know. Because of the large numbers of communicants, the mass took longer than usual. So when Father O'Connor said 'Ita Missa Est, *"Go, the Mass is over"*,' there was almost a stampede from the men standing in a group behind us to get out into the fresh air for a quick drag of their Sweet Afton cigarettes, before heading home for a much-needed breakfast; as all who had received communion that morning had been fasting from the night before.

For our Christmas dinner we ate the goose, with cabbage, turnip and mashed potato; for a drink, we consumed Maughan's ginger wine. Afterwards, the three of us sat in front of one of John's huge fires, with cups of tea and chunks of cake in our hands. The only decorations were the Christmas cards standing on the mantelpiece or propped up on the dresser. When these had begun arriving earlier in the month, John would call out from his chair, as his wife read out who they were from, 'Any money in them?' When the answer was invariably 'No,' he would tell her 'they were no damn good and to throw them in the fire.'

The big event of St. Stephen's Day was the annual hunt of the North Mayo Harriers through the fields of Carrowhubbock and along the shore to Lacken and beyond.

I stood at the kitchen door watching the horses and ponies go clattering past, the hounds, except for a couple that made a temporary diversion into our field across from the house, obeyed the shrill instructions of the *"Whipper In"*. Altogether I counted 42 animals trot by towards Orsmby's fort and their first obstacle. For a boy who had spent his childhood in the shadow of Govan's shipyards, it was a spectacle that I never thought I would see. My aunt pointed out any of the riders that she recognized.

We hadn't long sat down again, when there came a loud knock on the door. 'That will be the *"Wren Boys"*,' Aunt Nellie said, rising from her chair. I followed her to the door. Dressed in a variety of clothing, mostly women's, stood four young boys of around my own age, their faces disguised by veils. They began to sing:

> *"The Wren, the wren, the king of all birds.*
> *St Stephen, he was caught in the bush,*
> *And we have come here to your honour.*
> *Give us a treat to bury that Wren.*
> *And you know what that means,*
> *Don't you?"*

'Get me my purse from the dresser, Martin.' 'Now, there's sixpence for ye,' Aunt Nellie told our visitors.

'Thank you, Mam,' they said in unison, then turned and walked down the path singing, *"the Wren, the Wren…"*

What an easy way to make some money, I thought to myself.

Recently I read in a book, *"The Mayo Bingham's"*, that at the battle of the Boyne in 1690, while King William of Orange's men were resting at night, soldiers of King James crept up on them under the cover of darkness and would have overcome them had not the noise of a Wren fluttering about inside a drum alerted the drummers. The alarm was sounded and the battle was won by King William. Since then, the bird has become a symbol of 'bad luck' for Catholics and is remembered on St. Stephen's day to remind them of all past martyrs.

When I heard that the local branch of the Pioneer Total Abstinence Association was going to hold its annual social in January, I decided to become a member in order to attend the function in the Marine Ballroom.

Wearing my Probationer's pin, I hardly left the dance floor that night, as I guided my partner, Sheila Dunleavy, around the floor in almost every dance. Sheila, who had a nice smile and warm personality, was the daughter of Guard Dunleavy to whom the local farmers had given the Irish name *"Buachallan"*: the yellow Ragwort that grew in all the fields and was illegal. It was the guard's job to cycle around the countryside checking that the farmers were controlling the weed's growth.

Because of our constant presence together for most of the night, the adults present must have passed some comment. If they did, then Sheila and I were blissfully unaware of the interest being taken in us. Sheila was instrumental, at a later date, in having me chosen as goalkeeper for the Enniscrone Youth's Gaelic football team. Later on in life she married and lives in Co Wicklow. Her brother, Sean, who lives and works in Dublin, I have met most summers which he spends in his mobile home situated in the 'burrows' of Enniscrone. He tells me that Sheila always asks about me upon his return to Dublin.

The long, dark days of winter passed slowly, but I didn't mind as more new experiences came my way. I especially loved exercising the horse on the roads around the townland and up into the town itself. Sam was a gentle animal but nevertheless, John always advised me never to trust a horse; adding a saying of the deceased Major Mullaney: *"That no one should ever trust a horse's hooves until they're buried beneath the clay"*. The Major, retired as a Veterinary Surgeon from the British army, had committed suicide in the sand dunes by cutting his throat. Another winter pastime I was introduced to was going out in the evening with other boys to set rabbit traps; and before the sun had yet risen from behind the Ox Mountains, to crunch our way over the frost-covered fields, our footsteps sounding as if we were walking on broken glass, to check them for any kill. In a way I was glad that the snares were always empty.

By St. Patrick's Day the 'rambling' had come to an end for another year, as the farmers busied themselves preparing for the sowing of the crops. Because of the smallness of their holdings, each farmer teamed up with a neighbour to have a pair of horses for ploughing.

John's partner was *"Nigger"* Tighe. But before we put the animals to work, John and I had to take Sam to the Forge for a set of new shoes.

This small building in which the blacksmith 'Black' Eddie Dowd worked was situated down a slope off the main street and behind the Atlantic Hotel. I was fascinated to see a blacksmith ply his trade, especially to observe how he hammered home the nails into the horse's hooves, puffing and blowing as he did so. In between these exertions, he spoke soothingly to the animal. But before giving the it the new shoes, the blacksmith first used cutters to remove any surplus hoof growth and then ran a rasp over it to ensure that it was level. Behind him glowed the fire in which he softened the metal to enable him to work the new shoe into the shape he desired. Satisfied that he had got it right, his next action was to plunge the shoe into a trough of water for about a minute to cool it down, before driving home seven nails to secure the shoe to the animal's hoof.

When he had finished with Sam, the blacksmith and John left me in charge of the horse while they climbed the slope to the hotel. It was nearly 30 minutes later before both men reappeared. In the meantime, two more clients had arrived with horses and were waiting patiently for the blacksmith's return.

On the way home, I asked John about the small, round holes in the Forge's roof. They were, he told me, caused by the Black and Tan's indiscriminate firing one day as they drove through the town. When the ploughing began, both horses were so experienced that, despite John's poor eyesight, the furrows were reasonably straight. Occasionally, I took over from him when we moved into the 'far field,' where the land did not contain so many stones and had a deeper and richer soil. When the time came to do the harrowing, John entrusted me with the job on my own.

"Only a man harrowing clods
In a slow silent walk
With an old horse that stumbles and nods
Half asleep as they stalk".
"The Breaking of Nations"
by Thomas Hardy.

In following the plough or harrow for a whole day, one must have walked anything up to 15 miles in that time. But though tired when evening came, I always felt relaxed and happy in myself as Sam and I walked slowly back to the house in the gathering dusk; sometimes just as the Angelus bell rang out from the chapel in the town, recalling the words of a poem I had come across in St.Gerard's:

"The curfew tolls the knell of parting day,
The lowing herd walks slowly or the lea.
The ploughman homeward plods his weary way
And leaves the world to darkness and to me".

The two cows dropped their calves into the world with the minimum of help from John and his wife. I was an interested but fascinated bystander watching John tie a rope round the calves two feet once it they emerged from its mother, and then pull ever so gently until the new arrival lay wet and shivering on a big bed of straw. I was old enough to realise that this was, in a way, how I myself had come into the world.

The bucket of the cow's 'beastings' - the first milk after calving - Aunt Nelly threw out in a field behind the house; the afterbirth she hung up on the whitethorn bush that stood on the highest point on the farm: this was to placate the 'wee folk.'

Having slept during the summer and all that winter in the same bedroom as the married couple, I became aware of what took place between a husband and wife, but it wasn't until I accompanied John to have one of the cows serviced by the local bull, that I actually saw how the sex act was performed. While John stood in Tony Leonard's field behind the chapel, doing his best to restrain the restive cow, I climbed the hill to let the farmer know that we were there. As I approached the ivy-covered house, I could hear our cow bellowing at the bottom of the hill. 'Tell John I'll be with him in a couple of minutes,' Tony Leonard said.

Standing alongside John I watched with trepidation the approach of the bull, *"Frankfort the Third"*, Though he looked ferocious at a distance, as he drew closer I was surprised at how small he was. But it was the red, moist, carrot-like thing protruding from underneath the animal's belly, and growing bigger by the second, that really caught my attention.

By now the cow was frantic, turning and twisting and doing her best to break free from John's restraining hold. The bull's owner led his animal up onto a low earthen bank to the rear of the cow, and then pulled aside the cow's tail. Satisfied after a few stiffs, *"Frankfort the Third"* reared up on its hind legs, and spread-eagled himself on the cow's back and began thrusting and thrusting into her with ever increasing force until at last he gave one mighty plunge which moved the cow a few feet forward. Satiated, the animal slowly lowered itself of its mate, his member still swollen and dripping semen onto the grass, and was led away to await his next client.

As I had looked forward to my first Christmas in Ireland, so now it was with anticipation that I awaited the arrival of Easter, 1946; especially since my aunt had reliably informed me that the Sun danced on Easter Sunday morning. 'But have you seen it?' I queried. 'Many a time.' 'I've seen it too,' John added. 'It dances for joy at the Resurrection,' my aunt explained.

Rubbing the sleep from my eyes, I awakened to the touch of a hand on my shoulder. 'It's a fine morning, thanks be to God,' Aunt Nellie said. John was already up and kneeling on the bed, peering out of the small, back window; his wife, clad only in a medium length cotton vest, knelt beside him. She was right, it was a fine morning. There wasn't a cloud in the sky as I took my place alongside her on the bed. Amazingly for such a beautiful morning, there was no birdsong to be heard.

'Look, the sun is coming up,' she exclaimed. I looked towards the Fort. Sure enough, there was the first edge of the sun peeping over the Fort's rim. I watched expectantly as the orb began to inch its way ever so slowly higher and higher. Then just as I began to think that I had been woken up for nothing, the sun suddenly shot high up into the sky as if propelled by a rocket. I gave an involuntary gasp. Aunt Nellie squeezed my arm reassuringly. To my amazement, the sun began to cavort all over the sky, as I continued to gaze wide-eyed at what I was seeing. For a moment I thought that I was still asleep and must be dreaming. But as I watched I knew that the performance in the sky was real alright. The sun was now at the top of one of its crazy cartwheels. It stopped for a second or two before plunging earthwards. 'Aunty Nellie,' I cried out in terror. 'It's all right, Martin, just watch,' she said reassuringly. Then just when it seemed that our planet was doomed, the sun very slowly came to a halt and took up its original position above the Fort. 'Now, what did I tell you,' my aunt said, making no attempt to hide the note of triumph in her voice. What could I say? I just smiled and climbed back into my bed. Before falling asleep I heard that glorious singing of countless birds.

What the atheist, Richard Dawkins, will make of this, heaven only knows. In his book, *"The God Delusion"* he dismisses the occurrence by the sun at Fatima, Portugal, in 1917, when a similar celestial display took place to convince people that the Virgin Mary had really been appearing to three child visionaries.

Mr. Dawkins' incredulous attempt to dismiss the miraculous nature of the event that morning is not only feeble, but an insult to the many members of the International Press and the many thousands of people who were unbiased witnesses. *"If you have had such an experience, you may well find yourself believing firmly that it was real. But don't expect the rest of us to take your word for it".* Page 92 *"The God Delusion".* What arrogance, you might well ask?

But one must in, Christian charity, make allowance for the Atheist Mr. Dawkins. For if he doesn't believe in the existence of God, how can he accept that such a being can intervene and suspend the very laws that He created?

Another matter that caught my attention in Dawkins' book is on the dedication page, where he uses this quotation: 'Isn't it enough to see that a garden is beautiful without having to believe that there are fairies at the bottom of it too? 'My, my, Mr. Dawkins, may we not ask the obvious question as to how the garden became beautiful in the first place? The gardener must be very upset at not receiving the praise he so deserved for his creation. But then, Mr. Dawkins doesn't believe in 'creation.' Things just happen.

Finally, a last comment on this brief flirtation with Mr. Dawkins: he dismisses the conversion of the renowned atheist, Anthon Flew, to a 'believer' in *"some sort of deity"* as being that of an *"Old Man".* So, in Mr.Dawkins' weird mind, a renowned philosopher loses his mental capabilities overnight and becomes *"An old man"* without the ability to reason anymore. When Mr.Dawkins cannot come up with an explanation to support his argument, he resorts to ridicule.

English poet Thomas Traherne wrote: *"Those whose Eyes are Sealed up with Rust, whose Dirty Hearts are filled with Earth and Interposing Grit, they cannot see Him"*. Might not that be the problem with Mr.Dawkins?

As the days grew longer, so then did the hours we spent in the fields, which were being rapidly prepared for the sowing of the crops. But first, we had to transport 'dung' which had accumulated from the stables. Using the ass and cart, John and I've moved it to the two back fields to await the opening of the potato, cabbage and turnip drills. In the meantime, we put a light scattering on the meadow to promote it's growth. At a later stage fertilisers would be added to all the crops. Once the potato drills were opened, John gave me the task of spreading the manure along the length of each drill, while he set to work to cut the seed potatoes into individual sections, making certain that there was an eye in each one. In the planting, we placed them about seven inches apart. At the end of the day, we harnessed Sam to the plough and covered them.

To sow the cereal crops, John summoned the help of Jimmy Tighe, *"Nigger's"* son, who did the job with a 'fiddle:' so called because the equipment, was made up of a small, wooden box and a canvas bag containing the seeds, which were then scattered in a wide arc by means of the bow that Jimmy moved horizontally back and forward like a talented violin player. When the job was finished, I moved into the field with the horse and harrow to cover the newly sown seed with a light sprinkling of soil. Once the crops were in the ground, John and I took on the next job in the farming calendar: the cutting of the turf. Again, the donkey transported us to the bog. My first task was to go to the spring well for the day's supply of water. While I was away, John set to work lighting our fire.

Before we got round to cutting the turf, one had to clear the 'scraws' of heather from the top of the turf bank; this was done by using a hay knife to cut the top into sections that would easily come away when the spade was slid underneath them, to reveal the dark, brown, soapy peat. The depth of a turf bank was measured in 'spits:' the length of an average sod of turf. John's two biggest banks were four 'spit' in depth; the third one, whose turf was almost as black and as hard as coal, was only two 'spit' deep. I took a couple of turns at using the 'slean' - a type of spade with a wing on one side. But by early every afternoon, my wrists were killing me so much from the unaccustomed labour that I had to return to spreading the sods instead. But even this took its toll on my weakened wrists.

Despite all the farm work, the boys of Carrowhubbock and I still found time to meet in the evenings for an occasional game of football, or if we had worked hard that day, just to sit on a wall and talk about nothing in particular, until it was time to go indoors. It was on one of these evenings that I had a fight with Peter O'Neill, John's nephew. Like all such happenings, it is difficult to say how it began or who began it. All I remember is deciding that the fight had run its course and lowered my guard only to be knocked to the ground by a vicious and cowardly punch on my right eye. But from the start it was no contest, with my opponent towering above my meagre 5'3" inches.

When Aunt Nellie saw the damage done to my eye, she rushed up to O'Neills and berated Tim O'Neill and his son for attacking her beloved nephew. John said nothing. But I could see out of my one good eye, that he was angry about the affair. For my part, I knew that the O'Neill's hated me because, up to my arrival, they were certain that Peter would inherit the farm from his uncle.

During a spell of fine weather in June, my aunt and I began whitewashing and painting the exterior of the house in preparation for the coming holiday season, when she hoped that she would have as many visitors as the previous year The barn too, now empty of grain, turnips and assorted debris which had accumulated during the winter, was cleaned out and given a coat of whitewash. John, meanwhile, was busily thinning the turnips; with his poor eyesight, he had to rely mainly on touch to perform this task.

The turf had been long enough on the ground for us to spend a few days 'footing' it: gathering individual sods and propping them up against one another to promote the drying process still further. It was backbreaking work and hard on my tender fingers. Despite

My mother Elizabeth Gordon(nee Hackson)

After my baptism, being held my father's lovely niece, Margaret Gordon.

A bonnie wee bairn.

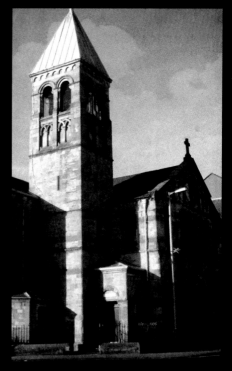

St. Anthony's Chapel, Govan.

Aunt Annie and my sisters Betty, Sadie and I.

Granddad James Hackson.

Govan Road.

riel view of the shipyard district of Govan.

Pearce Institute

Here I am in Ireland alongside our stack of turf.

Dad and John McGowan digging up the spuds.

African Mission's College, Cork.

Enniscrone United. 1957.

oan, her father George and I, sailing down the Moy river to Bartra island.

oan and her mother, Madelaine.

Joan Conboy and a young clerical student. Circa 1953.

The Pallottine college Gaelic football team 1956. I am the goalkeeper.

In the play, "Tons of Money". I am the actor with the moustache.

Ordination Sunday, 12th. June, 1960.

The breakfast table that morning.

With a group of Parishioners at Catholic Stage Guild Ball in the Dorchester Hotel London.

the tiredness and pain, the bog was still a wonderful place to be on a fine summer's day. I had not been in Ballina since Christmas, but had not forgotten Joan. Indeed, I was counting the days until the August, now just six weeks away, when I would welcome her back to Enniscrone and a resumption of the previous year's relationship Excited at the prospect, I just had to call and see her and discuss our plans.

During the visit to Morrison Terrace, Mrs. Conboy told me that after the summer holidays Joan would be boarding at Gortnor Abbey, on the shores of Lough Conn, the convent school run by the same order of nuns as in Enniscrone. Joan and I had barely two minutes to ourselves; but we did manage a quick kiss in the hall as I left to catch the bus. Like me, she too couldn't wait for August to arrive, where the family would occupy the same house as last year.

The final important task John and I had to do was to spray the potatoes: in the moist climate of Ireland, this was vital if the crop was not to be damaged, or indeed destroyed completely, by blight. Firstly, we had to fill two large wooden barrels with water, already standing in the horse cart, and then cover their mouths with sacks to prevent as much of the contents as possible from splashing out, while the cart made its way to the potato field. Once there, John made up a mixture with soda crystals and bluestone. I then poured this concoction into the sprayer strapped on his back like a rucksack. Shoulder straps and a waist band held it in position; attached to its left hand side was a handle that John moved up and down to direct a fine spray on to the crops green foliage by means of the copper pipe and a rubber tube that he held in his right hand. At the end of the operation, light, blue spots covered John's clothes and face.

On one of the hottest Sunday of the year, I joined a group of the lads from the town in an expedition to the 'burrows.' Our purpose was to seek out courting couples and to spy on their activity. It was not long before we encountered a man and woman in their late twenties dressed in swimming costumes and passionately engaged in their amorous activity. It was only when the woman, who until then had been on top of the man but now turned over onto her back and looked up at the ridge above, did the couple realise that eight pairs of eyes had been watching them. We scattered as the man came running angrily after us.

Aunt Annie arrived from Glasgow accompanied by her neighbour and workmate, Peggy Gray: the mother of my companion in the Govan graveyard. The first thing Annie told me, as we walked from the bus, was that she was taking me back to Glasgow with her at the end of July. When I protested and said that daddy wanted me to remain in Enniscrone, she replied that he didn't mind one way on the other. When I got Aunt Nellie alone I told her that terrible news. She was furious: 'He has no spunk,' she said angrily.

For the next two weeks I went about as a man condemned to death. I thought of running away; but to where? And what about Joan? I couldn't bring myself to call and say goodbye to her. I even asked Peggy Gray what I should do, after I came upon her unexpectedly one morning as she crouched down pissing on the spot where we had piled the stable manure during the winter.

'Martin,' she cried out with embarrassment.

'Sorry, Mrs Gray,' I mumbled. But instead of retracing my steps, I simply turned away to look at the barn wall and waited until she had finished and pulled up her nickers. My face was burning. Now I have seen both mother and daughter with their knickers down, I thought.

'Mrs. Gray, will you walk back the fields with me, I want to ask you something?' She looked at me suspiciously. 'It's about going back to Glasgow,' I added, as she gave me a suspicious look.

The morning I left Enniscrone, the fog that enveloped the resort did nothing to assuage my sadness. Peggy Gray had been of no assistance; well it was naive of me to expect her to be on my side: she was, after all, my Glasgow aunt's friend. I thought of Joan arriving in two days time only to find me gone. What was she going to think of me, leaving without saying goodbye?

'Be sure and write to Joan, she's very fond of you,' were Aunt Nellie's last words to me, as I walked away from the house. I fought hard to restrain the tears.

As the 8 o'clock bus to Sligo came to a halt outside Eamon Rafter's pub, the Pilot Bar, I thought of the year that I had spent in Enniscrone as part of a small community: I even had a nickname: "Scotty". But above all else I had fallen in love with the most adorable girl. Now I was leaving all that behind me. 'It's not fair,' I almost shouted in anguish, as I boarded the bus ahead of the two women whom I now regarded as my enemies.

When the bus neared the top of Cowel's Hill, I turned around in my seat to have one last look at Enniscrone. There was still no sign of the weather clearing. But I knew that by noon at the latest, the sun would emerge to disperse the mist and that the waters of Killala Bay would sparkle in its light. A great sob rose within me: 'Joan,' I whispered. Like my father 23 years previously, I too was leaving with a broken heart to make the same journey to Glasgow.

A Glasgow Interlude

Upon my return to Glasgow, I discovered that the year spent in Ireland, and more especially my meeting Joan, now made me look at my native city with a jaundiced eye. It was no longer the exciting playground of my childhood. I had experienced a vision of what life offered in another land, and I had fallen in love.

"We love but once, for once only are we perfectly equipped for loving: we may appear to ourselves to be as much in love at other times-so with a day in September, though it be six hours shorter, is seen as hot as one in June. And on how that first true love-affair will shape, depends the pattern of our lives".

Cyril Connolly's "The Unquiet Grave".

Granddad was naturally pleased to have me back again with him; so was Annie. Uncle Jimmy, now a foreman in Fairfield's shipyard, suggested that I become an apprentice welder. I knew that as a Freemason he would be in a position to advance my career once I entered the yard. I politely declined the offer and instead went to the labour exchange and was given a card to attend an interview for an office boy's job with a company at Shieldhall. The two men, whom I met in an upstairs office overlooking the docks, questioned me on my time in Ireland and then asked me what schools I had gone to in Glasgow. When I said St. Anthony's and St. Gerard's, a look passed between them. I didn't get the job.

The next interview was at the Clyde foundry, Helen Street. Again, the vacancy was that of an office boy; this time in the foundry's progress department. The manager who interviewed me was Mr. Ninian Lapsley: a tall, slightly stooped figure, he was kindness personified during the 20 minutes or so I was with him. I was given the job at a salary of four pounds a week and told to start work the following Monday at 9 a.m., at which time I would join the other three men and three women whose task it was to ensure that work in the foundry moved smoothly through all its various stages of production.

My main task was to visit the foundry twice daily with a list of castings, check on their current state in the production line and then write up a report on standard index cards which were already illustrated with drawings of the objects in question.

Amongst the men in the office was a handsome young man who had flown a Spitfire during the North African campaign. The two others had also been in the war, but they never talked about their experiences. Of the three women, Mr Lapsley's secretary, Mary, was the nicest to me. Even in her mature years, she was still very attractive looking and with a warm, cheerful personality to match. Her desk was alongside mine, which made it easy for me to seek help whenever I encountered a problem with my work. But a tall, thin-faced woman didn't like me, I believe, because I was a Catholic.

Walking around the factory in those first weeks, I recognised some of the Irish men among the workers, including my own father: only a few by name from meeting them after Mass on Sunday, as they stood talking across from the chapel. Many of them were natives of County Donegal.

When I made my afternoon visit to the foundry, it was always around the time that casting took place, and the giant containers of molten metal were being poured into the moulds lined up on the factory floor. The size of these moulds ranged from relatively small items to ones weighing a couple of tons, which would require correspondingly long, supportive, road transporters, or in some cases, a steam engine, to move them to another part of the country or to the docks for shipment overseas.

There was excitement in the office one morning, when one of the ex-soldiers gave us all a fright when he suddenly began to moan loudly and sway back and forward on his chair. The youngest of the three women screamed with fright and ran to the other end of the office where she stood sobbing, while Mr. Lapsley and Mr. Sneddon, the poor man's colleague, helped him to his feet and assisted him to the sick room.

After about a half an hour's absence, Mr Lapsley returned to the office and asked me to accompany the man in a company car that would take us to his home. Fortunately the man's wife was in the house when we got there and took charge of her husband. 'It's that war,' she said sadly, and thanked me for my help. A few days later she contacted Mr. Lapsley to say that her husband would not be returning to his job.

The staff in the office expected a new man to fill the vacancy. Instead, Mr. Lapsley gave the position to me and recruited a new office boy to take my place. I noticed that although I was going to do a man's work, there was no mention of my receiving a corresponding rise in wages. I think that soured my relationship with my employers. For from then on, I thought of little else but returning to Enniscrone and Joan.

I had little social life apart from attending the odd football game at St. Anthony's, Ibrox or Parkhead. Occasionally I went to one of the local cinemas. It was at the Vogue I saw the most talked about film for years: *"The Outlaw"*. The story didn't matter: it was the size of Jane Russell's breasts supported by a bra designed by Howard Hughes and their partial exposure up there on the screen that attracted audiences in their thousands.

The night I saw the film the cinema was packed. As the film rolled on at a languorous pace, I couldn't really understand what all the fuss was about. Sure what about it, I thought, if one could see a little bit more exposure than usual of a bigger than ordinary female breast. But there were two scenes in the film, however, that made me squirm a little in my seat. One was when the outlaw was ill and had to be kept warm at whatever cost. The character, played by Jane Russell, gallantly offers her services as a human hot-water bottle and climbs in beside the sick man. But it was the second scene that really stirred the audience. The outlaw finds himself in a dark barn with Jane Russell. In the darkness, he pins her to the ground. After seconds of struggle, one hears the woman's assailant threaten: *"If you don't lie still, I'll tear your dress off"*. Women squealed around me and in every part of the cinema, as if they themselves were somehow vicariously enduring the sexual assault being perpetrated on the actress.

In the succeeding months of 1947, I had become friendly with Reggie Fitzgerald, second son of the Janitor at St. Anthony's School, Reggie was around the same age as me, but was taller and heavier built than his new friend. His most striking feature was his thick, sensuous lips: an attribute he used to great effect with the opposite sex.

I accompanied him one night as part of a foursome that he had arranged. I don't know where he led us but I found myself with this girl in some back court, the two of us just standing there not knowing what was expected of us, while Reggie and his partner went off into the darkness. If we kissed, I can't remember doing so. With Joan still a vivid memory, I doubt whether even a chaste embrace was exchanged between the girl and me.

In early June, with the annual Glasgow Fair holiday looming nearer, I gave in my notice to Mr. Lapsley, who was clearly upset at the news of my impending departure. He told me that he had arranged for me to start attending the apprentice's school after the holidays. In that way, I would be able to progress up the management ladder within the company. I thanked him for all his kindness to me. - I thought especially of how he used to allow me to slip down to St. Anthony's Chapel to attend Mass on a Holyday of Obligation - and his interest in my future. I must admit that the thought of being given technical training with a view to entering the ranks of management was very tempting. But in the end, it was no contest against the attraction of living once again in Ireland and meeting Joan.

On the second Friday in July, I bade farewell to my colleagues in the office and sailed that night from the Broomielaw, accompanied by Reggie Fitzgerald. As the Burns and Laird steamer glided past the Govan Ferry landing stage, I saw granddad standing with his back to Harland and Wolff's Wall anxiously scanning the decks for a wave of my hand. When, I wondered, would I see him again, as he spotted me and raised his arm and I waved back. I could just about see him as a small speck as the ship approached Fairfield's shipyard. I turned my head away from my companion as a small tear defeated my efforts to control it.

On the overnight journey to Derry, Reggie wasted no time in trying to seduce a pretty young woman, urging me to do the same with her companion. But I wasn't interested in following his example. Instead, I found a quiet corner in the saloon and settled down for the long night ahead.

A Welcome Return

My aunt and John were overjoyed to see me again and gave a warm welcome to Reggie. 'You haven't grown very much, Martin,' was Aunt Nelly's comment the first moment we were alone. 5'4": no wonder a girl I knew from my school days and a sister of Reggie had both referred to me as *"Little Martin"*. I had not been conscious of my height until then; now it was something that irritated me. I was still only 16 years old, so there was plenty of time for me to add another few inches to my stature, I thought hopefully.

When I arrived in Ballina to visit Joan and her mother, I first called in to Lipton's to say hello to George Conboy, who, learning that I was on my way up to the house, gave me a small parcel of groceries for his wife. Joan opened the door and stood in the hall for a few seconds. 'James, it's you,' she eventually exclaimed with obvious delight. 'Hello, Joan,' I said, as she stepped aside to usher me into the living room.

Joan was changed: but in what way I couldn't say. Physically, she still looked the same; but there was a certain reticence in her manner that had not been there a year ago. She would be 15 years of age in two months time; perhaps that had something to do with the change in her, I thought, as I continued to answer the many questions about my year in Glasgow.

Before leaving, I learned that Mrs. Conboy was removing Joan from Gortnor Abbey, where she had spent the last year, and was sending her to a convent in Co Tipperary that had a good reputation for achieving excellent results in civil service examinations. For many years afterwards, Mother Loyola, who had taken a special interest in Joan during her time at the school, blamed Joan's mother for destroying her daughter's future life.

The following day Reggie Fitzgerald and I accompanied John to the bog to help clamp the turf. Also there on that same day was our neighbour, John Leonard, and his vivacious daughter, Peggy, who was then about 20 years of age. While I assisted both men to light the fire Peggy asked Reggie to go with her to the well.

When my help was no longer needed, and the water carriers had still not returned, I decided to go and meet them. Walking through the knee-high heather, I almost stumbled across the recumbent figures of Peggy and Reggie in a passionate embrace. Even though I was that close to them, they were so busy with what they were doing I was able to retrace my steps and wait until

I heard their voices and judged that they had completed their activity.

Within a few days of my return, I heard that Peter O'Neill was telling everybody he met that I had brought Reggie Fitzgerald as my bodyguard.

The Conboys came to Enniscrone for the month of August. But even though Joan and I did spend a good deal of time together, we never managed to recapture the experience of two years previously. I expect that being older we were more aware of our sexuality by then: not that I personally had any problem in that area. To me Joan was not someone who attracted me sexually. She was still the girl of 13 who pushed me into the sea and whose company I enjoyed more than anyone else. It was a great disappointment that we felt so shy with each other during those weeks, that we never exchanged even so much as one chaste kiss.

But one major event did it take place. One day, our mutual friend, Mary Kilcullen, challenged me as to what was really my true Christian name. Under pressure from her, I eventually had to admit that my first name was indeed Martin. From then on, that was how I came to be addressed. I didn't mind once I heard Joan pronouncing it. On her lips Martin sounded so musical, that I wondered why I had ever bothered discarding it in favour of my second name.

Amongst the 'canters' who stayed with us that year was Mrs Adams and her son, John. Another son was married in the home place, Carrowbehy, Co Roscommon, and the third son, Joe, was a priest ministering in the diocese of Alabama.

John Adams was about 35 years old and of a fun-loving disposition. While staying in the house, he used to get up to all sorts of tricks with the women. One of his favourites was to place strange objects in their beds to frighten them when they retired for the night. One habit of his I found strange was his kissing me on the cheek when we first met and when he was returning home at the end of the holiday.

Mrs. Adams was a lovely person who mixed easily with the rest of the women. She told a slightly risqué story one night, and ever afterwards when John McGowan repeated the same story, he always laid great emphasis on the fact it was a priest's mother from whom he had first heard it. Before mother and son left at the end of their holiday they invited me to come and stay with them after Christmas. Although I didn't miss the absence of a radio in the house, it was a great delight when in that year, 1947 The Society for The Blind presented John with a Bush battery-operated radio.

In October, we sold the two young cattle and John bought a suit from the proceeds. He paid £5 to gent's draper, Ned Queenan, who came from Carrowhubbock North, which lay beyond Ormbsy's fort. Ned was a daily communicant and a member of the Pioneer Total Abstinence Association.

That evening, as John sat by the fire examining his purchase, I heard him swear. 'The bastard, he's sold me a second-hand suit. Look at the grease marks on the inside of the cuffs,' he called out to his wife. She confirmed his suspicion, as I did too. Next morning John and his wife took the first bus into Ballina and got the money back.

When he died, a relative wrote a lengthy obituary of Ned praising him for his religious devotion and how he used to have many priests come to visit him in his home above the shop in Bridge street.

When a brother of Ned Queenan married and he and his bride spent the first few days of their honeymoon on the penitential island of Lough Derg, Father Gallagher said; 'I never knew that there were double beds on Lough Derg.'

The Town Hall Theatre changed its name to that of 'cinema' on the 8th. Of December, when Mr. Llewellyn showed the film, *"Dodge City"* starring Errol Flynn, Olivia de Haviland, Ann Sheridan, Bruce Cabot and Ward Bond, all in glorious technicolour. The hall was packed. But within minutes of the film beginning to roll, the screen went white and there was no sound. After fifteen minutes, the hall's owner appeared and apologised for the breakdown and told the disappointed audience that their tickets would be valid for a reshowing of the film the following week. It was later discovered that the cause of breakdown had been a failure to degrease the new projector. My aunt did not allow ne to attend the opening night as she was afraid of something happening on the 'first night.'

On Christmas Eve, when we finished our simple supper of boiled eggs and soda bread, I switched on the radio and found on the

B.B.C. a broadcast of the Merry Widow Opera from Sadler's Wells in London. Sitting at the fire that was now blazing merrily in the hearth, I listened entranced to the music of Franz Lehar and tried to visualise the theatre from which the opera was being broadcast. It made such an impression on me, that even to this day the strains of the Merry Widow waltz almost bring a tear to my eye.

After Christmas, I accepted the Adams invitation and took the bus to Castlerea, where John Adams was waiting with a Hackney car to take us the few miles to the Adam's home.

Most of the farmland was of the poorest quality and sloped away from the house in the direction of a small lake. Their original home, into which Mrs. Adams had come as a bride after returning from working in the United States, was situated in a hollow and now served as stables. As well as the mother and John the eldest son Michael, and his personable wife Delia, also lived in the bungalow. To augment the meagre income from the farm, John and Michael worked repairing roads for the County Council.

Around the house were to be seen photographs of Father Joe Adams in his seminary days at St. Patrick's College, Carlow, as a scholarship student in Summerhill College, Sligo, and as a newly ordained priest. He was handsome and very intelligent looking.

Amongst the other memorabilia, I found a wooden chalice, painted silver, which Joe Adams had made himself, when the time came for him to practice the saying of mass. Once I had seen it and held it in my hands, hardly a day passed during the two weeks I stayed there, that I didn't go through the motions of celebrating mass, using an every-day missal from which to read the words. When I left that lovely family, I'd had within me the first stirrings of a desire to be a priest, like Father Joe Adams.

During Lent of that year 1948, I persuaded some of the boys in Carrowhubbock: Tommy Ford; Paddy Devaney and the two Kelly brothers, Eamonn and Paddy, to follow me to the chapel each evening to do the stations of the Cross; but only after we had clustered around John McGowan's radio to listen excitedly as Charles William's thrilling music, the *"Devils Gallop"* introduced that evenings episode of *"Dick Barton - Special Agent"* and his able assistants, Jock and Snowy.

In addition to my regular churchgoing, I became an avid reader of religious magazines such as those of the Mill Hill Fathers, The Society of African Missions and the Far East of the Colomban Fathers. If that were not enough, there were also the little Sacred Heart Messenger and from Canada, the Annals of Anne de Beaupre. My imagination was stirred by the many pictures of bearded priests on horseback travelling through mountainous terrain in Kashmir, canoeing down a swiftly flowing river in Borneo or walking miles along a jungle track in Nigeria in order to get to the next village, where an expectant congregation would be waiting for him to say mass and baptise their children. Could I ever be one of these men, I often asked myself, as I eagerly awaited the arrival of the next batch of magazines.

The local clergy were not models who would inspire a young man to become a priest: both men were in poor health, especially the curate, Father James Gallagher, of whom it was said that he had only one lung: the parishioners excused his frequent bouts of bad temper on account of this. I knew that I could never discuss my thoughts about becoming a priest with either him or the parish priest, Father Munnelly, who had served for some years in Glasgow and was also in ill-health.

Around this time, a great change in the lives of the people of rural Ireland took place, when electricity was installed in their houses. My aunt opted for having just the single bulb in the kitchen. On the first occasion she pulled down the switch, and for many years afterwards, she would cry out 'Jesus Mary and Joseph protect us.'

During the next two years, various jobs were offered to me. The first one was when Frank Maughan wanted to know if I would like to go into business. But I turned down his offer: a decision which surprised the businessman; for at that time there were very few jobs to be had and emigration from Ireland was the norm for most young men. The next offer of work came from the Misses Kenny who wanted me to work for them in their Seafield Hotel. I think it was the picture they painted of me dressed in a short, coloured jacket and bow tie and serving tables that dissuaded me from even contemplating the offer. The last offer, and the most attractive, came early in the winter of 1949.

One week I read in the local newspaper, *"The Western People"*, that a cottage in Enniscrone was for sale. It was one of eight two-story council houses situated across from the convent. My aunt agreed that I ought to contact my father in Glasgow to see if he might be interested in buying the property, since he had just married a widow a couple of weeks previously and perhaps they would like to live in Ireland.

In response, Father sent a telegram telling me to make an offer of not more than £2000 for the house. I was sorry that he had made public the amount of money he was willing to pay: for we were to learn soon afterwards that the postmistress, a Mrs. Burke, went to the vendor and revealed the contents of daddy's telegram to her.

On my father's instructions, I took the bus to Ballina to instruct solicitor, John 'Jackie' Gordon, to handle the legal aspects of the purchase. It was while I was with him that he enquired if I were looking for a job. Although he didn't actually specify what the job was, I instinctively knew that it was more than likely that of a junior clerk in his own firm. Again, as in the two previous cases, I politely declined.

In January of 1950, my father arrived to complete the legal formalities of the purchase. The morning we were to go in to Ballina was bright and sunny. But as we walked along the Cliff road and had just about reached halfway to the square, we saw the bus pull away from Hopkins pub. My father simply said: 'it's a fine day for a walk.' The distance was 9 miles. Fortunately his appointment with the solicitor wasn't until midday.

While my father was with Jackie Gordon, I took the opportunity to visit Mrs. Conboy, who was delighted at my unexpected visit and told me that a Joan had got the civil service exam and was going to start working temporarily in the Ballina telephone exchange in March. She invited me to stay for lunch. I would have happily accepted, had I not arranged to return home on the 1 o'clock bus with my father.

Between my father's departure that January and his return in early June with his new wife and her youngest son, a boy of around 11 years, my desire to become a priest had grown stronger by the day. I even sent for a booklet on the monastic life to Mount Saint

Joseph's, a Cistercian monastery in Co Tipperary. When it arrived and Aunt Nellie saw it, she was horrified at the thought of losing me to the strict life of a Trappist monk. I must admit that when I examined the details of a typical day in the monastery, I did not find it too difficult to put the idea of joining the Cistercians out of my mind, for good.

I was still doing the *"Nine Fridays"*, a very popular devotion in Ireland at the time. What it entailed was attending Mass and receiving Holy Communion on the first Friday of nine consecutive months. This duty fulfilled, one was promised the gift of heaven. Many of the devotees of this practice were young women who were not so much interested in the happiness of the next life, as the pleasure the present one that would provide in the form of a good husband with a job and pension or a bit of land. Somehow, I hoped that my *"Nine Fridays"* would afford me the opportunity to commence my studies for the priesthood. Not even the experience I had with my aunt during a spell of unusually hot weather did anything to make me change my mind.

John was in the fields and I was in the kitchen tidying up after baking a couple of soda scones, when Aunt Nellie returned from having bathed with some of her neighbours on the shore below Devaney's field. She stood at the fireplace wearing a black, crochet style skirt and a blouse, when to my amazement she removed the blouse and let drop her skirt to reveal her nakedness. 'Look at the difference in colour between my face and neck and the rest of me,' I heard her say, as if from a far distance. I didn't know what to do or where to look; but passing within inches of her on my way to the dresser, I noticed the smallness of her breasts. As she pulled on a short, cotton vest, I observed a nipple peeping through a small hole in the material.

In the days that followed, I found it difficult to get rid of the image of my aunt as I saw her on that afternoon. But what made her do such a thing, I kept on asking myself? One thing I was certain of was that there was no sexual motive in her action. Even at her age and being married, there was still an aura of innocence about her. The only conclusion I could come to was that, being without a son of her own, she was somehow trying to show me that there was now a physical bond between us.

A few weeks later, I found myself with my aunt and other women, including young Bridie O'Neill, on the shore below Devaney's field. How the women arranged to meet and how they tolerated my presence amongst them, I cannot explain. But within minutes they had discarded their upper clothing and were splashing themselves with sea water that had gathered in small pools amongst the rocks. The only one not to engage in this activity was Bridie, who smiled shyly over at me, as we turned to look at my aunt who was squealing excitedly as the water ran down her chest.

About a week after that incident, I was sitting one evening at the fireplace reading, when Aunt Nellie called out: 'Martin, come here and see the sky. Across the Bay the sky looked as if someone had taken a gigantic tin of scarlet paint and hurled the contents against a white wall. What I was looking at was not the usual red sky heralding another fine day, but a sky streaked with a redness I had never seen before. 'The last time I saw a sky like that was before the 1914 war broke out. There's going to be a terrible war,' was her conclusion. Just over four weeks later, on 25 June, 1950, North Korea invaded the south.

Austin Clarke, in his book, *"A Penny In The Clouds"*, also witnessed this strange phenomenon prior to the outbreak of the Great War in 1914, while on holiday in Co Wicklow, and remembered the misgivings of the local farmers upon seeing it.

In more recent times, Herbert Dohring, who supervised most of Hitler's domestic arrangements, tells of how on the night of August 23. 1939, while standing with his employer and senior Nazis on the terrace of Berchtesgaden, they witnessed the night sky suddenly in turmoil: it was blood red. And that was the very moment Hitler's foreign minister, Von Ribbentrop, was signing the infamous treaty with Russia. A mysterious Hungarian woman in Hitler's entourage subsequently approached him and warned:

"My Fuhrer, this augurs no good. This means blood,
blood and more blood".

Father and his new wife and her son arrived in Enniscrone the same week to take possession of what would always be referred to in the family as *"the town house"*. They stayed a few days with us in the farmhouse until their furniture arrived, two days later from Glasgow. I still dreamt of becoming a priest. But the more I looked at myself in the mirror, the more despondent I became when I compared my looks with those of the seminarians in those photographs in the Adam's home. They were all so good-looking and of intelligent appearance: as evidenced by their high foreheads. Even by pushing my hair back with my hand, I still failed to see a sufficiently high enough forehead for it to indicate that I had the requisite intelligence to become a priest. Then there was the question of money; not to mention the *"Curse"*.

'I don't know what I'm going to do with you, Martin,' George Conboy said one afternoon in August. It was his half day and only he, young Frank and I were in the house. 'Would you like to be a mechanic or a carpenter?'

Me with greasy, dirty hands, or worse still, with no hands at all, given that my track record in using sharp tools? No thank you, I thought.

'Daddy, Martin would like to be a priest,' his son called out from the scullery where he was helping himself to a piece of his mother's baking. His father put down the paper he had been reading and looked at me as if he were seeing me for the first time.

'Is that correct?' He wanted to know

'Yes,' I mumbled shyly.

George removed his spectacles and began wiping them with his handkerchief. Satisfied that they were clean, he put them back on and looked long and hard at me. 'You know that you will need a lot of money to become a priest. And then there are the long years of study.'

'I know,' I replied.

'And of course you can never marry,' he added, sternly.

I thought of Joan. To give up any chance of marrying her was going to be hard. 'I would still like to be a priest.'

The man's face relaxed into the nearest it could come to a smile. 'Alright, Martin, I'll speak to Madeleine about it when she comes back from the cathedral.'

Three days later, at Mrs.Conboy's suggestion, I accompanied her husband to a meeting with the Rev. Dr. Loftus, president of St. Muredach's College, where my uncle James was a border when it first opened in 1906. George did his best to persuade the priest to accept me without any fee. This, the President refused. Instead he advised me to apply to one of the Missionary Orders which were always seeking recruits to continue their work in Africa and the Far East. With them, no fees where required, as they were well supported by the devout people of Ireland.

Madeleine Conboy was angry, with Father Loftus. 'What do you think of going on the missions, Martin?'

'That's what I really want, 'I said truthfully.

'I don't blame you. After all, what is there for a young priest to do stuck in some country parish in Ireland?'

Eventually, through a priest friend from her hometown of Kiltimagh, she arranged for me to have an interview with the Rector of the junior seminary belonging to the Society of African Missions, which was situated about 35 miles away.

The college of Ballinafad had been built around the original home of the wealthy, land owning family of the Blakes. It was a big house, the sort the Land League had ushered out of existence and in the struggle for independence was often ear-marked for burning. It was Llewellyn Blake, uncle of the Irish literary figure, George Moore, who had gifted the property to the Missionary Society: for this act of generosity he was created a Papal Count.

The Rector, Father Tobin, was a softly spoken man of medium height and sallow complexion and with a friendly smile. During tea in the Refectory he told me a little about the Society's work in Africa, where he had spent a number of years, before illness had forced him to return to Ireland. 'But I was one of the lucky ones. Many of our priests are still out there never to come home,' he said sadly.

Before leaving to get my bus back to Ballina, the priest reminded me to send my baptism certificate and a letter from my parish priest to Father MacKay at St. Joseph's college, Wilton, Cork, where I would join their Late Vocation's Class that was due to commence in a week's time.

'One week, it doesn't give you much time, Martin,' was Mrs. Conboy's comment when I told her about the class I was to join in Cork. Joan wanted to know at what time the students had to get up in the morning. All I could tell her was that it was early, very early, some time before seven o'clock. After helping Joan to wash and dry the supper dishes that evening, I sat down with her mother to discuss what we were going to do about fitting me out for college. A list would be forthcoming from Cork, but in the meantime Mrs. Conboy decided that she would start asking her friends in the town to contribute either cash or clothes. The thought of her going round Ballina begging on my behalf was a source of embarrassment to me; but it had to be done. There was no other way if I were to begin my studies for the priesthood.

My father was relieved that Mrs. Conboy was taking on the responsibility of collecting all the clothes I required. But my stepmother was furious at my decision; even though she was at Mass every morning. 'If I had known that you were going to do this, I never would have left Glasgow. I thought you would be here all the time and get a job.' She told me angrily. My aunt was equally annoyed, but for a different reason. 'Oh, the climate out there is cruel. Sure how many young priests haven't I heard about going there and dying within a few weeks or months,' she said. 'But that was years ago,' I responded. She gave a snort. 'Go ahead, then, have it your own way. But you will see that I'm right,' she concluded.

By the time of my departure, two weeks later, Mrs Conboy had two of every item of clothing on the college's, list; including the present of a fine dressing gown from the nuns at Foxford Woolen Mills. Every item had to be labelled in the traditional manner. Mrs. Conboy did that task as well. For football I chose a black and white jersey, white shorts and black and white stockings.

Leaving Enniscrone was not too difficult. The summer was well and truly over and the small resort preparing for its long, winter sleep. Any visitor still around was usually some elderly 'Yank' who had found a home for himself until the following spring.

The one person most upset by my departure was John McGowan, who, when I went down to the small room to bid him goodbye, found him close to tears. He begged me not to leave and promised to give me the farm. I explained to him that I wanted to try my vocation, but if it didn't work, I'd come back. However, even as I said those words, I knew in my heart that there would be no coming back. I would be a 'spoilt priest,' and knew what that meant in rural Ireland. 'I must go now, John,' I said gently.

My aunt was standing at the kitchen door. She pressed two 1 pound notes into my hand: 'I wish it could be more, Martin, but when we sell the cattle out here, I'll send you something.'

'Thanks, Aunt Nellie, God bless.' I was going to miss her, I thought, and went to open the front door. 'Wait!' She commanded, as she walked towards the dresser, returning with a small Paddy whiskey bottle in which she kept holy water. As the drops fell on my head and shoulders and I dutifully blessed myself, she prayed that Jesus, Mary and Joseph would protect me and bring me safely to my destination.

'You look very nice, Martin, Black suits you,' Mrs. Conboy told me when I arrived that evening to stay over the weekend in order to catch the train to Cork on Monday morning. The two boys looked at me with a degree of awe on their faces. Joan greeted me shyly when she came in from work. Her father asked if I were all set for the great adventure: a remark which made his wife pull a face. After supper, Madeleine suggested to her husband that they take me to the cinema. George declined and Joan wanted to stay at home and wash her hair in preparation for a dance the following night. In the end, Mrs. Conboy and I went on our own to the Astoria cinema.

Dressed in my clerical black I followed her down the steps to seats in the balcony, conscious of the many eyes that were watching us, including two of the priests from St. Muredach's College.

As we walked home afterwards, I linked an arm through that of Mrs. Conboy's for the first time and was gratified when she held my hand tight against the side of her breast; only disengaging our arms as we reached the top of the lane leading down to Morrison Terrace.

The following afternoon, Joan and I were alone in the house. She asked me if all my clothes had my name attached to them. I told her that they had with the exception of the underpants I was wearing at that moment. 'Take them off, Martin, and I'll sew on the label,' she said, blushing furiously and not daring to look at me.

When I was carrying my underpants downstairs, after having removed them in the bedroom, I was conscious of the fact that Joan would be about to handle a garment I had just removed from my body and would feel its warmth and above all smell the body odor coming from it.

As I handed the garment to Joan, she busily rummaged in the sewing box. Her cheeks were fire red. 'Thanks, Martin,' she whispered hoarsely, as I placed the still warm underpants in her hands.

The morning of my departure, when I went upstairs to get my suitcase, Joan was standing on the landing with a black object in her hand. 'I'd like you to have this, Martin,' she said, holding out what I saw to be a 'missal.' Aunt Peggy bought it for me, but I know that you will make better use of it than me. ''Thanks, Joan,' I said debating whether in my new role as a clerical student I could kiss her.

'I better go now or I'll be late for work,' Joan said. Then she stepped forward and kissed me lightly on the cheek, before running down the stairs. I stood there with her gift in my hand and vowed that every time I opened it at mass, I would say a special player for its donor.

As I said goodbye to Mrs. Conboy I felt the first pangs of loneliness, and also the realisation of what this woman had come to mean for me. 'You will write, won't you, and let me know how you are getting on?'

'Of course I will, Mam,' I assured her.

'Goodbye then, Martin. God bless you.'

I kissed her tenderly on her proffered cheek and followed her out to the front gate, where she was still standing when I looked back before turning into the laneway that led up to the station.

I Have A Dream

The platform station was crowded. It was my first time there, and I was surprised at the number of people traveling that late in September. I was fortunate to find a window seat from which I could observe the little knots of people standing on the platform. Whole families were crying, even stalwart, elderly men, as parents bid farewell to sons and daughters, many of them around my own age and even younger, who were emigrating to the industrial cities of England and Wales. Most of them would weep all the way to their destination, I thought.

Two blasts of the guards whistle brought about a fresh outpouring of grief amongst those still remaining on the platform. One young woman had to be forcibly detached from her mother's arms and hauled aboard the train. 'Stand back there,' a voice called out. The engine gave three sharp blasts of its whistle and ever so slowly the train began to move out of the station, accompanied along the length of the platform by the younger members of the emigrant's families. As the train cleared the station, I caught a brief glimpse of 23 Morrison Terrace.

At Limerick Junction, while waiting for the Dublin to Cork train, I stood talking with a young commercial traveller who told me that he at one time had thought of becoming a priest, but had changed his mind and was now working for a tea importer. He was on his way to Dublin. 'Here is my train now,' he said, as a whistle sounded in the distance. Through the milling crowd changing trains I hauled my suitcase until I came to a carriage door that was clear of people and climbed aboard. Seated and ready for the second part of the journey to Cork, I waited for the ticket collector to approach.

'You are going to Cork?' He queried, as he examined my ticket.

'Yes,' I replied, puzzled by the question.

'I'm afraid you're on the wrong train; this train is going to Dublin.'

I was stunned. How could I be so stupid? More importantly, what was I going to do now? 'Can you get the train to go back?'

The conductor smiled. 'I'm afraid we can't do that son,' he said kindly.

'What am I going to do then?'

The man looked thoughtful. 'the best thing to do is get off at

Thurles and wait for the next train down from Dublin,' he advised, 'and that will be at...' he opened a well thumbed timetable.

I groaned inwardly. All those hours I would have to wait; and what about the college; I was expected there in time for supper?

With the help of the station master of the Co Tipperary town I sent a telegram to Father McKay advising him of my late arrival but leaving out the reason. That task finished, I entered the dimly lit and unheated waiting-room, where I bemoaned my stupidity and wished that I had never left Ballina that morning.

As darkness fell, rain splattered in heavy drops against the windows. From the direction of the town came the sound of a church bell. I felt lonely and hungry, and was feeling very sorry for myself. A teardrop trickled down one cheek. A railway employee looked in on me: 'You won't have long to wait now,' he assured me.

During my wait, I had wondered what Cork was like? Recently, I read this description of the place around 1940:

"It's very continental; or rather it's so un-English (more un-English than Dublin) that there is nothing to call it but Continental... It has a long and animated river front, lined with puce and pistachio-coloured buildings, several small steamers, with guns still mounted, along the docks. A long wide Serpentine Main St, which used to have beautiful buildings, but they were all burned down by the Black and Tans or the I.R.A. during the troubles, and have now been replaced by vast modern stores, Burtons, the 50-Shilling-Tailor, Woolworths etc. However, most of the older part of the towns intact; it is criss-crossed through with canals and small hump-back bridges. The houses have steep roofs, and many of them are painted; there is a very dashing Opera House, overlooking the River. Across the river from the main part of the Opera House is a very steep hill, rather beautifully plastered over with houses, some of them elegant terraces and trees. The whole place has a sultry, sweetish smell, which I'm afraid arises from its being imperfectly clean; a slightly Italian smell, except for the absence of garlic. One can smell the incense out of the many churches, and the slight saltiness of the tidal river".

The train for which I had so anxiously awaited pulled in. Within minutes of taking my seat, I was fast asleep, cocooned in the warmth of the carriage, and woke up only when we reached Mallow: the last stop before Cork.

As I walked along the station platform, a small, slightly built priest approached me. 'You must be Martin Gordon,' he said. I put down my suitcase. 'Yes, Father.' then apologised to the priest for being so late.

'Good man, I'm Father Kenny. If you follow me I have the car outside.'

During the time that it took us to reach the College, the priest spoke only once to ask if I were hungry. Father Kenny steered the car between massive stone pillars each topped with large, decorative acorn. Up ahead the cars head lamps picked out a long sloping Avenue lined on either side with triple columns of tall trees. A sharp right-hand bend gave me my first sighting of the college. No light shone from any windows. With the exception of two small buildings and of what was clearly a church, the college itself stood on the left-hand side of the avenue.

Through a door that opened directly off the Avenue, Father Kenny took me into a large room which, when he switched on a solitary light, revealed that we were in the refectory. The priest sat me down at the table nearest the kitchen, while he went to organise my supper. In his absence I surveyed the room. Three long tables were placed across its width, while two steps led up to another table placed lengthwise: all were set for breakfast. A small desk with a chair was positioned next to a frosted glass door. A big crucifix, a couple of religious paintings and one of a distinguished, bearded man all in heavy, ornate frames decorated the walls I stifled a yawn as the priest reappeared and handed me a mug of cocoa and a plate of ham salad. Not having eaten a decent meal since breakfast, I devoured the repast in a matter of minutes, and then followed the priest upstairs to the dormitory where, from the light of a solitary bulb outside the door, I saw the bed waiting for me just inside the partition. 'Be sure and switch off the light before you get into bed,' the priest said. 'I nearly forgot. You don't have to get up until 7:30 Breakfast is at eight o'clock.' He whispered.

Within minutes of climbing into the narrow, iron bed, whose springs sagged badly in the middle, I had joined the ranks of the other sleeping students.

Upon entering the refectory the following morning, a well-built student of swarthy appearance approached and nodded to me to follow him to the table at which I had sat the previous night, and indicated to me that I should occupy the last remaining place. There was no talking. Priests and students stood silently until a priest said 'grace' in Latin.

The breakfast, eaten in silence, consisted of porridge, tea, bread and butter; and although the bread was fresh and plentiful, the small roll of butter on each one's side plate was totally inadequate. The priests were served cereal, rashers and eggs. Once the meal was eaten, the students were free until classes commenced at nine o'clock. As I stood on the avenue wondering what to do next, one of the students came towards me. 'I'm Ricky Devine,' he told me,

'Martin Gordon,' I responded.

'Are you really from Enniscrone?' I confirmed that I was.

'I'm from Ballymote,' the smiling student said, a small town near Sligo.

'I haven't met Father McKay yet,' I said. Ricky Devine looked around.'See that priest coming towards us?' I looked in the direction he was indicating. 'That's Father McNamara, he teaches Latin; ask him about seeing the Superior.'

'Thanks,'

'Excuse me, Father, I'm Martin Gordon. I arrived late last night.' The tall, sturdily-built priest looked at me through gold-rimmed spectacles before removing the pipe from his mouth. 'So, you are the fellow, who went gallivanting off to Dublin,' he said, with just the trace of a smile. I could feel myself blushing.

'Well, what can I do for you, sonny?' I explained that I wanted to see Father McKay The priest looked at his watch. 'Come this way with me.'

The room in which the genial priest deposited me looked out over a wide expanse of lawn which was divided by a flagstone path about 6 feet wide; an ornamental balustrade fenced off this area from the football pitch, which had a slight incline until it reached the far touchline; from that point the field sloped away dramatically until it reached marshy ground at the bottom. To the left, a large mansion stood in a valley, smoke rising through the surrounding trees from its chimneys. Across the valley a few farmhouses, just about visible in the greyness of the autumn morning, dotted the hillside, along which a goods train huffed and puffed its leisurely way. The room itself was the biggest and grandest I had ever been in. It was furnished with two high, wide bookcases; a magnificent, highly polished table with a set of eight matching chairs; a white marble fireplace with a delicate scrollwork; and on the wall above it a portrait of the Virgin Mary.

With still no sign of the Superior appearing, I began a cursory examination of the contents of the bookcases. In one of them I came across a folder containing personal details of priests belonging to the Society of African Missions. I hurriedly closed it and put it back in the bookcase. Next item was a small book with the title *"History of The Society of African Missions"*. This looks interesting, I thought, and sat down and began to read.

The Society had been founded in France by a bishop Melchior de Marion Bresillac in 1856. The Bishop soon gathered around himself a devoted band of followers, chief of whom was Father Augustine Planque, who became the first Superior of the new Society, whose aim was the evangelization of Africa. Their third member of the infant Society was a seminarian, M. Alba.

On the eighth of December, 1856, the three men went to the shrine of Notre Dame de Fourviere, one of the oldest shrines in France, to make their formal consecration. It is this date that is rightly taken as the date of their Society's foundation.

The first group of missionaries consisting of Fathers Louis Reymonde, Baptiste Bresson and Brother Eugene Reynaud left Marseille for Sierra Leone on November 3rd. 1858. Its leader was Father Reymonde. Bishop Bresillac was to join up with them a little later when he had completed some urgent business on behalf of their Society.

Eventually the Bishop, accompanied by Father Louis Riocreux and Brother Gratien, arrived at Freetown on 14 May 1859. But their happy reunion was of short duration: that terrible scourge of the white man, 'yellow fever,' soon attacked them, and within a few short months they were all already dead or dying. The recently arrived Father Riocreux died two weeks after his arrival; Father Bresson was buried three days later on the 5th. of June and Brother Gratien on the 13th. Bishop Bresillac lasted until the 25th of the month, when Father Reymonde had to be carried on a stretcher from his own bed to administer the Last Rites to the Bishop who, in turn, did the same for the dying priest, who followed him into eternity three days later. All the others were already dead. The only survivor from the original six members of the Society of African Missions to return to France was Eugene Reynaud, whom the Bishop had sent home as unfit for the climate.

When Father Planque, Superior of the infant Society back in Lyon, got the catastrophic news, he said:

"if we have lost our father and elder brothers, yet have we not the agreeable certainty of advocates in heaven who will be able to pray for our case more effectively now that they are near God".

He then went on to consult the saintly Cure d'Ars, who advised the missionary priest to continue the work and that God would bless it and prosper it. His words were prophetic. For now, I read, the Society of African Missions is one of the most flourishing Missionary Societies in the entire Catholic Church. The book then went on to relate how the Society came to be set up in Ireland.

An Irish priest, by the name of O'Haire had worked in Africa for a number of years. His experience had convinced him that the best way to convert people there was to have a special Society entirely devoted to that work. Accordingly he got in touch with Father Raymond Bosion in France, impressing on the French cleric the desirability of establishing a house of the Society in Ireland. The Irish priest then rented a house in the city of Cork in 1877. Soon afterwards, two priests arrived from France to take charge of the new Community.

A Mr. Himsworth, a wealthy Yorkshire farmer and a convert to Catholicism, supplied the Society with £10,000 to purchase the ground on which the present Provincial House on the Blackrock Road now stands. A college and a church were added between 1880 and 1881.

The Wilton College property, in the Western part of the City was purchased as a fine, old Georgian house, built around 1796 and with 72 acres of land for the princely sum of £100. But when the Society acquired it in July 1888, it was in a bad state of repair. Renovations soon began, and on Saturday, 23 March, 1889, forty students moved from the original foundation on the Blackrock Road to the new College, where the Coach House was converted into a chapel after a sacristy and sanctuary had been added.

In September 1894, building work began on the construction of a proper church and the foundation stone was laid on May the Sixth

1895. It is said that the Superior, Father Zimmerman, a native of Switzerland, placed to fistful of sovereigns underneath the stone as it was being laid. The church has a few Swiss features such as its red brick walls and the snow-shedding steep roof angle.

The church could never have been built without that financial support of Count Llewellyn Blake of County Mayo, who donated £20,000 to the Society. He had served for 15 years in the Connacht Rangers. After the death of his wife and without any children, he began to look around for suitable Catholic charities to endow in 1891. One of them was the infant Society of African Missions. His grave, I was to discover, is on the grassy slope outside the sanctuary wall of the Wilton church, and is well cared for by the Society.

Father Zimmerman's Superiors in Lyon, for some unknown reason, took a dislike to their priest and sent him to Savannah, Georgia, where he died in 1921. Perhaps he had become too successful and popular.

About five minutes later my vigil came to an end when the priest who had said 'grace' at breakfast stood in front of me. 'Come into my office,' he told me. Once inside he motioned with a wave of the hand for me to be seated. Nothing was said as the priest stared at me across the desk. There was a smouldering intensity, almost a hint of great passion in the deep, dark eyes studying me. Under such scrutiny, I lowered my own eyes to look at the desk.

'Mrs. Conboy has written to me about you.'

The voice startled me. Slowly I lifted my head.

'I hope you won't disappoint her, Mr. Gordon.'

'I'll try not to, Father.'

The Superior continued to study me closely. 'Good man,' he eventually said. He looked at his watch. 'The Latin class has just started. But before I take you down to join your classmates, there are a few rules you ought to know about if you are to be a good student.'

I listened intently as the priest went through a list of do's and don'ts governing the student life in Wilton. 'Nunquam unus, Rarum duos, Semper tres,' he told me, the trace of his Ulster accent coming through the Latin. 'Never one, rarely two and always three' the priest translated; 'In that way there is less danger of forming particular friendships.' 'Students are not allowed to smoke or read newspapers,' he continued. 'When writing letters the envelope must be left unsealed. Finally, there is no talking after night prayers. Do you think you will be able to keep these rules, Mr. Gordon?'

'I think so, Father.'

'Now let me take you to the Latin class.'

My classmates came from all over Ireland, even from Malin Head, and like myself had worked in a variety of occupations. One red-haired chap had been a soldier in the Irish army another had been a civil servant. In age we ranged from 19 to 40..

One of the students who fascinated me in the early weeks at Wilton was Joseph Devine. Girlish in appearance, with wispy, blond hair swept to one side, high colouring and deep, sunken eyes of a brilliant blue, he was regarded as someone special by Fr. McKay. Intense and serious at all times, the student's intensity reached its peak each morning in the chapel after he had received Holy Communion. Returned to his seat, Joseph placed his head in his hands and began rocking back and forward so convulsively that students in the same pew could feel it moving under the student's emotional onslaught.

I noticed a plaque dedicated to a Sir. Richard Gordon attached to a wall of the chapel, and made a mental note to find out more about this man.

In the first letter to Mrs. Conboy, remembering to leave the envelope open, I gave her a full description of my typical day in the College.

'The bell to waken us is rung at six o'clock, accompanied by the cry of the Bellman, 'Benedicamus Domino,' to which we all respond, 'Deo Gratias.' Priests and students then assemble in the semi darkness of the side chapel for morning prayers and meditation, followed at seven o'clock by the community mass. After mass the students gather on the Avenue, for a few minutes of physical exercise, followed by a gentle jog down towards the main gate. Then it's a mad race back to the college. After this, each one of us goes about his allotted ask of housecleaning and making one's bed. Did you know that cold tea leaves are good for cleaning carpets? Breakfast at eight o'clock is

eagerly awaited, as you can guess, since we have been up for the past two hours and not having eaten since seven o'clock the previous evening. We then have some time before classes begin at nine o'clock. We 'Late Vocations' finish classes at lunchtime, while the rest of the students continue with their studies until afternoon tea; we do manual work in the farmyard, or orchard or in the fields; except, of course, on half-days when we play football, hurling or soccer. I have been selected as the goalkeeper in a Gaelic team and as outside left in soccer. After tea at 4.30, we go into study until 6.30, when there is a break for recreation and the rosary, before having our supper; usually mashed potatoes and scraps of whatever meat has been left over from lunch. To drink we have large mugs of cocoa. Study resumes at eight clock for an hour and a half, then it's night prayers and lights out at 10. As you would expect after such a long and busy day, Mam, I have no problem in falling asleep.'

To end the letter, I asked about George, the two boys and Joan. *'Tell her that I use her missal every morning at mass,'* I added.

Those 16 hours of non-stop activity were obviously intended to sublimate our sex drive: in my case it worked. Not that I was, up until then, aware of any great stirring in my loins, even at the age of 19 years. But as I listened each lunchtime to the reading of the Martyrology, I began to feel embarrassed at the number of times the word 'breast' was mentioned. Each day the names of those heroic men & women killed were remembered for the way in which they endured the most horrific tortures and agonising deaths for the sake of Christ. The young virgin girls in particular had a most difficult time: having their breasts cut off was just one of the things they had to endure. Their other sufferings were never mentioned. Suppose on the day it was my turn to do the reading and had to tell the tale of some poor virgin...? My worst fears were realised on my debut at the lectern, when I had to mention that dreaded word 'breast' no fewer than three times. I could feel my face burning and imagined that every eye in the room was looking in my direction. Then to my utter humiliation, when I had only gone about four paragraphs in the book that was currently being read to the community, the tinkling of a bell brought my reading to an abrupt end. Conversation was then allowed until the end of the meal. None of my classmates passed any comment as I sat down at the table to begin eating my lunch; but I knew that I must have been reading too fast making it difficult for the community to understand my Scottish accent.

Between the end of September, when I first arrived at the college and Halloween, we had not been outside the grounds except to attend the *"Farewell Ceremony"* held each year on the feast of *"The Little Flower"*, Patroness of the Foreign Missions; even though she herself had never left France, and died at an early age in the Carmelite convent, at Liseux in Normandy.

The ceremony took place in the small church attached to the house on the Blackrock Road, site of the original Foundation. Dressed in white albs and stoles the priests who were departing for the missions, a number of whom had been ordained in June, ranged themselves around the altar facing the packed congregation. We students were positioned in the gallery from which vantage point we had an unobstructed view of the proceedings. As the liturgy progressed, I found myself being more and more moved by it all; especially when choir and congregation joined in the singing of the *"Departure Hymn"*:

"Go forth, ye heralds of God's tender mercy;
The day has come at last, the day of joy!
Your burning zeal is shackled by no fetters,
Go forth, O' brothers, happy you go forth.

How beautiful the feet of God's Apostles,
We kiss those feet with loving, holy awe.
How beautiful are they on hills and valleys
Where errors darkness reigns with death!

The winds will howl and tear the sails asunder,
The waves will foam and dash against the ship.
But go in Jesus' name to preach his gospel!
And fear not, Him the winds and sea obey.

When Jesus seems asleep and the nights are stormy,
Gaze on yon gentle, glittering star and hark,
Your brothers sing the "Ave Maris Stella"
That you may reach the distant shore.

Go forth, Farewell! For life, O' dearest brothers
Proclaim the sweetest name of God.
We meet one day again in heaven - land of blessings,
Farewell, brothers, Farewell".

Many of the women in the congregation were weeping; even some men dabbed at their eyes with handkerchiefs. I found the whole experience highly emotional, and a little misty eyed, but was able to preserve my manhood.

The ceremony concluded with the Missionaries imparting their blessing on the congregation. As I made the sign of the cross I thought of the day, eight years away, when 'I' would be part of the *"Departure Ceremony"*.

Halloween arrived and with it parcels of food from home. There was a tangible air of excitement about the college as we anticipated a special supper for the feast. When the Prefect, Donnie Cassidy, handed me a parcel I knew from the handwriting that it was from Mrs. Conboy. Once I had opened the cardboard box, I found in it fruitcake and a letter written on her favourite Basildon Bond.. The letter told me about the present state of her arthritis and that Joan was being transferred from Ballina to a town in the neighbouring county of Galway. George was rehearsing a Gilbert and Sullivan production with the musical society. She wished me a nice time at Halloween, reminding me that Christmas was not too far away and asked me to give her best wishes to Father McKay.

Inside a letter from Aunt Nelly was a 10 shilling note. Her words were few: *"spend the money wisely and tear up this letter when read".* I looked at the money in my hand and recalled her words as I went out the door on the first leg of the journey to Cork.

Mrs Conboy was correct; Christmas hadn't been that too far away as the weeks sped by and there I was on the Galway bus, where a group of us from the West had to stay overnight as the trains were on strike.

'You have grown, Martin, Mrs. Conboy told me; but you could do with a bit more flesh on you,' she said.

After her husband at eaten his lunch and returned to Lipton's, the two of us sat in front of the range with cups of tea in hand. I took my first cigarette from her, 'just to keep you company, Mam.' She was especially pleased that I had learned to serve Mass. About Father McKay I wasn't able to say much when she enquired about him, except that he was a strict disciplinarian.

The longer we sat together that afternoon, the more I wished that I didn't have to leave that woman in a few hours time. I leaned across and took one of her hands in mine. It was soft and warm; she looked at me and smiled. I wanted to tell her how much she had come to mean to me. But all I could do was to smile shyly and release her hand, noticing the spots of colour that had risen in her cheeks.

When the packed bus reached the top of Scurmore Hill, I saw the lights of Enniscrone: - all seven of them. The conductor was the same one as on that first Christmas Eve and was still singing *"I'm Dreaming of a White Christmas"* when the bus halted in the Square. A light drizzle was falling as I stepped down from the bus and began my walk towards Carrowhubbock. I could have stayed with my father and stepmother in the town, but decided that my home was still the farmhouse.

One thing that was expected of a clerical student while at home from the seminary was daily attendance at Mass. To accommodate the nuns the daily liturgy was celebrated at eight o'clock each weekday morning. So it was at that hour the morning after I arrived home that I gave the good sisters and a couple of dozen pious women their first glimpse of Martin Gordon in his new role as a clerical student.

Christmas passed without my seeing Joan. The weather was very inclement and I was glad when the holiday ended. But when kissing Madeleine Conboy goodbye I felt lonely and hated the thought of leaving her to return to the all-male environment of the African Missions College and the getting out of bed at six o'clock on a January morning.

With Easter Sunday 1951 falling on 25 March, the term was going to be a relatively short one. But unfortunately we students were not permitted home for Easter as we were required to participate in the ceremonies of Holy Week. Naturally, I had attended the Holy Week ceremonies in Enniscrone, but now I was to witness them carried out in a more impressive manner. The theatricality of Tenebrae; the solemnity of Good Friday and the joy of Easter were conveyed in the most exemplary fashion by priests and students in the presence of the huge congregations who attended each and every liturgical service between Wednesday night and Sunday morning

After our exertions during Holy Week we were treated to an excursion to the picturesque western part of Co Cork. On the actual day, the weather was sunny but with a bitterly cold wind blowing down from the Arctic, reminding one just how early Easter was that year. First stop on the journey was Glengariff, famous for a small island off its shoreline.

Surrounded by the wild Atlantic and in one of the most remote parts of the country, Garnish Island contains a perfect Italian Garden, complete with pergolas; rock gardens; eight marble ponds full of goldfish; Roman statues on marble pedestals; cypress trees and an amazing collection of flowers and shrubs. The whole thing might have been blown over from Tuscany by some preternatural wind.

Reading a small guidebook I discovered the island had been bought by the brother of an English Viscount, because the man's wife fell in love with the place. Together, husband and wife set out to create a 'Garden of Eden' in a wilderness, employing a Signor Pineto to give the project an authentic Italian flavour. The hour that we spent on the island left me full of admiration for the English couple who had accomplished so much.. If Faith can move mountains, then love cannot be very far behind.

Lunch was taken at a local hotel, then it was back on to the coach to move on into the beautiful countryside. Finally, as the clouds began to gather and the sun to dip behind the mountains, we arrived at Gougane Barra: our last stop of the day and where we were to have supper in Healy's Hotel.

Gougane Barra is a wild, desolate place where, legend has it Finbarr, the patron saint of Cork, lived and died. It is also the source of the River Lee as it starts is torturous journey towards the city of Cork and out to the open sea.

Sitting in the hotel dining room enjoying a supper of a mixed grill, across the lake the shape of the mountains were still visible in the gathering darkness, the lines of a poem we had been learning in Dr Alfie O'Shea's English class came to mind:

137

"There is a green isle in lone Gougane Barra,
Whence Allua of song rushes forth as an arrow;
In deep valley Desmond a thousand wild fountains
Come down to that lake from their home in the mountains".

The wind was blowing strongly and the first spots of rain were beginning to fall, when we emerged from Healy's Hotel. All things considered, the day had been an enjoyable one; though it hardly compensated for not being with Madeleine and Joan over Easter.

There was no study that night, and we were free to do whatever we liked until night prayers. I chose to go to the library, loving the quiet of the room with its subdued lighting and shelves packed with a catholic selection of books and magazines, amongst which were copies of their National Geographic. This fine magazine contained superb photography; especially the colour plates of young, native women in the Far East or Africa, their breasts glistening tantalisingly in front of the camera lens. I gazed in fascination at the diversity in shape and size of those female protuberances, and wondered how priests working amongst them coped with such sexually stimulating displays of nudity?

With two thirds of the college year over, I was reasonably pleased with my progress in all of my subjects: Latin and English being personal favourites. The many hours of reading since childhood gave me a slight advantage over my classmates when it came to answering questions in class or writing an essay. Father Alfie O'Shea who taught English, used to embarrass me when he would say:

"Mr. Gordon, if I were you I wouldn't let anyone of these 'yobbos' tie my shoelaces. You come from one of the princely families of Europe".

Can you imagine how one felt in a room full of traditional Irish family names? But I can never recall any of my classmates resenting what the priest had said about me and them.

Father McNamara had by then replaced Father Morton as Latin teacher 'Sonny,' to give the priest his nickname, was a good teacher. But whenever a student irritated him with what he considered a stupid answer, he would turn on the hapless young man and tell him:

"Sonny, go and get a job in Board Na Mona - the State Peat Producing company - you don't have to become a priest to save your soul. You can do that just as well cutting turf on the bog".

Father Harmon, the oldest priest on the college teaching staff instructed us in the rudiments of book keeping. He had a Master's degree in science. The only thing I can recall learning from him about bookkeeping was, as he announced with monotonous regularity at the start of each class *"Whatever goes out is placed on the left-hand side; whatever comes in on the right-hand side".* End of lesson

The priest had one trait that endeared him to us all: his sense of humour. Repeatedly he would tell his classes that he regarded the students from Galway as the lowest form of the human species. *"Why, you may well ask, do I hold this opinion?"* the priest would say, as he surveyed his audience like a detective trying to recognise a suspect. *"For years, those fellows have been stealing my books and pawning them when they get home to Galway. But don't worry; I'll get every single one of my books back soon".* Father Harman would then pause and look at us with a calm expression that displayed confidence in his ability to outwit his sworn enemies. Then he would continue: *"I am perfecting a giant magnet and when it's ready I'm going to turn it in the direction of Galway and all my books that are lying in the pawn shops up there will come flying back to me in Cork",* he would growl; a sound which from one of such small stature gave rise to his nickname, *"The Bear".*

His humour, I learned, was also directed at his fellow priests. For example, whenever the bursar, Henry Kenny, took to his bed with a recurrence of malaria, Father Harmon would stand at the patient's bedroom door and say: *"I don't know how we are going to get your coffin out of this room".* What a lovely saintly man he was.

Most afternoons after tea, one would catch sight of him, wearing an old gabardine coat that had turned a mouldy blue with age, wheel his bike around by the church on his way to visit the sick. Years after his death, people who remember him visit his grave in the Community Cemetery.

With the arrival of the Month of May came the college custom of the student body gathering around the statue of the Blessed Virgin standing on its pedestal overlooking the football field, to sing such hymns as: *"I'll Sing Hymn To Mary"* or *"The Loveliest Flower of The May"* in her praise, before we resumed our last session of study for the day. Under the evening sky our voices floated Heavenwards in this simple act of devotion. But the feeling that there was something mawkish about virile young men engaged in this act has never left me.

The long, hot days of the month were a joy; but with them came the realisation that exams were looming; I was studying hard and felt confident that I would do reasonably well.

When the results were eventually announced, my confidence had been justified, passing all the subjects. But it was Father McNamara himself who told me that I had passed in Latin: 'You got 68%,' he whispered to me when we met on the Avenue after breakfast one morning before he resumed his stroll, puffing contentedly on his pipe.

On the last day of term, I was busily engaged in chopping blocks in the farmyard, which I then wheeled up to the cellar underneath Father McKay's office. I was on my third load when the priest appeared on the steps above me.

'Make certain that you brush up all those chippings when you finish.'

'Yes, Father,' I dutifully answered

I was enjoying afternoon tea, when another student approached and told me that the Superior wanted to see me immediately.

As I emerged onto the Avenue, I could see Father McKay standing on the steps like some Roman Emperor waiting to signal whether a Christian was to live or die. My eyes focused on the ground underneath the cellar window. I had swept the place clean of all traces of wood chippings. But there was no mistaking what now littered the ground. How could this happen, I wondered, as I arrived in front of the priest.

'Mr. Gordon, what did I tell you to do?' I repeated his instructions.

'Then how do you explain this?' He asked, indicating with his hand the debris. 'What have you to say for yourself?'

'I did as you told me, Father.'

'You are a lying, Martin Gordon,' he thundered. He continued to glare at me, then without saying another word he went back into the building, leaving me still standing angry and bewildered. He is crazy, I decided, as I went to collect a brush and shovel.

As our taxi left St. Joseph's College, I looked back on my first year there with mixed feelings. On the one hand I enjoyed the studies, spiritual exercises and the sporting activities; and the food was of an acceptable standard. But there was something joyless about the life. Now whether this was due to Father McKay's regime, to the effect of the Society being a French Foundation or had something to do with its dramatic beginnings, I couldn't tell. But whatever the cause, I felt that there was something missing from our lives in that institution.

In the first weeks of the almost three month vacation, I helped John with the saving of the hay and on the bog. My hands, softened by college life, suffered for a while until they became accustomed to the work.

Though I was enjoying life, it wasn't until Joan arrived for her two weeks holiday that I felt my own holiday had begun. During the two weeks she was at home, we managed to swim a couple of times and go to the cinema. But as a man with a 'vocation,' I had to be most circumspect in my behaviour; never at any time or in any way giving the impression that Joan and I were 'going steady.' When we visited the cinema, Mary Kilcullen was usually present to act as a chaperone. But with Joan's mother there was no such problem because of the difference in our ages. We still continued to link arms on the way home from the Ballina cinemas.

When I saw Joan off on the bus at the end of her holiday, I found it difficult to believe that there were barely 3 weeks of my own holiday still remaining. But with Joan no longer around, the thought of returning to Cork aroused in me no feelings of homesickness.

Walking around the grounds of the college on that first night back, I was given a message that Father McKay wished to see me in his office. As I made my way along the Avenue, I recalled how he had been giving me long appraising looks during supper.

'Well, Mr. Gordon, had you a nice holiday?'

I assured him I had.

'Now, I suppose that you are wondering why I have sent for you?'

Well, the question had crossed my mind in the last five minutes.

'Yes, Father.'

'I have decided to appoint you bellman for the year. 'I don't have to tell you that being bellman is a very responsible position. Do you think that you can do the job?'

'I'm sure that I can, Father,' I assured him, with more conviction in my voice than my innermost feelings warranted.

'Here is the watch. The bell you will find out on the landing next to the clock.' I took the watch and slipped it on my wrist.

'You duties will commence with the ringing of the bell for night prayers.' I mumbled a 'thank you, Father,' and staggered from his presence, wondering what in God's name had I done to deserve such a fate.

From that first moment when I swung my arm back and forth sending out loud peels from the wooden-handled bell, the daily life of Wilton College was in my hands. From 6 a.m. until 10 p.m. every student and priest alike, even Father McKay had to answer the summons of the bell.

Up until shortly before Halloween I had encountered no problems as bellman. But waking up with a start, one night, I thought that I had overslept when the illuminated hands of the large alarm clock indicated that it was about three minutes past six o'clock. Jumping out of bed as if catapulted from cannon, hurriedly put on my dressing gown, slipped feet into slippers and grabbed the bell. *"Benedicamus Domino"*, I cried out, shaking the bill with enthusiasm and raced out of the dormitory to arouse the inhabitants of the small dormitory next door and the priests at the other end of the building. Funny, I thought as I sped along the corridor ringing the bell and crying out for everyone to *"Bless the Lord"*; there wasn't the same volume of response usually heard. The door opened to my left and Father Harmon appeared with his dressing gown thrown over his shoulders and a night cap on his head, looking like one of the Seven Dwarves.

'Paddy, what time is it?' He asked crossly.

'About five minutes past six, Father.'

The priest held out his pocket watch: 'well, Paddy, what time is it?'

'It's 12:35, Father.'

The priest looked sternly at me for a couple of seconds: 'Paddy, boil that alarm clock.'

I had to run the gauntlet of angry scowls from other priests as I retreated back to the dormitory, where I found most of the students were back in their beds; but a couple of conscientious souls were sitting on the edges of their beds wondering what to do next. The devout Joseph Devine was in the washroom washing in cold water. I broke the news gently to him. What I found strange about the incident was the silence of Fr. McKay, the next day.

That term Father McKay introduced a two hour reading period on Sunday mornings when we were allowed to read any book of our own choice from the library. To a reader like me the news was most welcome.

One night when in the library selecting reading matter for the following Sunday, I was turning over some pages of the book I was contemplating as my choice, when I was astonished to find a postcard size photograph of a young, smiling, well-built woman, some of the buttons of whose dress were undone to the waist, unashamedly displaying one very large breast for the delectation of whoever was taking the photograph.

Looking over my shoulder, I saw that I was alone. Quickly, I slipped the photograph into an inside pocket of my jacket and hurried away.

In the recreation hall, I gathered some of my fellow students around and produced the photograph for their viewing; once they all had a look, and in a few cases is second look at the buxom wench, I took the photograph to the nearest toilet, tore it into little fragments and flushed them into the river Lee. If I had been familiar then with the poetry of D. H. Lawrence, I might very well have quoted his lines:

> "Then her bright breast she will uncover
> and yield her honeydrop to her lover".

How on earth, I have often wondered since, did a photograph like that get into a seminary library?

That Christmas of 1952, I enjoyed the Festive dinner with the Conboy family for the first time. Joan looked more of a woman now; she wore loose fitting jumpers so as not to accent her figure. She and I continued our practice of washing and drying the dishes after each meal. Oh, how I enjoyed those moments of domestic life as we stood side-by-side in the scullery talking about films and books or about her life in Dublin, where she now worked in the Savings

Department of the G.P.O. When occasionally our hands touched, spots of colour would appear in Joan's cheeks.

When I carried her suitcase up to the railway station on the morning of her departure, my heart went out to her when I saw how sad and lonely she looked at having to leave home.

The morning I had to say farewell to Madeleine Conboy I was comforted by the knowledge that in five months time, I would finish my course in Cork and move on to the Society's Novitiate in Co Galway.

On Easter Monday, 1952, we were allowed out of college to visit the Savoy Cinema which was showing the Film *"The Student Prince"*. Next morning, with the sun shining warmly for the first time that year, I was busily performing my allotted house work for that week: cleaning the outside toilets and was singing *"When it's Summertime in Heidelberg"*, when Father McKay walked in.

'What is the meaning of this, Mr. Gordon, he thundered, his eyes blazing with fury. Well what was I to say? I was happy; it was a beautiful morning and the birds were singing in the trees. Better not, he might think I was a little bit simple and ought to be carried off to the big red brick building on the other side of the river Lee.

'This is not good enough,' he shouted. 'This is a black mark against you,' the stern faced priest told me as he continued to glare at me.

A few weeks later I had another confrontation with the Superior when, according to him I rang the bell too early for afternoon tea. When I defended myself that I had rung the bell at the correct time, Father McKay accused me of moving the hands of the watch forward. I couldn't believe what I was hearing. Was the man completely mad? By now I was angry really angry: 'No, Father, I didn't do such thing,' I said slowly and deliberately while staring him in the face. My spirited response took him by surprise. But he quickly recovered and told me 'I believe that you did; and that is another black mark against you,' he announced before turning away and entering the building.

The only logical explanation to explain the priests irrational behaviour must have had something to do with whatever happened to him while serving as a chaplain with the British Army in the Far

East. So now I had two 'black marks' against my name. At this rate, I judged, I would never be ordained. Fortunately there was only a few weeks left of the term, I thought with some relief.

Many years late Father McCarthy, a priest of the Society who was working then for Vatican Radio, told me during the visit of Pope John Paul 2 to Switzerland, it was his opinion that Father McKay ought never to have been put in charge of students.

Despite Father McKay's inadequacies as a college President, I left St. Joseph's College with a feeling that my two years there had changed me: I had a new found confidence in myself, for one thing. Fathers O'Shea; 'Sonny' McNamara; Harman - hope you got all your books back - and Father McKay, killed in a car crash in Nottingham in 1972,Aged 61, Requiescant in Pace.

June and July slipped by quickly and soon it was August. I became apprehensive when no letter had arrived to confirm my entry into the Novitiate. When I spoke to George Conboy about the matter he allowed me to use the telephone in Lipton's to speak to someone at the Ballinafad College. From the priest I spoke to at the junior seminary I learned that a new Provincial had been elected, and he had decreed that every student from then on must obtain a university degree. In order to obtain this one must of course have passed the leaving certificate; which none of us in the late Vocation's class had obtained.

I stood there are in the backroom of Lipton's, with the receiver still in my hand, and feeling and emptiness at the bottom of my stomach. A *"Spoiled Priest"* that's what I am, I thought with horror. When George appeared at the door I explained what the priest had told me. 'The bastards,' George said, and apologised for his 'French.' He suggested I better go up to Morrison Terrace and tell Madeleine.

The key was not in the front door, indicating that Mrs. Conboy was either downtown or taking her customary afternoon rest. I put my hand through the letterbox and withdrew the key to the front door. 'Is that you Martin?' Madeleine Conboy called from upstairs. 'Yes, Mam,' I answered, as I climbed the stairs with the realisation that I would be going into her bedroom for the first time

On entering, I went straight over and sat down on the bed. A statue of the Virgin gazed out at the room. Madeleine smiled up at me, the whiteness of her bare shoulders showed tantalisingly above the bedspread. 'Have you decided what you're going to do now, Martin?' I hadn't given any thought to what I might do with my future. Flight to England seemed the only alternative at that moment. Then I thought about the clerical student I had met during the summer, who lived outside Enniscrone and was only two years away from ordination. When I told Madeliene about this student, she immediately suggested that I write to him without delay. 'You can use my writing paper downstairs,' she said. Before taking the bus back home, I posted my letter to: Mr. Michael Timlin, Pallottine College, Thurles, County Tipperary.

A week later a reply from the college arrived. At the top of the sheet of notepaper was a crest with a motto in Latin, which, with my newly acquired proficiency in the language was able to translate as *"The Love of Christ Spurs Us On"*. The letter was from the rector of the Pallottine College.

Dear Mr. Gordon,

Michael Timlin gave me your letter to read enquiring about the possibility of your entering the Pallottine College. I hope to be in your part of the country in about three week's time and will call to see you. In the meantime, I enclose a small leaflet which will tell you something about us.

I remain,
Yours sincerely in Christ,
Daniel Hayes, S.C.A

Reading the small leaflet, I learned that the Pallottine Fathers - The Society of the Catholic Apostolate - was founded in 1835 by a Roman priest, Vincent Pallotti, for the purpose of mobilizing lay Catholics to become involved in the work of the church. *"God"*, he wrote, *"Asks you to become a saint in the world, in ordinary life... Sanctity consists in doing the will of God"*.

Eight days later at around nine o'clock in the evening, I was sitting by the fireside reading *"At Sundown the Tiger"* by Ethel Mannin, when a knock sounded on the front door. I hastily slipped on my shoes while Aunt Nellie went to the door. Two tall, distinguished looking priests entered the kitchen. 'God save all here,' said the younger looking of them, even though he had a shiny, bald head.

'God save you kindly,' my aunt replied.

I rose from my chair to greet our visitors. 'You must be Martin,' the same priest said as he extended a hand. 'I am Father Hayes and this is Father Hedderman,' introducing his companion.

For the next half hour the two Pallottine Fathers questioned me on my standard of education and the reason for my rejection by the African Missions. When I showed them the Latin grammar used at Wilton and how far the class had progressed in it at the end of two years, they appeared genuinely impressed. I noticed that Father Hedderman was having a good look through the pages of the novel.

'Well, Martin, I think you can come to us,' Father Hayes at last announced. 'What do you think, Father?' 'I think that he'll do very well with us,' the priest replied, as he laid down the book.

One week later I was again on the train traveling South to a new beginning with a Society which, if it's two priests were an example, would be a transformation from the African Missions as represented by Father McKay. As the train pulled into Thurles station, I recalled that occasion almost 2 years to the day when I had arrived in that county Tipperary town by mistake. Mistake? I wondered.

Following directions, I made my way along a narrow street of unimposing shops and houses that lead eventually into a wide square that was quite clearly the commercial heart of the town. After crossing a bridge from which I noticed a large institutional type building surrounded by trees, I walked on past the Ursuline convent adjacent to the Cathedral, whose facade and 150 foot campanile are modelled on Pisa Cathedral. Directly opposite were the entrance gates and a long, tree-lined avenue sloping gently up to the large building I had seen earlier from the bridge. Some yards farther on stood another convent, this time of the Presentation Order. The novelist, R. H. Benson, had used all these ecclesiastical buildings grouped in such close proximity to one another as a setting in one of his books. A few minutes later I reached the Pallottine College.

The two story edifice was set well back from the street and surrounded by a 7 foot wall. High above the front door a statue of the Virgin Mary stood in a niche looking out over the garden to the street beyond. Somewhere within the building a bell rang when I pushed the large, bass doorbell. Footsteps sounded from the other side of inner doors, one of which swung towards me to reveal a black-cassocked figure.

'Hello, you must be Mick Timlin's friend. He told me to expect you,' the, broad-shouldered man of about 25 years said. 'I'll put you in the parlour and then tell Mick you have arrived. Let me take that,' he offered, as I went to pick up my suitcase.

I had been in the room only about five minutes when there was a knock on the door and Mick Timlin's smiling face appeared. 'You're heartily welcome, Martin, how are they all in Enniscrone? I expect you're hungry.'

After eating my supper of ham and tomatoes, we collected the suitcase and walked through the college grounds, passing on the way a small building that looked like it was meant to be a chapel, but obviously was not used as such, as I could see a tennis table standing just inside the door. Michael Timlin saw my puzzled look and laughed: 'that's the *"Ark"*, we use it as a recreation hall.' Near the top of the garden was a tennis court, with a cluster of apple trees at either end. Eventually we came to a building of more recent origin, but smaller than the one we had just come from. 'We call this place *"Bethany"*; it's where the postulants sleep and study. You are upstairs in the big dorm,' my guide told me.

'And the building we've just left?' I asked.

'That's called *"Jerusalem".*'

I counted 12 small beds in the dormitory. My one was placed to the left inside the door

At 9:50 I joined the community in the large upstairs room in 'Jerusalem' that served as a chapel. Each of the students had his own prie-dieu: I recognised Father Hayes, the rector, kneeling inside the heavily curtained door; his head buried in his hands. Mike Timlin came towards me and indicated in a whisper that I could occupy a vacant prie-dieu to the left of an antiquated looking organ. The priests and seminarians rose at 6.30 a.m.; the rest of the community at 7 a.m.

The breakfast that was served up the following morning came as a shock. The tea was watery - hence its nickname, 'scald.' But it was the porridge that really took my breath away. Not only was the portion small, but one could turn the spoon almost upside down and the substance would do is best to stick to it. Like the tea, the milk was weak; and although there was plenty of bread to eat, the tiny role of butter was sufficient only for one slice.

There were three other students in the class preparing for the Entrance examination to St. Patrick's College, where the Pallottine students attended lectures prior to ordination. This was a prerequisite imposed on the Society by then Archbishop of Cashel, prior to its being allowed to open a house in his diocese. My classmates, Paddy O'Dwyer from Co Waterford, Tim Twomey from Co Cork and Christy Maher a native of Dun Laoghire, Co Dublin, were cheerful characters and accepted me immediately as one of them. We had to study only three subjects: English, Latin and math's. Father Hayes, or 'Big Dan,' as he was popularly known, took us for Latin in the 'End Room' - so called because it was at the end of the corridor and had a dual purpose as his living room and community room. Father Gormley, who suffered from nerves, held his English class in the parlour; Flor Carroll, a small, chirpy theological student from Co Kerry, and who had a brother already a Pallottine priest in Africa, tried to teach us math's in the cold, dusty library: the billiard table serving as our desks.

During the first few weeks in Thurles, it was noticeable that the rector never had any direct dealings with the students; unlike his counterpart in the African Missions College, Father Hayes appeared to rule through the prefect, Paddy 'Simon' Ryan, who had a slight speech impediment and along with my friend Michael Timlin, was due to be ordained in two years time. Some years ago Paddy 'Simon,' gained world - wide notoriety when Belgium police arrested him on being in possession of a false passport; charges he strenuously denied; he was also suspected of training terrorists in the use of electronic explosives equipment and carrying cash and orders to provincial IRA units on the continent. If that were not enough, he was also linked with setting up weapons shipment networks in partnership with Colonel Gaddafi. The newspapers claimed that Paddy was proficient in a number of European languages. However, his Pallottine colleagues who worked with him in Tanzania will tell you that he was one of the worst linguists amongst them. Prior to all this happening, the Pallottine Fathers had already expelled the priest from the Society.

Following the disappointment of breakfast an attempt was made at lunchtime to serve us a decent meal of soup, meat, vegetables and potatoes, followed by a pudding. But despite its plenitude, most of the food was badly cooked and in the case of the meat, of the poorest quality. Our daily sustenance finished at seven o'clock in the evening with 'scald' and again as much bread as one could eat; but most of it dry.

However with the arrival of Halloween, we gave ourselves up to an orgy of eating for about three nights as we devoured the contents of the numerous parcels that poured in from all around the country. Mrs. Conboy sent me her usual fruitcake and my aunt a ten shilling note.

When we filed into the refectory for supper on those blessed nights, our faces lit up at the sight of plates piled high with a variety of food that one or more of the students seated at a particular table had laid out: thick slabs of butter; wedges of cake; even sausages and pieces of chicken lay tantalisingly in front of us as we waited impatiently for Father Hayes to finish the saying of grace. Once seated, a plague of locusts could not have done a better job on all those tasty morsels.

Six weeks had passed since my arrival and I found life much more relaxed than in Cork. There were rules to be obeyed, of course, but looking back I can't ever recall being as conscious of them as I was in the African Missions College. For example, smoking was forbidden, but the more senior students visited a shed behind 'Bethany' for a quick 'drag' after meals and sometimes between classes. 'Big Dan' had to know about this practice, but ignored it as long as he felt that it was not being abused, and that younger students were not involved.

Unlike at Wilton in Cork, the college had no farm surrounding it. Apart from the football field and another large field beyond 'Bethany,' the only other land was a small patch used to grow vegetables near the tennis court. A narrow laneway ran along one side of the college and continued past the side entrance used by the seminarians to gain access to Saint Patrick's College. This laneway was known locally as *"Lovers Lane"*? Before the winter nights arrived, one would occasionally catch a glimpse of courting couples passing by the study hall windows, the girl shyly averting her eyes from the curious gaze of the student priests.

Three days prior to the Christmas vacation, I found myself involved in an unexpected trip to Dublin. The community had just begun night players when there came the most unearthly of moaning sounds from one of the deacons due to be ordained the following June. Some of the young postulants shouted with fright, one leaped to his feet and knocked over his prie-dieu. Still the awful sound continued. Paddy 'Simon' and Willie Burke's classmate, Seamus McGuire, took the afflicted deacon by the shoulders and led him gently from the chapel, followed by Father Hayes.

Next morning, the Prefect approached me and told me Father Hayes wanted to see me. I knocked. 'Come in,' Father Hayes looked up from his desk where he was writing. 'Sit down for a moment until I finish this letter.' Copies of the day's newspapers lay on the carpet. Father Hayes turned from the desk to face me. 'I have to take Willie Burke to Dublin and I want you to come with me. Christy Maher will be coming along as well. So go and pack your suitcase and be ready to leave by 9:30.' 'The suitcase?', I queried. 'Yes, seeing that there are only a few days left before the holidays, you can go home from Dublin,' the Rector said.

A very obviously heavily sedated Willie Burke sat by my side in the backseat of the car. My classmate occupied the front passenger seat. There was very little conversation on the incident - free journey to Dublin, where the patient was admitted to a psychiatric institution on the south side of the city. Afterwards, Father Hayes took Christy and me to lunch in the restaurant attached to the Savoy Cinema. Before leaving, he gave each of us a five pound note and wished us a Merry Christmas.

On the train home to Ballina I thought of the student left behind in the Dublin hospital. There was no chance of him ever being ordained: church law in the matter of mental illness in a candidate for the priesthood was very precise, and extended even to relations. As it so happened, the unfortunate Willie Burke had a cousin who was around 15 years of age in the college. I wondered, at the time, what action Father Hayes would take in regard to him? In the end, to my amazement, the boy was allowed to continue to ordination only to be institutionalized within a couple of months of his becoming a priest. I happened to meet him a few years ago when I visited Bruree House in Co Limerick: one of the centres that Sister Consilio, a Mercy nun, has opened up in Ireland for the treatment of alcohol and substance abuse.

Bruree House itself was once the home of Lady Ursula Vernon, a noted beauty and second daughter of the Duke of Westminster. She and her husband, Major Stephen Byrne, who had polio and was confined to a wheelchair, had a racing stables attached to the house. Elizabeth Bowen, the Anglo-Irish novelist, who had a home in nearby County Cork, was a frequent visitor to the couple.

That Christmas holiday was uneventful. I met Joan only once and noticed she wore a little more makeup and looked even more grown-up; was there a boyfriend in Dublin, I wondered; and felt the first pangs of jealousy.

All too soon it was time to return to college; and even though this was my third time leaving home in January, it got no easier. In 'Big Dan's' classes he had given me the nickname of; *"the Full-back from Scotland"*. I never did discover how he came to call me that. One morning he asked me 'what part of speech is that?' I looked at the sentence, 'Gerund of Attraction, Father.' Behind his glasses the priest's eyes opened wide with a look of disbelief. 'By the hockey' - a favourite expression of his - 'I have studied under the greatest Latinist in the world and I have never heard of-what did you call it?'

'Gerund of Attraction, Father.'

'Next sentence, Christy Maher,' the priest barked, while still staring at me.

A few weeks later during evening recreation, the Rector stopped me on the walks. 'You were right' he said, and continued on his way.

Father Gormley, who taught English, was tall and thin and with a most ungainly walk; like a sailor who had tried too often to walk on the heaving deck of a ship. His hair was ginger coloured, flat, brushed back straight and parted down the middle. His nickname was *"The Lank"*. Serving mass for him was something we all tried to avoid as much as possible, because he suffered from scruples. This meant that if he did not pronounce a word or a phrase in the liturgy to his own satisfaction, he would continue to repeat the offending words until he was fully satisfied. An invalid from the Pallottine missions in Africa, he now edited a magazine to promote an awareness of the Society's work and also had the responsibility for collecting money from the hundreds of boxes placed in shops and pubs around Ireland.

Again, as in Cork, reading was customary at mealtimes. This was no hardship for me, as I liked to hear a good book being read, especially if it were of the quality of Axel Munthe's *"The Story of San Michele"*. Munthe was a Swedish doctor who gained worldwide fame when this book was published. He told his London publisher, Jock Murray, that he had become bored by his weekly audiences with King Gustav. When the King arranged for him to be buried in the royal mausoleum, Munthe was horrified to think he might continue to be bored by the sovereign for all eternity. After his death, his son secretly disposed of his father's corpse at sea, and an empty coffin was interred in the mausoleum.

In my private reading one book I recall with affection was Halliday Sutherland's *"The Arches of the Years"*. In it he tells the story of a factory in Spain, whose weather vane was in the shape of a cockerel. The local folklore was that the cockerel would crow the first time a virgin went through the factory gates. Nobody had ever heard it crow.

The year passed quickly and soon I was on the train heading homewards for the long summer months. On that journey, I thought of the tale still current amongst the people of Enniscrone, that there was a curse on the seaside town which said that no priest would ever come from there. I am not certain who was supposed to have laid the curse, whether it was St. Patrick or a 'whiskey priest,' cursing the local people for their lack of Christian charity towards him.

Canon James Greer, in *"The Windings of the Moy"*, relates how he used to hear it said that a Priest Hopkins, who had fallen foul of his Catholic bishop and had then become the Protestant curate of the Union of Castleconnor and Kilglass, and had, as he neared the end of his life, pronounced maledictions on the parish. One of them was that no priest before God would ever arise from the parish of Kilglass. It was certainly a fact that at the time of writing his book, Enniscrone was the one place that had failed to produce a priest. Some young men had tried only to give up long before their ordination. Now here I was following in their footsteps. Would I succeed where others, with the advantage of wealth and a superior education, had failed? If I passed the entrance exam to St. Patrick's and got through the Novitiate year successfully, then I thought I stood a good chance of reaching ordination: after all, I wasn't a native of the town, was I?

As usual my holiday began when Joan came home. We spent as much time as we could with each other. But she was changing into a woman extremely conscious of her own sexuality and my vocation. I sensed a barrier between us that had never been there before. But we still enjoyed the moments we shared together.

In the few remaining weeks of the holiday I worked hard in studying for the entrance exam. I was very confident about my English and Latin; but the math's...?

My classmates and I sat the exam on 6 September and were passed intellectually fit to begin the study of philosophy the following year. But first we had to be invested in the habit of the Society of the Catholic Apostolate, and then spend the full year isolated in the Novitiate situated at Cabra, a few miles outside the town of Thurles and separated from the sugar factory by a small river. A local priest had bequeathed the house and farm to the society. A large portrait of him hung in the hall and his name featured high on the list of benefactors regularly prayed for in the Pallottine community.

The actual clothing ceremony was a relatively simple affair conducted by the new novice master, the Reverend Dr. John Hassett. In giving the habit, he prayed:

"May the Lord clothe you with the new man who has been created according to God, in the justice and holiness of truth".

When he handed us the Roman collar his prayer was that *"Your servant may so wear this that he may obtain your grace in this life and your glory in the next".*

On giving us the cincture, Father Hassett asked *"May the Lord gird thee with the cincture of purity and extinguish in thy loins the fire of lust, so that the virtue of continence and chastity may ever abide in thee".*

Finally the priest presented each of us with a candle saying, *"Receive, dearly beloved brother, the light of Christ as a pledge of your immortality, that being dead to the world you may live to God. Arise from amongst the dead and Christ will enlighten you".*

We were now to be addressed as *"Brother"*.

The Novitiate's extensive, fertile farm on which we were to work for the next year was under the supervision of a lay-brother, Willie Murphy; one of three Lay Brothers at Cabra who had dedicated their lives to serving God through their manual labour.

After morning Mass, each of the novices had an allotted half-an-hour's work to do before breakfast: my daily task was to bring in the herd of cows for milking along with 'Charlie,' the bull. A dog always accompanied me just in case 'Charlie' decided to take an interest in me instead of 'Josie,' his constant companion. The remainder of the day we spent doing seasonal work on the farm, keeping the main house, the chapel and corridors of the novice's quarters clean, and attending lectures on the spiritual life or the rule of our Founder. Prayer, spiritual reading and long periods of silence took up the rest of our time until 'lights out' at 10 o'clock.

On speaking about the Rule, as laid down by Vincent Pallotti, Father Hasset emphasized that it was to be regarded as the presence of the Founder amongst us. Some of the things we listened to struck me as very odd, to say the least. For example, it was suggested that when drinking wine, his followers should dilute it with water lest it to lead to unrestrained behaviour. Concerning contact with females he was very clear in his instruction: no undue familiarity with women, especially young women. This was to be avoided at all costs. But the rule which, or so it seemed to me, to contradict the Society's motto: Caritas Christi Urget Nos, was that in which Pallotti commanded his followers to shun any member who has left the Society for the love of a woman. I could understand the reasoning behind such an injunction, but still thought it extremely harsh. Would Christ act in this manner? I didn't think so.

In more recent times, when the many illicit sexual relationships of priests and sometimes even bishops have been revealed, it is quite hypocritical of the Catholic Church to reject those priests who have left the active ministry, but allow clergy who have given scandal to remain. I personally know of three priests who are involved with women. Not only have they been allowed to remain in this situation, but successive bishops in this particular diocese have promoted them. One is believed to have a son. The Catholic Church is therefore seen to condone lust but condemn love.

Our first break from routine came, when on the Feast of All Saints, we went into the college to attend the annual Gaelic football match between St. Patrick's and the Pallottine's: a match we usually lost. The college had picked me to be its goalkeeper and I gave an inspired display to keep my goal intact. The result: Pallottines one goal. St. Patrick's three points: a draw. My friend Mick Timlin said after that game that I ought to be playing for the County Sligo team.

Early in December, the Christmas cards began to arrive; this was to be our first experience of being away from home at the Festive season. I wondered how I would cope without Joan and her mother, with whom I'd spent such a wonderful time the previous Christmas.

Father Hassett celebrated a Missa Cantata at midnight, during which Christy Maher and I did our best to lead the small congregation in the singing, despite the attempts of the celebrant to lead us into different keys. Afterwards we gathered in the refectory for tea and currant cake. The Novice Master showed his head around the door to wish us a *"Happy Christmas"* and to remind us that we didn't have to get up in the morning until nine o'clock.

Back in my cubicle, I stood at the window looking out to the moonlit football field and thought of Joan. I picked up her Christmas card from its prominent position on my locker and read for the umpteenth time the words of greeting. I felt moistness in my eyes as I lifted the card my lips and kissed her name. 'Happy Christmas, Joan, I whispered.'

Everything possible was done to make our Christmas Day as pleasant as it could be: the lunch was excellent; after it, we were given the use of a downstairs room where, for the rest of the day, we sat around a blazing fire listening to the radio and eating our way through a couple of boxes of chocolates. Father Hassett had left soon after he had eaten with us to visit his family in nearby Toomevara.

Undressing for a bed that night, I had to admit that the day had turned out better than expected.

Once the winter was over, work on the farm began in earnest. Added to my morning work of the cows was caring for the newly-hatched turkeys and chickens. Out in the fields we helped Brother

Murphy prepare the ground for the cereal crops, and in the garden we did some weeding and planting.

For the third time that year, we made the short journey into the college: the previous two trips had been to attend the St. Patrick's night play, and to watch the hurling match between the two neighbouring colleges. But on that second Sunday in June we attended the ordination of Michael Timlin and his classmates, including Paddy 'Simon' Ryan, in the Cathedral of the Assumption. Afterwards, we knelt on the tennis court to receive the traditional blessing of the newly ordained.

'Pity you can't get home to serve my first mass,' Father Timlin said, as I stood up to shake his hand. I was sorry as well.

In August, when Brother Cleary went on holidays, the Novice Master appointed me in his place. I knew the kitchen routine from the weekly stints that each novice had to do as assistant to the brother; but to be in sole charge of preparing meals for the whole community and the occasional visitor: was this not a chef too far?

At the end of the first week no complaints about my culinary skills, or lack of them had come my way. Encouraged by this, I began to bake soda bread much as I used to do in my aunts, but with an Aga cooker at my disposal I found the work a good deal easier than on an open turf fire.

The Novitiate year was slowly coming to an end. In a couple of weeks time, we would be leaving Cabra to begin two years of philosophy and four years of theology at St. Patrick's. So what, if anything, had I personally gained from the relative seclusion of the past 12 months? For one thing, I had learned to value silence. Another was in the area of prayer where I'd always thought of it as a one-way conversation. Now, however, I learned that if one listened there was always the chance that the Person at the other end of the line could be heard. Was there anything else?

I think that the year also taught me that a priest is a man alone. He is, as the definition puts it:

"A man chosen from among men for the things
that appertain to God",

and hence can be in the world but not of it; a quality well summed up in the following quotation familiar to most priests:

"To live in the midst of the world without desiring its pleasures,
To be a member of every family without belonging to any,
To share in all sufferings, to penetrate into all secrets.
To heal all wounds,

To go from men to God to offer Him their prayers,
To return from God to men, to bring pardon and hope,
To have a heart of bronze for chastity and a heart of gold for charity,
To console and to pardon. To bless and to love.
What a life!
And it is yours, Oh priest of God".

Pere Lacordaire.

Two days before we were due to move back into the college to begin our philosophy course, Father Hassett sprang a surprise: we were to be allowed home for one week. No explanation was given, nor did it we seek one. A suggestion was made that the decision had something to do with the recent death of his mother.

Enniscrone was quiet when I arrived home that day in September. My aunt was very worried at my unexpected arrival, until I assured her that I would be returning to Thurles in a week's time. Mrs. Conboy looked well and was delighted to see me after an absence of one year. We went to the cinema the night before my return to college.

There was no sadness on the day of my departure; for the first time I really felt like a clerical student and thought of the exciting years ahead, at the end of which would be my ordination as a Pallottine priest and a new life in England, Argentina, Africa or the USA.

A Seminarian

There were 17 of us 'first philosophers' gathered in the classroom of St. Patrick's seminary waiting for the first of our professors to arrive. Two large windows were set high up in the wall. Facing us was a dais on which were placed a desk and a chair. A blackboard occupied part of the wall behind, while the rest of the walls were bare except for a large, wooden crucifix and a sizeable map of the holy land.

St. Patrick's seminary, whose motto was, *"May their Youth be Renewed Like that of the Eagle"* was founded in 1837 to prepare students for the foreign missions; which was why most of those standing around us Pallottines were destined for parishes as far apart as Brighton in England, Glasgow, Auckland in New Zealand and San Diego, California. In the years since its foundation, 1250 priests had been ordained before the college closed as a seminary in 1987. And at the time of writing, 80 former seminarians held a reunion in Thurles. In a photograph of the event in the *"Irish Independent"*, I was able to identify one of my classmates, Joseph Quinn, even though I had not seen him since the morning of our ordination, 50 years ago.

The shrill ringing of a bell ended what muted conversation had been taking place. Seconds later, a small, portly priest, a bundle of books under one arm swept into the room, knelt down at the dais and made the sign of the cross. *"Veni Sancte Spiritus"*, he intoned. We to a man prayed with great gusto for the Holy Spirit to enlighten us during our two years of philosophy.

Father Jackie O'Neill stood at the desk and through gold-rimmed glasses surveyed our anxious faces. 'Now, gentlemen, let me have your names starting here in the front.' 'Paddy Feeney;' 'Gus Tobin;' 'Sean Quinn.' since the Pallottines traditionally sat at the back of the room I was the last to give my name.

The hour passed quickly as the priest talked with enthusiasm about logic, and other constituent parts of the philosophy course he would be teaching us; he left us in no doubt that there would be no daydreaming in his class.

Next to appear was the English professor, Father Ryan, the antithesis of the previous man. His face was tanned and weatherbeaten, almost like that of a sailor or a fisherman; he spoke slowly and deliberately with only the occasional smile flickering around his mouth.

We attended two more lectures that day: physics and modern history. But since they were regarded as 'minor subjects' not too much attention would be paid to them, except by the 'swots.'

Apart from the statutory subjects to be studied at St. Patrick's,' we Pallottines had our own requirements: for example, learning to preach. This took the form of a twice yearly appearance in front of the entire student body to deliver a five minute homily on that Sunday's Gospel. On my own debut I spoke on the parable of the Good Samaritan. When I had finished, old Father Boyle, who was presiding that day, congratulated me and said that I would be a great asset to the Society. As one can imagine, I had to endure a great deal of leg pulling for the rest of that week. But inwardly I was pleased, recalling that lunchtime in Wilton when my initial attempt to read in public was brought to a humiliating and abrupt end.

One well-loved face was missing from the college: 'Big Dan' had left the previous year and gone as parish priest to Our Lady Star of the Sea, in Hastings. This church in the pleasant English seaside resort had been founded by the English poet Coventry Patmore. In his place was James Daly, who had worked in Argentina and Texas. He was a handsome looking man but reserved.

In her first letter of that term from Mrs. Conboy told me that she had been in touch with a Mrs.Gordon, who lived in Ballaghadereen, where she owned a large business; she was also a widow who had buried her husband and all of their seven children. The last one to die was a daughter of 19 years. The widow gave financial help to a number of clerical students in Ireland and abroad, and Mrs. Conboy was hoping that she would add me to that list. Mrs. Gordon had agreed to meet me during the Christmas Holiday.

A very popular tradition in the college was the walk to Ballycahill, a village a few miles from Thurles. The outing usually took place on one of our free days during each term and was always looked forward to with eager anticipation. Before setting out, we assembled in the oratory to pray to God that he *"Turn away our eyes that they may not behold vanity"*. Upon our return *"Turn away, Oh Lord, thy face from my sins, create a clean heart in me Oh God"*.

Upon arriving at our destination, the custom was to take over Mrs. Gleeson's little grocery store and home for a couple of hours, during which we managed to consume almost her entire stock of cakes; eat innumerable loaves of bread layered with a thick covering of butter and jam, and drink gallons of strong, sweet tea. The inner man well and truly satisfied, some sat down to play serious games of cards, while others gathered around a slightly out of tune piano to sing with Paddy 'Doon' Ryan . Paddy was a brilliant musician; much loved by the nuns whom he entertained in the front parlours of many a convent in Counties Limerick and Tipperary. Sadly Paddy's life ended tragically in 1981, when he was found murdered in a motel bedroom near Denver city, USA. The police arrested the handyman employed at the church for the crime.

Mrs. Conboy and I took the early morning bus to meet Mrs. Gordon in the second week of my Christmas holiday. The husband of the woman I was on my way to meet and the father of their seven dead children had been a successful businessman, but died in his early 50s.

With her silver, coloured hair and kind, intelligent face, Mrs. Gordon was easy to converse with. She and Madeleine Conboy seemed to get on well together as they sat by the fireside and chatted away about people they both knew. From time to time they looked in my direction and gave me reassuring smiles. There was no trace of bitterness or indeed of sadness in Annie Gordon's face; but then, according to my aunt, she was a woman of great faith.

A housemaid who had worked in the Gordon home for a number of years, called while we were there. She was now a nun in Australia. While Mrs. Gordon was upstairs, she told Madeleine how she had entered the upstairs drawing room one day to find her mistress standing in front of a large picture of the Sacred Heart offering up the dying infant she held in outstretched hands.

Before leaving, Mrs. Gordon promised she would be delighted to give me some financial help while I was a student. 'It must have been my singing,' I said jokingly to Madeleine on the bus home. It was she who had asked me to sing for Annie Gordon, and I obliged with a rendition of *"A Gordon for Me"* and *"My Ain Folk"*, much to the delight of the widow.

Once we had settled back into college in January of that year of 1955, the rest of the year passed so quickly that it came as something of a surprise when the final week of classes arrived and there were just the exams to overcome before we all went home for summer holiday. A new experience for all of us in the first philosophy class was the oral exams; especially those in which Latin was the language used.

On the August Bank Holiday, I made my first trip on the River Moy to Bartra Island. Joan's father had managed to borrow a boat and an outboard engine to take the three of us for a pleasant day's outing. We began the 30 minute cruise from Bachelors Walk on a morning which, to judge by the sky, promised a fine day ahead.

After passing the Quay two miles downriver where, in years gone by, large numbers of ships had tied up there but in more recent times was rarely used, the first landmark of note on the River was the ruins of Moyne Abbey. This religious foundation had come into being around the year 1500, and belonged to the Franciscans. Built close to the shore, it allowed the monks easy access to the salmon fishing for which, up to the present day even, the river is noted. For this facility the Franciscans had their brother Franciscans in the nearby Rosserk foundation to thank. It was they who cut a channel through the sandbank at the river's mouth, thereby allowing the Atlantic salmon easy access to the River Moy. In time, this channel was widened to permit steamers to sail up the river to within 2 miles of Ballina.

As we chugged past the ancient ruins, the words of Collins's lament on the Abbey of Timoleague sprang to mind:

"Lone and weary as I wandered
By the Black shore of the sea,
Meditating and reflecting
On the world's hard destiny.

Forth the moon and stars gan glimmer
In the quiet tide beneath,
For on slumbering spray and blossom
Breathed not out of heaven a breath.
Still the ancient seat was standing,
Built against that buttress grey,
Where their clergy used to welcome
Weary travelers on their way.

Deserted aisle, deserted chancel,
Tower tottering to your fall,
Many a storm since then has beaten
On the grey head of your wall.

Gone your Abbot, rule and order,
Broken down your altar stones,
Naught see I beneath your shelter
Save a heap of clayey bones...

Oh the hardship, Oh the hatred,
Tyranny and Cruel war,
Persecution and oppression
That have left you as you are".

After beaching the boat on a narrow strip of sand, we unloaded the rugs and boxes of provisions then carried them up to a grassy hill that would afford us shelter from any sea breeze that might spring up later on in the day.

'Mam made certain that we wouldn't go hungry,' Joan said, as we set up camp and examined the boxes contents.

Bartra Island was owned by the actress, Joyce Redmond and her husband, who came each summer for a long holiday and who telephoned George Conboy from London in advance of their arrival with orders for groceries. The English couple allowed the local people to use the island, provided they kept a respectful distance from the house.

'I'm going out to do some fishing before lunch,' Joan's father called out, as he eased the boat back into the water.

Joan and I decided to take a short stroll around the island. When occasionally we crested a sand dune, we caught a glimpse of the house and most of the time we could see George fishing out in the middle of the estuary where, by then, he had a couple of other boats for a company. Along the way we picked a dozen mushrooms.

'They'll go well with the trout when we get home in the evening,' I said. Joan laughed. 'Yes, provided daddy catches them.'

I looked up at the sky and felt the sun's warmth on my face and estimated that the temperature must be at least 70 degrees: and it was still only mid-day. Already my thoughts were turning to the afternoon, when Joan and I would swim together for the first. time in a number of years.

We lunched on chicken salad, brown soda scone, Madeira cake and cups of tea from one of two large flasks. There still remained for later, if we were hungry, egg and onion sandwiches. After the meal, the three of us lay down on the Foxford rugs, Joan between her father and me, and promptly fell asleep. I was the first to wake up. George was turned on his left side with his back to Joan and me. She was lying on her back. I watched the gentle rise and fall of her breasts until I realised what I was doing. 'Martin, how long have I been asleep,' Joan's soft voice asked. I squinted up at the sun. 'About forty minutes I would guess.' I turned around to face her as she sat up, pulling down the hem of her dress which had climbed above her knees. George gave a yawn and turned on to his back and glanced at his watch. 'Have I been asleep that long,' he said between yawns. 'Dammed bad day for fishing,' he growled, looking up at the cloudless sky. Bad day or not, the river produced six lovely sea trout, that along with the mushrooms would provide us with a most tasty supper when we returned to Morrison Terrace around seven o'clock in the evening.

That day was to be one of the most enjoyable days of the summer; spoilt only by Joan's absence when I went swimming late in the afternoon. 'I can't, Martin; not today,' she told me, her cheeks and neck colouring as she spoke.

After Joan left at the end of her two weeks vacation, I decided that it was time to visit Glasgow and spent an enjoyable two weeks there. On the homeward journey from Belfast to Dublin, I shared a railway carriage with a party of cattle drovers. Dressed in the clerical black it was obvious to them that I was a seminarian. Eventually one of the men asked me what I would do as a priest if someone came to me and confessed to having stolen some bread to feed his starving family. I answered that he had the moral right to take that course of action. 'You'll never be a bishop then, because you think with your heart not with your head,' the drover said. I smiled and thought of the tinker woman's prophecy to my father that his son would become a bishop.

In September I returned to college to begin the second year of philosophy. As second year students my classmates and I took up residence in the smaller of the two dormitories in 'Jerusalem,' where each one had a cubicle to himself; but unlike in the Novitiate, these had no doors. One could, if they so wished, hang a curtain to provide some degree of privacy: hardly anyone bothered. The year passed with only one thing of note taking place: our class suffered its first casualty.

January was always, in my estimation, going to be the month when 'drop-outs' would occur. Our fellow student, a St. Patrick's man, returned with the rest of us, but after about six days he slipped quietly out of our lives and returned to his home in Connemara. Nothing was said about his absence; it was almost as if he had never sat amongst us for close on a year and a half. Weeks later, we heard that our classmate on arriving home late that night and naturally tired, probably hungry, had been refused entry into his home. His mother told him that he had brought shame on the family by becoming a 'spoilt priest.' Turned away from his own front door, the poor lad had to seek shelter in a neighbour's house, and with some financial help from them left the following day for England. We were to lose another one of our number the following year, but in much more tragic circumstances.

At the end of those two years of philosophy, my Pallottine classmates and I made our First Profession. To prepare for this, we had to cut short our summer holiday by a month and return to the Novitiate at the beginning of August, where, on the eighth of September, we knelt once again in front of Father Hassett and formally pledge allegiance to the Society of the Catholic Apostolate. We signed the documents which were then taken from us and placed on the altar. Prior to this, the Novice Master had presented each of us with a metal crucifix hanging them around our necks and saying:

"Receive the cross and image of our lord Jesus Christ and follow Him according to His holy vocation, denying yourself and taking up your cross: in the name of the Father, and of the son, and of the Holy Ghost. Amen".

I still have that crucifix and it lies on my bedside table.

During that summer, Madeleine Conboy and I grew closer together in what had become an intense mother-son relationship. I began to sense that she was finding in me someone to fill the void in her life caused by the friction between herself and her husband. I never did discover what the cause was, but I was aware that I was being placed in a very delicate, if not dangerous situation, and resolved that I was not going to be seen to be taking sides between husband and wife. They slept in separate bedrooms and hardly spoke to each other. But as a 'Good Catholic Wife,' Madeleine never refused her husband his 'conjugal rights:' no matter how distasteful that was to her.

Six years on the road to the priesthood had now passed by in the course of which I had found myself a family that had welcomed me as a son and loved the daughter. Now, in a week's time I would be heading back to college to begin the last part of our studies: the four year theology course.

Returned to the seminary, I found that our own Pallottine class was reduced to three: Paddy O'Dwyer was being sent to Rome to do his theology course at the Gregorian University. This came as a surprise to his classmates.

We moved from the small dormitory in Jerusalem to the larger one where most of theologians slept. On the second night I was woken up by a loud Spanish voice going on with the rapidity of a machine gun. Loud groans rose from every cubicle. Then following a loud banging on the flimsy, wooden petition separating the dormitory from the rooms occupied by Father Gormley, the intrusive noise immediately became a whisper, and we all went back to sleep.

There was never any complaint, however, whenever the priest had his radio turned on to the Irish Hospitals Trust Programme. On those nights, we let ourselves be lulled to sleep by the voices of Bing Crosby, Doris Day or Perry Como singing the songs we had become familiar with during our holidays.

Our food was still of poor quality and badly cooked. None of us blamed poor Sarah, who was old and barely able to hobble around the kitchen, never mind cook for a large community. The blame, we all to a man agreed, lay with the Rector. A number of the senior students decided to present a petition to Father Daly. My classmate Christy Maher was one of the delegation that went to confront Father Daly, who received it with cool politeness: such an event would have been unthinkable in his student days. He listened intently as 'Bunny' Quinn spelled-out the students complaints. 'Is that all?' The priest politely asked when his prefect had finished. 'Yes, Father, 'Bunny" answered. 'Very good, I'll look into the matter immediately. You may go,' the rector told him. The five students mumbled their thanks and turned to leave the room. But just as Christy Maher reached the door, he stopped and asked: 'Have we your word for that, Father?' The priest sat for a few moments with a look of disbelief on his face. Then as if sprung from a trap, he leapt to his feet and pointed at the door: 'get out,' he roared.

At lunchtime the following day, Father Daly went around the tables examining the contents of our plates. There was a noticeable improvement in our food, but all too soon, things returned to normal and the porridge started sticking to the spoon again.

Were we to know it, salvation was at hand for those of us who would survive Sarah's best efforts to send us to an early grave. Rumours began to circulate that a new college was to be built to replace the cramped, unhygienic quarters in which we had to spend six years of study. If a new college was really on the way, then more than likely, we all concluded, Pallottine sisters would take charge of the domestic arrangements; and that would include the cooking. The decision to build the new college was made by the Society's newly-elected Superior General, William Mohler, a German, after he had seen for himself our living conditions. Father John Bergin, who was Provincial of the Anglo-Irish Province at the time, always maintained that it was he who decided to go ahead with the building project. Amongst us, however, the 'smart' money was on the German.

At the start of a theology course we were introduced to three new professors: The Rev. Dr. Thomas Morris; the Rev.Dr. Michael Russell and Father Seamus Ryan, the youngest of the three. Tom Morris, known amongst the students as the 'Duck,' lectured on dogmatic theology. He was later on to become Archbishop of Cashel and automatically, Patron of the Gaelic Athletic Association. Michael Russell, a shy, handsome priest took us through the minefield of Theology and Sacred Eloquence. Later on he was appointed Bishop of Waterford; Father Seamus Ryan took us for Sacred Scripture. He was given the nickname, 'Jam Jars,' because of the thick lenses in his spectacles. They would attempt to teach us moral and dogmatic theology; scripture; sacred eloquence and canon law; in which I would be startled to come across a prohibition against a priest hearing the confession of his mistress, but thought the law would only apply to those hot-blooded priests of Italy and Spain.

The term was progressing smoothly when, in late November, Madeleine Conboy wrote telling me that Joan was coming home in two weeks time to prepare for her entry into a convent on 8th of December. I read and re-read that paragraph I don't know how many times. I always knew that Joan was religious; but a nun? I sensed that she was fleeing from life; from the worry of making decisions, especially about men, sex and marriage. Another factor contributing to her decision would have been her parent's own loveless marriage. The habit also of her father waking everyone up during the night by flushing the toilet and coughing, as he made his way to his wife's bedroom, troubled Joan a great deal. Once in her flat in Dublin she suddenly said to me: *"Don't they ever think of a third person"*. It was only some days later, reflecting on these words, that I came to realize to what she was referring.

In writing to her the following day I begged her to postpone her entry into the convent until sometime in the New Year. She owed her parents, I told her, one last Christmas at home. Naturally, as a student for the priesthood, I could not very well include my own desire to spend that time with her as well. But I did write a poem in which I poured out some of my affection for her. It began: *"Joan her name is, sweet it sounds but sweeter still to all is she"*. In bed that night, I tried to visualise life without Joan. It was too terrible to contemplate; even though I realised that once I was ordained, it would not matter where she lived or what her estate in life was, I would no longer be in Ireland. But as a nun, we would never have the freedom, whenever we did meet, to walk on Bartra Island; to go swimming together; or to walk down Morrison Terrace to fetch a bucket of drinking water from the pump. I must have given a loud, involuntary sigh, for Connie Ramirez from Texas, in nearby cubicle called out: 'Martin, You're in love.'

When I reached Ballina that Christmas, Joan was already a Postulant in the order of St. John, whose convent was situated a few miles outside the town of Kiltimagh, her mother's birthplace, in County Mayo. Madeleine was grieving as if her daughter had died. Because I sensed that she needed me; and if the truth be told, I needed her, I stayed with her for the entire holiday.

On St. Stephen's Day, we traveled to the convent to join other parents waiting in the parlour for the arrival of their daughters. Joan entered wearing a long black skirt, black cape and a short, black headdress. She looked pale. It took a supreme effort on my part not to shout out: 'Joan, you don't belong here.' Instead, I went shyly towards her after she had kissed her parents, and holding her hand said 'Hello, Joan.' 'I'm glad you came, Martin,' she said softly, as we continued to hold hands until her mother's cough made as separate.

At 5 o'clock the nuns served their visitors with tea, cakes and sandwiches. But Joan and her fellow postulants were not allowed to eat with their families. Instead, they had to excuse themselves and go to the refectory. I thought this a very inhuman act on the part of the Order. Later, we all trooped into the Chapel for Benediction. I knelt at the back alongside Madeleine. 'Join in the singing,' she commanded me at one stage. But I was too sad to comply with her wishes, and continued to kneel in silence, my eyes fixed on the back of Joan's head, as she knelt in a pew up near the altar.

Afterwards, when we gathered in the hall saying our goodbyes, I noticed Madeleine's eyes were filled with tears. When it came my turn to say farewell to my beloved Joan, I leaned forward and kissed her tenderly on the cheek. 'By, love,' I whispered softly. Then on a sudden impulse told her: 'Remember, Joanie, if you have any doubts don't stay a moment longer than you have to.' I thought she was about to cry. Instead, she gave a slight nod of the head and turned away to answer a bell summoning the community to its next devotional exercise of the day.

In a letter Joan wrote to her mother a week later, she said that *"I was very nice"*.

The three weeks of Christmas vacation passed swiftly and in many ways happily for me. For it was the first time that I had stayed for so long in a home other than my own, and with the woman who had, during those weeks, become more and more of the mother I missed in my own life. Her husband, I sensed, was not altogether happy with my lengthy stay. Whether this was

171

because my presence curtailed his visits to his wife's bedroom, or because I was another mouth to feed, I could not be sure.

Back once again in college to face the bleakness of January, our moroseness gave way to feelings of joy when news spread amongst the student body that a new college was indeed going to be built on the site of the football field, and that work on preparing the ground would begin later that year.

The weeks seemed to fly by, as we settled into the rhythm of college life. For those involved in the production of the annual St. Patrick's night play, and for the first time I had a part, each day came too quickly as we approached opening night. Fortunately, the college's choice of play never proved too much of a strain on the student's acting abilities, as they were always of the Irish Kitchen comedy type performed by every rural drama group the length and breadth of Ireland. I was cast in the role of a solicitor: a part I was to play in two further productions. St. Patrick's College, on the other hand, aimed for a much higher standard and staged such plays as Journeys End and Harvey.

On Shrove Tuesday, we walked out to Mrs. Gleeson's shop. This time, there was no Joan to telephone. But I still enjoyed the day as we prepared for Lent by storing up enough food for the arderous 40 days trek across the desert of Sarah's cooking, during which the only Oasis along the way would be St. Patrick's Day.

One night that term, as we sat in the study hall, a mouse ran out from the fireplace. 'Bunny' Quinn, gave a squeal and jumped up onto his chair, gathering his habit up around his knees like a woman. The little creature tried in vain to find a hiding place until its sojourn amongst us was terminated, when Joe Harris used his expertise with a hurling stick to kill it.

Much moved by this episode, I composed a poem in the manner of my fellow countryman.

> "O thou wee sleekit timorous cowering beastie
> What foolishness was in thy breastie
> That made thee, on this night of nights,
> Come up frae thy wee hame into the light?

But sure who could blame thee:
Thou must live as well as we.
But why o why did you no wait
Till we were gone and night was late

Then frae thy wee hoose beneath the floor
Roam frae thy wee corner tae the door
To search for food, ere long you may
Till we return the following day.

But you could no longer bide to wait
So along you came into the grate;
There to find your butter and breed
Till someone saw and now you're deed".

With apologies to Robert Burns.

Near the end of February, Madeleine wrote that Joan had left the convent and was now at home, and would remain there until well after Easter. The news made me happy and I wrote immediately to the poor girl, making certain to emphasise the fact that she had made the correct decision, and telling her how much I was looking forward to being with her in a few weeks time.

When I entered the Conboy home on that Easter Sunday afternoon and saw Joan looking so sad and timid, it was difficult for me not to rush forward, take her in my arms and tell her that she would never be without my love. Instead, I could only give her the slightest of embraces as I kissed her tenderly on the cheek.

During the days that followed, I learned from Madeleine that her daughter had not just simply left the convent, she had fled from it wearing her postulant's clothes and without shoes, and had walked the couple of miles into Walsh's shop in Kiltimagh, where one of the family immediately telephoned Lipton's for George to come and collect his emotionally disturbed daughter.

Thanks to the Grant I was now receiving from the Corporation of Glasgow for being in Third Level Education, I was able to hire a car for the Easter vacation. The money was paid directly to the college; but Father Daly gave me a substantial part of it for my own use.

To try and discover what exactly was troubling Joan, I suggested that the two of us drive out to Loch Talt.

While sitting in the car looking out at the lake, I asked Joan if there was anything she wanted to tell me. She blushed 'I can't, Martin, I know you too well.' All the more reason, I thought, for her to confide in me. But sensitive to her fragile state of health, I did not press the issue. Without anything definite to go on, I could only guess that her problem was of a sexual nature: a theory I had put forward a couple of times when discussing Joan with our mutual friend, Frances Heffernan, still studying medicine in Galway.

Many years later when staying with Joan in her Dublin apartment, I discovered holy pictures and medals attached to the underside of her pillow. There was only one reason why they were there: to ward off sexual thoughts. So my analysis of Joan's problem had been correct.

During the summer holiday of 1957, I began playing soccer with a group of the local boys whose game I had watched down in the 'hollow' one night, as I stood alongside Owen Shevlin on the Cliff road.

'Why don't you go down and join them. I'm sure they would love to have you,' he said, in his distinctive Belfast accent. Owen was a civil servant. In response to his suggestion, I told him that my football boots were left behind in college. 'Send for them,' he ordered.

In July, we formed Enniscrone United F. C., and as a team played our first game against Ballina Town F.C. in a field situated immediately behind the chapel and belonging to Peador Kilcullen, who, sporting a distinctive moustache, resembled an R.A.F. type from the Battle of Britain, and who was one of Ireland's greatest Anglophiles. I was chosen as captain and centre-half.: a position I hated but had to remain in because of my height, and the fact that I was the only player with any expertise in heading the ball.

Staying in Enniscrone: at the time of the inaugural game were Seamus O'Connell, who had just won a championship medal with Chelsea, and had played for England's amateur team, and Frank O'Callaghan of Scottish team, Dundee United. The opportunity of using their talents was too good to be missed. But first we approached our opponents for permission to play both men. It was readily given, even though they suspected that they were probably going to lose the game.

A big crowd turned up on a warm, cloudy July night. The news of the presence of the two 'guest players' had attracted them. The result was Enniscrone United five Ballina town one. In the following six weeks, Enniscrone United played further matches against Castlebar Celtic, Westport United, Quay Hearts and a return match against Ballina Town that we lost 3-2 on a hot, sultry afternoon at the town's greyhound track.

When the term of 1957 began, our class was looking forward to having the first of their Minor Orders conferred on us. In ancient times each of them was of some importance. For example, in the case of 'door – keeper,' he had to prevent the heathen from entering the church and thereby disturbing the service; another of his duties was to separate the men from the women. The Order of Exorcist still gives power to drive away the devil; but this power is restrained, and the Order has come to be regarded as chiefly a stepping-stone to the priesthood. The remaining ones, Lector and Acolyte speak for themselves.

By now, I was not the only clerical student in the town. Garda Sgt Henly's son, Ken, was in Clonliffe College.

As that year's Christmas holiday was coming to an end, and the area was experiencing wonderfully crisp, clear days and severe frost at night, tragedy visited the resort when Ken's younger brother, Barry, drowned at the pier. He always seemed to be on his own. And many a time I watched his solitary figure go past my home and wondered about him. On the day of his death, the sea was dark and threatening looking, with a heavy swell running. Father Willie Moyles, the curate, had gone down to the pier with his two gundogs, and had just got out of the car when he spotted a figure standing at the end of the pier and recognised it as being Barry Henly. Almost at the same moment, the horrified priest saw the boy topple into the wintry sea. Immediately the curate began running, at the same time looking around to see if any other person was on hand to assist him in a rescue attempt. But he was alone, and arrived just as the unfortunate youth was being swept around the head of the pier and moaning like the sea itself. The body, badly cut and bruised, was found two days later wedged between rocks about a mile along the Carrowhubbock shore. One of the stories that soon began to circulate in connection with the death was that he had told classmates in Saint Muredach's College in Ballina that he wasn't coming back after the Christmas holiday. I felt certain that Ken's days as a seminarian would soon come to an end, due to the circumstances of his brother's death.

On the night of February 6, 1958, as I walked around the gardens with two fellow students, Father Gormley approached and in a solemn voice told me 'the plane with the Manchester United team on board has crashed on take-off at Munich airport. There are some deaths. I'll let you know if there is any further news.' After lights out that night, the inhabitants of the big dormitory listened to the news reports coming to us courtesy of 'Lancs' radio. By then the world of soccer knew that many of the Busby Babes had played their last game. Roger Byrne, Tommy Taylor, Eddie Coleman, Mark Jones and Dubliner, Liam Whelan, died in the wreckage and snow that awful night. Their manager, Matt Busby, himself lay seriously injured in a Munich hospital. 16 days after the crash, one of the greatest of young men ever to stride across a football pitch, Duncan Edwards, died from his own appalling injuries.

The world-wide support that Manchester United enjoys today stems in many ways from that dreadful event at Munich airport. It was the day the team died... but a club was born.

In the days following the crash the Munich tragedy dominated all our conversations. Even the St. Patrick's professors were not unmoved by the scale of the tragedy and kept as fully informed by reading out excerpts from the newspapers.

On my way home at Easter, I visited a jeweler's shop in Limerick's O'Connell Street and purchased a silver trophy with a lid on which stood a female Grecian figure. I requested that the trophy be engraved with the words *"Manchester United Memorial Cup".* I would collect it, I told the shopkeeper, early in June on my way home for the summer holiday I cannot recall the exact purchase price, but I think it was no more than £12. When I met up with the Enniscrone lads and told them what I had done and proposed that we organise a summer tournament to play for the trophy, they accepted the idea with great enthusiasm, especially the McGowan family, two of whom, Tom and Bill were both by then clerical students.

I had to cut short my stay in Enniscrone by one day to join up with some of my fellow Pallottines. We were 'booked' to appear at Sean Ross Abbey, Co Tipperary, a home for unmarried pregnant women, run by the Order of the Sacred Hearts of Jesus and Mary. Our contact with them, naturally, was Paddy 'doon' Ryan.

Before presenting us to our audience, the good sisters fed us with a hearty meal of rashers, sausages and eggs, home-made bread and chocolate cake, washed down with tea served in bone china cups.

Like most of Ireland's homes for unmarried mothers, the abbey was attached to a much older convent. When it was taken over by the sisters of the Sacred Hearts of Jesus and Mary in 1932, Shane Ross occupied an imposing Georgian mansion with extensive lawns and walled garden. The remains of a mediaeval monastery still stood in the grounds.

When a girl arrived at Sean Ross Abbey they gave up their own clothes. For the rest of the time they spent there, they wore a regulation uniform of coarse denim a loose smock-like garment to disguise their swollen stomachs that we're a shameful manifestation of their sins. The girls were forbidden to talk among themselves and were warned not to reveal their real identities or where they came from. They had been put away to spare their families. Few, if any, had visitors. The fathers never came. The nuns took in laundry from the nearby town of Roscrea, surrounding villages, boarding schools and state institutions. The resident women were then put to work washing and ironing for many hours a day. The money earned from this enterprise helped to support the community of nuns and expectant mothers and their babies.

After we had eaten our supper we walked onto the stage of a spacious Assembly Hall and looked down on the faces of about 40 women aged between 16 and 40 years of age, most of them at different stages of their pregnancy. Others amongst them would have recently given birth to their infants. With the knowledge we now possess today as to the widespread incidence of incest, I would deduce that a percentage of the Abbey's audience that night were there as victims of a father, brother, uncle or some other close relative; and who is to say, perhaps even a priest too may have impregnated some of them.

While visiting Chicago some years ago, I met a man who had actually been born in Sean Ross Abbey; and given his age, it was quite possible his mother was in the audience that very same night. More recently, I have met another person in Ballina, Co Mayo, who was also born there. After the concert we drove back to college to begin the last term of that year 1958.

'Big Dan is dead,' called out 'Bunny' Quinn to a dozen or more of us sitting in the study hall. There was a shocked silence while we absorbed the news. Then a barrage of questions was flung at the Prefect. How did it happen? When? Where? We listened intently as 'Bunny' gave us the details of Father Hayes's death. He had gone out to play a round of golf on the Hastings course on Easter Monday morning, and as he swung his club on the ninth tee, he suffered a massive heart attack. He was only 48 years of age.

One new record was added to the miniscule College collection. It was Doris Day's rendition of *"The Black Hills of Dakota"* and *"Secret Love"* At every available opportunity that record was on the turntable, with some us providing a 'backing group' to the glamorous Miss Day. Father Daly must have grown tired of hearing the latter too often, and told the Prefect: 'Andrew Quinn, no love here.'

Work on the foundation of the new college was making steady progress; supervised on a daily basis by the entire student body, which had its own ideas as to the final shape the building would eventually take. The debates that took place, as we stood on the concrete and tried to visualise the edifice of our dreams, were long and imaginative. But we had to wait until we were given a sight of the plans by the friendly Clerk of Works, to confirm where every facility was going to be placed within the confines of the four walls. Some aspects of the building met with instant approval: for example, the individual rooms and adequate toilets and showers. We all agreed that by the time we returned in September, the building would be up to the first floor, and then a year after that we would be able to take possession of our beautiful new college.

The end of term exams took place in lovely, warm weather. For my elocution piece, I chose *"The Presence of God"*, written in Dublin's Mountjoy prison by Joseph Mary Plunkett, while awaiting execution for his prominent role in the 1916 Irish rebellion. A few hours before he faced the firing squad, the poet married his sweetheart Grace Gifford, who was already pregnant.

THE PRESENCE OF GOD

I see His blood upon the rose
And in the stars the glory of his eyes;
His body gleams amid eternal snows
His tears fall from the skies.

I see his face in every flower
The thunder and the singing of the birds
Are but His voice; and carven by His power
Rocks are his written words.

All pathways by His feet are worn;
His strong heart stirs the ever beating sea;
His crown of thorns is ever thorn,
His cross is every tree.

It was during that summer, our class lost its second member when Gus Tobin died from injuries he sustained in a Gaelic football match. A St. Patrick's student, he was slightly built with a friendly smile, crowned by wispy, blonde hair, and was one of those I was closest to in the class.

I was soon immersed in the preparations for the commencement of the inaugural Manchester United Cup competition, which, from the moment it was first announced in the press, attracted entries from all over the province: even from towns and villages that had never fielded a soccer team.

Enniscrone United reached the semi-final; and despite having what, at least on paper, looked like the strongest team ever to represent the club, went down 7-3 to Castlebar Celtic, whose Scottish junior player, Peter Duke, playing at centre forward, scored four goals. I was at centre half. Need I say any more?

All our goals came in the second half, when I moved rugby international player, Hubbie O'Connor, into my position and I went to wing-half: a position I was much happier playing in, because it enabled me to go forward in attack whenever the opportunity arose.

I refereed a thrilling final between Castlebar Celtic and Quay Hearts of Westport. Given that Celtic were leading 3-1 at half-time - that man, Peter Duke, scoring all three goals for the Castlebar side - the final score of 4-3 to the Westport lads was quite astonishing. Doctor O'Connor presented the trophy to the winners, and afterwards, we all went down to Mary Rafters. 'Long Room,' to celebrate what had been a wonderful tournament, crowned by a most exciting Final.

Next day I returned to college to begin the penultimate year on my journey to the priesthood; during which Archbishop Jeremiah Kinnane would confer the sub-diaconate on our class: the first of the 'Major Orders' that involved us taking the vow of celibacy and swearing the Oath against Modernism.

Despite my seniority in the student hierarchy, it did not prevent Father Daly from testing my humility, not to mention my patience, within a few weeks of the term beginning. On a fine October evening, while walking in the grounds with other students, I saw a large, galvanised, iron door that led into the yard of a house backing on to the college grounds, swinging back and forth and making an almighty bang when it crashed shut. I went forward and closed it, unaware that the Rector and a visiting priest were walking some yards behind me.

'Martin Gordon,' Father Daly called out.

I waited for the two men to approach.

'Martin Gordon, you did that to attract attention to yourself. You knew that we were behind you.'

I was unable to reply. I thought that all such unfounded accusations had been left behind in Wilton. From my experiences there with Father McKay, I knew that it was useless to offer any sort of defence.

I thought of some of my fellow students who were leading such invisible lives in the college, that when the Prefect mentioned one of their names to Father Daly he asked in surprise:' Have we a student by that name here?'

"A seminarian may be relatively incompetent, disinterested, or indifferent, but if he is. conforming, pliant, and above all, over docile, the seminary authorities will regard him as suitable for ordination". The old saying still had a great truth: *"The seminary makes boys out of men".*

With the confirming of the sub diaconate fast approaching, and with it, the taking of the vow of celibacy, it was surprising that no special talks on this major step were included in the curriculum. Indeed to be honest, I doubt if any of my classmates or I gave celibacy a second thought. We wanted to be priests first and foremost, and if celibacy was part of the package, then so be it. However, as recent events worldwide have shown, celibacy is something for which a seminarian may have little or no inclination. The priesthood is his goal, so he continues on the path to ordination in the mistaken belief that once he is a priest he will be protected by some sort of sacramental barrier to all and every sexual temptation. But, as the Catholic Church has learned to its cost in recent years, such is not the case; and I do not think that most of us were truly free in making the celibate decision. Our whole system of clerical education isolated us psychologically, spiritually, and physically from women. In such a climate a man is at best notionally free, but not experientially free. One final point: men today have neither the same outlook on sexuality, nor the identical affectionate needs of men in medieval Europe, from which times our legislation comes.

Candidates for the priesthood, used to be shut away in seminaries from as young as 12 years of age; away from all contacts with women and girls. Every sexual impulse, every budding friendship with a young woman had to be suppressed as a danger to their future celibacy. But no sooner were they ordained than these selfsame young men, now 23 or 24 years of age, were forced to listen in the stimulating darkness of the confessional to the most lurid descriptions of every form of sexual activity and deviance; young women, and not so young, would tell them of their innermost thoughts, deeds and longings. Is it surprising then that so many priests fail to remain celibate? If they do, that many of them fall into varying degrees of alcoholism and depression?

Sir Arthur Conan Doyle thought it immoral and degrading for celibate priests to hear the confessions of young women, which might contain sexual admissions.

The priesthood is the only life, these men know. The temptation, therefore, is for them to remain as a priest, even though they are unable to fulfil a necessary condition to being a priest. The result is, and has been for many years, that many priests live unchaste lives, thereby lowering respect for celibacy and causing countless problems in their own lives, and in those of the men and women who have become their lovers.

Hypocrisy became rampant within the ranks of the Catholic priesthood. I have been told, for example, that at least two of my former Pallottine colleagues ministering in Tanzania have fathered children with native women. Even in Ireland in recent times, a bishop and a well-known Dublin priest achieved notoriety when the press revealed the existence of children in their lives.

It was the council of Elvira in 305 A.D that passed the first decree on celibacy, requiring,' bishops, priests and all who serve the altar to live, even if already married, in continence.' Pope Siricius in 385A.D commended celibacy for all the clergy and separation if already married. But married clergy still remained, who in theory were continent. But it was the Lateran Council, 1123A.D., that absolutely forbade clergy to marry, and those who were to dissolve their unions. Therefore, celibacy for the Catholic priesthood is a clerical law, rather than a divine law.

Much of the legislation on celibacy grew from the austere practices in monasteries, which resulted in a growing demand for the absolute purity of a priest administering the sacraments, which was thought to be threatened by any form of sexual activity.

On a personal note, I had no problem at that time with celibacy. I knew that I loved Joan; but not in any sexual way. To me she was still that the young, fair-haired and laughing girl of 13 years of age, who had swam with me, picked the blackberries and stood in the moonlight of an August night to listen to the corncrake in Kilcullen's field. There was never occasion when I had to confess to a sexual thought about her.

A campaign for a change of tone in selecting our St. Patrick's night play for 1959, at last proved successful, when the producer and the committee chose the very popular English farce, *"Tons of Money"*. Conveniently, they discovered that a drama group in the neighbouring county of Kilkenny were doing the same play; and to confirm that it was suitable for his students to stage, Father Daly and the producer, a teacher in the local Christian Brother's school, attended the opening night.

When the cast held its first meeting with the producer, he confirmed that the Rector was more than happy with our choice of play. But, he added, 'I think you have bitten off more than you can chew.'

After the first few weeks of rehearsals, we realised that it was going to take a lot more effort than was normally required, if 'Tons of Money' was to be a success: for one thing, we all had to develop a suitable English accent.

Everything went well, up to the dress rehearsal, when after a long and frustrating evening; the situation was so bad the producer suggested that we cancel the show. However, good sense prevailed, comforted by the old show business saying: *"That a bad dress rehearsal makes a good performance"*.

But if we thought our troubles were over, we were sadly mistaken. For just hours before the curtain was due to go up on the most ambitious production ever staged in the Pallottine College, John Driver, from Hastings, and playing one of the female parts, took to his bed with stage fright. No amount of coaxing, pleadings or threats could move him; he was sick, he told us, and that was that.

When I looked in on him at around four o'clock in the afternoon, I couldn't help but smile, despite the gravity of the situation. The 'patients' close-cropped head just about showed above the bedclothes. There was no response when I called his name. John, I repeated. There was still no sign of life. With one last look at the recumbent figure, I went downstairs to the study hall.

'How much money do we have between us? I asked of some of the drama group. Half an hour later, I returned to John's cubicle to find that the patient had surfaced sufficiently enough for me to see his eyes. 'Here, John, take these and handed him a bottle of Guinness and a baby Power. A flicker of interest shone in his eyes as he struggled to free himself of the bedclothes. 'I'll be back in an hour's time to see how you're feeling,' I told him. When I returned, I found 'Lazarus' standing in front of a small, cracked mirror, raking a metal comb through the short stubble that served him as hair. He turned and smiled slyly at me.

Before going on stage three hours later, I poured another two bottles into the 'English Patient,' unrecognisable in his costume and make up as one of the female leads. He went on to give a fine performance.

For the occasion, we turned the spacious room that was going to serve as the Refectory in the new College, into a theatre; thereby allowing us to invite more of the St. Patrick's students and members of the public.

After the curtain came down, Father Daly came backstage to congratulate the cast. I noticed him give a sharp look at the two empty bottles on a chair, but he passed no comment. Instead, he was effusive in his praise for our acting talents, particularly for the lads who had to play the female parts. One old woman in the audience was overheard asking where we had got the girls from. Our producer was so moved by the performance and the reaction of the audience to Tons of Money that he suggested we ought to put it on for a week outside the college walls.

While learning my lines and rehearsing the play, I was at the same time deeply involved in writing and memorising a sermon, the first that I had to preach in St. Patrick's chapel to a congregation consisting of the entire class and the Rev.Dr Michael Russell. The subject, he gave me was: *"The Our Father in General; Who Art in Heaven"*, In particular.

I don't know where they came from, but somehow, I had in my possession two cassettes of talks given by the famous American television personality, Bishop Fulton Sheen. His television series, 'Life is Worth Living,' was one of the most popular shows in the United States and had won major awards. As I listened over and over again to that wonderful rich voice, to the imagery he painted with his words, and to the dramatic use he made of background music, I knew that somehow I wanted to preach my sermon, just like him.But first I had to write about 1500 words; and then memorise them.

Writing over the next three weeks, I found that the words came easily to me; and apart from opening the Bible, had little, any need to consult another book. But all the time my writing ear was listing to Bishop Fulton Sheen. The following passage from the sermon will illustrate how great an influence he had on me at that time.

"To apply this word, Father, to God, must have sounded strange, if not startling, to Jewish ears. Hitherto, God had been for, then someone to fear, to placate with sacrifices. The Jews knew of the God who had appeared on Mount Sinai amid a terrible upheaval of the

elements,, and of the God before whom their ancestors had cowered and trembled in terror; but they had still to see that same God nailed to a cross, his arms opened wide as if to embrace all of mankind".

Now that was pure Fulton Sheen. Near the end of the sermon, the bishop's influence appears again, when I wrote:

"The words of a modern song tell us 'That there's no place like home for the holidays.' But if that is so, then there is no place like Heaven for eternity". The sermon ended with a quotation whose source alludes me: *"The Saviour's words, the Saviour's blessed prayer have depths the human mind will never sound. Amen".*

Dr. Russell had only one comment to make when he handed me back my sermon 'You have spelt Hollywood wrongly.'

The day after I preached that sermon, many of the St. Patrick's students offered me congratulations; even fellow Pallottines who had heard comments from their own St. Patrick's classmates discussing the sermon, added their own tributes. It was the general consensus that the 1959 prize for sacred eloquence was mine.

Prior to ordination Sunday, the Archbishop conferred the order of sub-diaconate on our class. We were now entitled to wear the Roman collar and obliged to say the Divine office each day.

On ordination Sunday itself, when the prizewinners for the year were announced, I didn't even get a 'mention' in Sacred Eloquence. Since then, I have often wanted to ask, Doctor Michael Russell, why he didn't award me, at least a 'mention;' perhaps my effort was not dry and theological textbook enough for his ears and my delivery was too close to that of Fulton Sheen.

My arrival home wearing the collar was a great delight to my father and stepmother, my aunt and Madeleine; not to mention the people of Enniscrone, amongst whom the Sisters of Jesus and Mary who were really proud of their former pupil, claiming, I'm certain, some part in my vocation to the priesthood.

It was during that summer that Madeleine and I went into the 'burrows' for the first time, where she stretched out provocatively on the ground, while I changed into my swimming trunks.

When Joan eventually archived for her holiday, she too was thrilled to see me wearing the collar. But whenever we went down the river or walked on the Enniscrone beach, I discarded the collar and the clerical black for more appropriate apparel. Joan seemed to have fully recovered from her sojourn in the convent, and was slowly regaining her sly sense of humour. Her smile still captivated me.

Our friend, Frances Heffernan, gave the women of Morison terrace something to talk about over their cups of tea, when she had a visit from a young Dublin man, Tom Gunn, who worked as a sales representative for a continental camera firm. During his stay with Frances, he expressed a desire to do the Lough Derg pilgrimage, and I was encouraged to accompany him. Left to myself, I would never have gone near the place in a million years. But with all the women lined up against me, it was no contest.

Lough Derg is a remote, rocky island in Co Donegal. The landscape surrounding it has no appealing features; and the weather is very often windy, wet and cold, even in summer. Yet every year during the pilgrimage's short season, up to 30,000 people from all over the world elect to spend three days of prayer and fasting in this inhospitable spot.

Pilgrimages to St. Patrick's purgatory, as it became known, can be traced back to the 12th century. Its importance can be gleaned from the fact that it was the only place in Ireland deserving of a mention in a 1492 map of the world. In mediaeval times, a stone cave was where the Pilgrims congregated. It was not large, able to contain only a small number of people at any one time. But because certain abuses connected with the Vigil came to the attention of the church authorities, the cave was sealed up in 1492 on the orders of Pope Alexander VI, to be replaced soon after by a modest chapel called St.Patrick's. This in time gave way to the present church, upon which Pope Pius XI conferred the status of Basilica in 1931.

On 12 July, 1795, tragedy struck Lough Derg. At that time transport to and from the island was a matter of private enterprise. On the shore side near the ferry stood a 'shebeen,' and because it was a holiday, much drink, including 'poteen,' was being consumed that day. By 11 A.M, the boatmen where already drunk, or near enough to it. 93 Pilgrims embarked on the boat, which was old and leaking. Many of the passengers were already uneasy at its condition, not to mention that of the boatmen. Shortly before it pulled away from the jetty, one young passenger was hauled off the boat by his father, who arrived in a state of great agitation, saying that he had a most distressing dream the previous night. Halfway across the lake, the boat began to leak dangerously. Panic set in amongst the Pilgrims and within yards of the island, the floundering vessel capsised throwing everyone into the water. On the island itself, the Pilgrims already there could only watch in horror as the water filled with the screaming, struggling humanity. There were only three survivors. Since that day, every boat to and from the island is supervised by a priest.

The pilgrimage begins at midnight on the day prior to one's departure from home. From then until midnight on the third day, no meal is allowed, except that provided on the island. To fortify ourselves for the austerity ahead, Tom Gunn and I sat down in Heffernan's and feasted ourselves on huge steaks, mushrooms and chips, at around 11 PM.

Feeling fit now to face anything that Lough Derg could throw at me, I walked slowly up the terrace to Conboys and was soon in bed in George's room, with Joan and her mother sleeping in his bed, because Madeleine had taken in visitors who occupied the other bedrooms. George was camping on Bartra Island for a couple of days. Before falling asleep, I heard Madeleine say: 'Martin's bed is the only one in the house. I haven't slept in.' I was inclined to suggest that she come over then to 'my' bed.

The weather was cool and showery as the Pilgrims drove down Morrison Terrace, next morning, waved on their way by Frances, her mother, Joan and Madeleine.

Upon arrival on the island, one of our first acts was to remove shoes and socks. We would not need them again until the morning of our departure in two days time. Once allocated our place in the men's dormitory, we immediately began to do the 'Stations.'

An entire 'Station' consists of kneeling before crosses, circling the basilica a number of times, standing with one's back to the wall of the building, while renouncing the world, the flesh, and the Devil; walking round and up on the stone 'beds' of saints Brendan, Catherine and Columba; and finally kneeling on the shoreline, while one says five Our Fathers; five, Hail Mary's and the creed. Each station took about an hour to complete. Three of them had to be done before the night vigil commenced. I was half-way through my last 'Station' when the rain really began to pour down; since it didn't appear to affect my fellow pilgrims, some of them quite elderly men and women, I stoically kept on going right to the moment when I knelt at the lake's shoreline. By that time, I was so wet I might as well have been in the lake.

It was now time to sample Lough Derg's renowned cuisine, for which the place is rightly famous: or should it be infamous?

The small room that served as a refectory was crowded when Tom and I entered. Just after 5 p.m., neither of us having eaten since the previous night's meal in Heffernan's. On the table in front of us were plates of incinerated slices of bread. They were meant to be toast, but somehow along the way the process had gone into overdrive and produced the blackened objects we were expected to eat for supper. If a Pilgrim found this dish hard to swallow, they could then try the brittle oatmeal scones, which came with a health warning for those with tender gums or loose teeth. To wash all of this down, one could try 'Lough Derg Soup:' boiling water seasoned with salt and pepper; or drink strong, black tea. I tried them both and found them not too unappetising. But then I was hungry; and as John McGowan used to say: hunger is good sauce. That evening, I knew what he meant.

During the next nine hours, we prayed along with the rota of clergymen and lay people, who stood in the pulpit to lead numerous decades of the Rosary and other devotional exercises. Wearing the Roman collar, I was picked out to take a turn in leading my fellow sufferers in the Rosary.

As I stood high up in the pulpit, the rain still trickling down inside my collar, my greatest difficulty was trying to keep count of the Hail Mary's I was expected to say in each decade. At one stage, a sudden bout of coughing from the congregation warned me that I had said at least one Hail Mary too many.

All through those sleepless hours, the Pilgrims fought to stay awake by periodic visits outside the Basilica, seeking in the cold night air an antidote to their sleepiness. Inside the building, many a nodding head was revived by a friend's smelling salts or a good old-fashioned dig in the ribs. Sometime around 5 a.m., I sat with my eyes open, but I'm certain I was fast asleep.

The second and last full day of the pilgrimage was filled with all the repetitive devotions of the previous day, and ended for my companion and me at 10p.m., when we climbed between the cool, fresh sheets of our beds, and within seconds were sleeping the sleep of the just.

As the boat carrying us from the island late the following morning powered its way across the lake, I looked back at the Basilica and its adjacent buildings and wondered just what had I accomplished over the last few days by inflicting hunger and sleeplessness on my poor body? I didn't feel any holier; my physical health did not seem to have been affected by the harshness of the pilgrimage. But deep within me, I knew that the whole experience had been worthwhile.

September came, and I made my way South for the last time as a clerical student. For nine years, I had been making that identical journey, and now had almost reached the goal that I had set my sights on in September 1950. During the ten months which lay ahead, the diaconate would be conferred on my class and on the second Sunday in June 1960 would come our ordination to the priesthood.

As deacons we would be permitted to handle the sacred host, placing it, for example, in the monstrance at Benediction. We would also be given a greater amount of freedom from the college rules. But what was most exciting for us that year, was taking up residence in the New College, and having our own Pallottine sisters from their convent in Rochdale, near Manchester, to look after us.

Upon arriving at the college, my classmates and I, as the senior students, were given first choice of rooms and selected those on the first floor as our abode for our final year. My room was sandwiched between those of Tim Twomey and Christy Maher, and at the end of the corridor. The bathroom and showers across the way were spacious and well equipped, with large windows facing out onto the tennis court. Personal hygiene would now be the norm rather than the exception it had been for the previous seven years.

Our bedrooms were light and airy. There was a wardrobe, a desk and bookshelf, a wash hand basin and bed in each room. How, I wondered, as I hung up my clothes, had we ever endured the primitive conditions that had been our lot as lived in 'Jerusalem?'

After supper, cooked for the first-time by the nuns and eaten for the first time in the bright, clean and spacious refectory, our first task was to transfer our books from 'Jerusalem' to the New College. Funny, when one comes to think about it, the old buildings had all been christened with Biblical names, but the building that we occupied that night has never been known by any other name than that of the 'New College.'

That was not the only 'new' thing to greet the students that September: Father Jim Daly had gone to Rome to replace Father Ned Ryan at San Silvestro in Capite, the English National church. Father Ryan in turn became our rector.

A deacon's year is usually a hectic one. There are individual and class photographs to be taken - the latter to be hung on a wall in St. Patrick's College; ordination invitations to be printed and posted; measurements and fittings, for one's new soutane; hotel accommodation and meals to be booked for family and friends, an increasing amount of correspondence to be answered; one's ordination card to be designed and printed. But most of this activity would take place after Christmas. Of more immediate concern for the ordination class was learning how to celebrate Mass.

Although a student had probably served hundreds of masses and had certainly attended many hundreds more, it was quite another thing to be actually saying the mass. I had with me the wooden chalice given to me by John Adams, and now put it to good use.

By Christmas, I felt that I had achieved sufficient mastery of the rubrics of saying mass, and now began to concentrate on the administration of the sacraments. I would, of course, return to mass practice round Easter. In the meantime, I went home to enjoy my last Christmas with Joan and Madeleine.

Naturally, with ordination, only six months away, Madeleine Conboy was very involved with me in drawing up a list of those to be invited to the first mass. She had kept a list of all those who had very generously given me help when I first set out on my journey to the priesthood: each one of them was going to receive an invitation.

Joan looked lovely that Christmas, but very lonely. I still didn't know if she had a male friend in Dublin: and to be honest. I didn't want to know. I couldn't bear the thought of another man touching her.

I was returning to college for the last time that January of 1960. And as I kissed Madeleine before leaving for the railway station, I could not help but let my lips remain longer than usual on her cheek. We had come a long way together since August, 1945.

I declined to take part in the years play, *"Charlie's Aunt"*. Instead, I offered to provide background music in an attempt to give the production a touch of professionalism. Seconds before the curtain rose, I switched on the portable record player and the sound of *"Gaudiamus Igitur"*, went soaring out into the auditorium. During the romantic garden scene, the music was the slow movement from Bruch's violin concerto with Isaac Stern as soloist.

As the weeks of that term passed by, each one of us became acutely aware of the major event that was drawing closer by the day; an immediacy that was brought home to us after Easter, when Dr. Michael Russell began classes on the *"Dirt Tract"*. We had heard whispers of the contents of these talks from some members of last year's ordination class. They could be summed up in one word: Sex.

The professor tried to make his talks as light-hearted as possible, thereby lessening any possible embarrassment on our part. He did this by cracking jokes or telling humorous stories. One example I still recall:

"There was a young lady named Starkey,
Who had an affair with a darkie.
The result of her sins was quadruplets not twins,
One White, one black and two khaki".

A story, he told was one of two women who met in the blackout during the war. One woman says to her companion: 'isn't the blackout terrible. Yes, said her friend, you never know the minute you are going to be blasted into maternity.' On a more serious note, the priest told us that a woman can get a man to do whatever she wants, because she has what he wants; that there were 32 ways of having sexual intercourse. I counted up to 3, and then gave up. Finally, I recall, Dr. Russell, quoting from. The Fourth Earl of Chesterfields letters to his son referring to sex: *"The position is ridiculous, the pleasure momentary and the expense damnable"*;

that about sums up our sexual education for the hearing of confessions. One curious thing I recall from the talks was the day Dr.Russell told us that a priest ought not to go on a long car journey with a woman, because she could travel for hours without going to the toilet.

During the final session, Dr.Russell told us that at least one of us would leave the priesthood for a woman.

Now there was just one final hurdle to overcome before ordination: each one of us had to satisfy father Seamus Ryan that he was confident to celebrate Mass, according to the rubrics of the Catholic Church, and not introduce some words or actions of his own wonderful imagination. We therefore had to run through a 'Dry Mass' in the sacristy of St. Patrick's College, while the priest listened intently to our every word and watched each movement we made at the makeshift altar. 'Very good, Mr.Gordon,' was the priest's only comment when I had blessed the imaginary congregation and told them that they could go home. I was now ready for ordination to the priesthood: a journey begun in Cork, a few months short of 10 years, and one that almost ended there but for the fortuitous meeting with Michael Timlin.

On the eve of ordination and alone in my room, the magnitude of the step and I was about to take almost overwhelmed me as a shroud of blackness took possession of my whole being. For those few moments, I was not aware of where I was, or even of who I was. The only conscious feeling I had was that within a matter of hours Joan would be out of my reach forever. I do believe a groan escaped my lips, as I stood there unmoving as if in a trance. It was a frightening moment that I still recall vividly all these years later, and think of the words from a poem of W. B. Yeats:

"I became a man, a hater of the wind,
Knowing one, out on all things alone, that his head
May not lie on the breast, nor his lips on the hair
Of the woman that he loves, until he dies".

Many students were known to take a sleeping pill. I had one in my possession and slept through the night until it was time to rise on ordination morning.

nts and Peter and Paul's church, Amwell street, London E.C.1. My room marked with a cross.

With Sister Joan McKenzie in then Royal Free Hospital, Gray's Inn road.

A family group enjoying a day on rhe Enniscrone beach. Dad is wearing a cap and Joan had a hand to her hair. 1965.

On the way with Joan to visit our friend Mother Loyola at Gortnor Abbey.

n the canteen at Sadler's Wells.

Playing ... ... l for "Eamonn Andrew's Sport's Paraders". Rushing in is actor Brian Blessed

Louise and I emerging from S.James's church, Spanish Place. August 21st. 1971.

Louise and Katherine in our home in Cork.

Proud parents with our daughter Katherine after her baptism in St. Patrick's church, Cork. August 1973.

A group of Pallottine students. "Jerusalem" in the background.

My wife's parents, Bill and Ettie Kinmonth.

Join the Courage Light Brigade

Join the Courage Light Brigade

Join the Courage Light Brigade

Join the Courage Light Brigade

handled the printing of these posters for Benton and Bowles advertising Agency. L:R. Rod Soper and Terry Walker

The Gordons at home in Ballina. 1984.

After a Sunday session of the Humbert Summer School in Killala. Louise is second on the right next to her good friend, Greta Adamson, nearest camera. The couple with the dark glasses are our friends Susan and David Hedigan from Co. Dublin.

Martin Gordon, he with the cigar,and his good friend David Hedigan enjoying the final day of the 2007 Humbert Summer School outside Betsy's bar, Kilcummin Co.Mayo, the site of General Humbert's landing in 1798.

After showering and shaving, I dressed in my new soutane with its cape, and recalled the words of a woman on a Dublin bus when, while a student, she had said to me: *"Your mother must be very proud of you".*

The St. Patrick's students were already in the sacristy when Tim, Christy and I arrived. One of the cathedral priests instructed us to begin putting on the white albs, cincture and stole, all laid out neatly for each of the Ordinands; satisfied that all was in order, Father Jackie O'Neill, acting as Master of Ceremonies for the occasion, looked at his watch and said: 'Right, gentlemen, it's time to go, Good luck.'

From the opening peel of the mighty organ, the ritual of ordination moved smoothly through its successive stages to the solemn moment, when Archbishop Kinnane laid his hands firmly on our heads, followed by all the clergy present in the sanctuary, including my two clerical guests, Father Moyles from Enniscrone and the well-known Dublin Franciscan, Father Lucius McLean. Then kneeling once more before the Prelate, he anointed our hands with holy chrism saying *"The Father anointed Jesus Christ as Lord through the power of the Holy Spirit. May Jesus keep you worthy of offering sacrifice to God and sanctifying the Christian assembly".* He then proceeded to bind our hands together with a white linen cloth, while the choir sang the *"Veni, Creator Spiritus".* The stole that each of us wore in the manner of deacons was now rearranged over our shoulders as befitted a priest and the chasuble, which, up until then had been rolled up our backs, was lowered. We were now fully vested as priests, 'other Christ's.'

Back in the sacristy, the air was filled with 'Well Overs' and warm handshakes exchanged, as we congratulated one another on becoming priests. Never again would the class of 1960 be together in the one room, I realised, as with the final nostalgic wave of my hand, I bade farewell to my St. Patrick's classmates and went out into the cathedral once more to impart my blessing on my father and his wife. Dad, I noticed, was wearing a hair piece for the occasion.

The college laid on a fine lunch for its newly ordained and their families. But since the numbers were limited, the remainder of our guests had to be catered for in a local hotel. But before we all sat down to eat, I was kept busy blessing my fellow Pallottines, including a delighted Father Hassett, whose first novices we had been, to any of the students still remaining in the college and above all to Joan and Madeleine. That was a very special moment when the two women who meant most to me knelt down on the grass of the tennis court, while I prayed over them, and then offered the palms of my hands for them to kiss. There was a lovely moment later on in the day, when I imparted my blessing to old Father Boyle, while Joan, Madeleine, Annie Gordon, my step-mother and aunt Nellie looked on.

In the knowledge that we would have to say a few words at the lunch, I had prepared something in advance. After thanking my Superiors, my family and friends, I told the assembly that I felt like the young boy who had returned home sick from a birthday party to be asked by his mother 'If it had been too much ice cream.' 'No, not enough boy, mammy.' That is how I feel, for there is just not enough of me to give thanks for what I have become today. *"He that is mighty has done great things to me"*, I concluded, quoting the words of The Magnificat.

The one big disappointment of the day occurred when Joan told me she would not be attending my First Mass, her decision saddened me. She handed me an envelope containing a £20 note and a religious card with the inscription written on the back: *"to Martin on your ordination day. God bless you always, From Joan"*. Knowing her, I was certain she had debated with herself whether to put the word, 'Love' instead of 'from.' The verse on the card read:

"May Jesus support you al the day long.
Till the shades lengthen and the evening comes
And the fever of life is over, and your work is done!
Then in his mercy may He give you
A safe lodging and a Holy rest
And peace at last!"

The card is still with me, placed safely within the missal that Joan presented to me that September morning in 1950.

I had decided to stay that night with Madeleine and George, who, apart from the fact that the house in Enniscrone was full, had been my surrogate parents for over 10 years. But first, Father Moyles drove me to Enniscrone to spend the few minutes in my own home and to greet the neighbours who had been waiting patiently for my arrival. As the procession of cars made its way through the town, the drivers kept up a continuous blaring of their horns as a means of announcing the arrival of Enniscrone's first newly ordained priest in living memory. People came to their doors to wave, and I, like some royal person shyly, waved back. I found the whole thing very embarrassing and told the priest this. 'Sit back and enjoy it. The next time that this happens, you'll be dead,' he said.

As soon as I returned to Ballina and entered number 23 Morrison Terrace, Madeleine commanded her husband to kneel for my blessing. As I stood over his kneeling figure alongside the armchair, I thought of that moment ten years before when sitting in that selfsame chair, he had heard his son call out from the kitchen: 'Daddy, Martin wants to be a priest.' 'God bless you, Martin,' he said, emotionally, as I helped him to his feet.

Afterwards, alone with Madeleine in my bedroom, I presented her with a tissue-wrapped package. 'It's for you, Mam. It's the linen cloth the Archbishop used to wrap my hands in after consecrating them with the holy oil. 'Oh, Martin,' She said, visibly moved. She was aware that a newly ordained priest usually gave this cloth to his mother. It was my way of saying 'thank you' and of expressing my love for her. I kissed her tenderly on the cheek 'I'll treasure it always,' she whispered, as a tear slid down her cheek.

Enniscrone's small, stone-built church was packed, when I emerged from the sacristy, accompanied by the curate and four altar boys, one of whom was Roger Finnerty, a Pallottine student from an area between Ballina and Crossmolina. After his ordination three years later, Roger was appointed to a parish in Tanzania, where he was killed by an army lorry in 1975. My own classmate, Tim Twomey, was with him at the time, but he escaped with minor lacerations and bruises.

Looking neither to the right or left, I ascended the altars steps, arranged the chalice in front of the Tabernacle, and came back down to stand alongside Father Moyles, who would supervise me during the mass. From then until I gave the final blessing, I moved easily and comfortably through the liturgy, except for a slight hesitation when I came to the moment of consecration; but the pressure of Father Moyle's hand on my arm, reassured me, and I went ahead to pronounce the words slowly and distinctly. This is

My Body, repeating the words of Christ at the last supper. Behind me Rodger Finnerty rang the bell three times. When the mass was over, I returned to the sacristy to divest myself of the vestments. 'You did well,' the curate told me, before I went back into the church to give my individual blessing to members of the congregation. Young and old they knelt at the altar rails to receive the blessing of their newly ordained priest. If I knew them personally, and that meant most of them, I spoke their names, causing many of them to leave in tears. One of the last to appear before me was Paddy 'Monk' Mullaney, still dressed in clerical black and still intent on becoming a priest. Eventually he found a place in a seminary, but only as a worker in the library of St. Patrick's College, Maynooth. However, after spending about 25 years there, Paddy was at last ordained a priest for his own diocese of Killala, at 70 years of age. Four months later, he died suddenly as he knelt in the new Enniscrone church, prior to his celebrating Mass.

My traditional First Mass Breakfast took place in the Atlantic Hotel. Here gathered all the relations and friends, who could not be accommodated at the ordination. I was pleased to see amongst them many of the Ballina business community who had helped me 10 years ago.

But Joan, where were you? Happy and exciting as the day was, and surrounded as I was by so much love and sincere affection, it was your presence and it alone that would have made the occasion of my First Mass complete.

After leaving the hotel in the middle of the afternoon, I still had one more blessing to impart.

'Hello, John,' I said, as I entered my aunt's kitchen. John McGowan, who had been ill for the past year, sat hunched in a low armchair next to the fire. 'Is that you, Martin?' He asked in a weak voice, his sightless eyes turned towards the door. 'It is John,' I assured him. 'I've come to give you my blessing.' While I blessed him, he began to cry. His wife bent down and put her arms around his shoulders. 'There, there, now John, it's all right.' She told him soothingly. 'Do you remember how we used to work back the fields and in the bog?' the invalid asked me between sobs. 'I do very well, John. Weren't they good days?' Before leaving, I promised to visit often to have a chat with him.

Four days later, I traveled to Dublin and stayed overnight in Joan's flat at 48, Upper Drumcondra Road. The next morning, accompanied by her flat mate, Maureen Hannifin, Joan served my Mass in a local convent before going to work in the G.P.O. We arranged to meet there and have lunch in the canteen.

As we ate, she pointed out some of Ireland's well known broadcasters, one of whom was Philip Green, whose thrilling commentaries of the big soccer games at Dalymount Park I had listened to over the years. Before leaving the building, Joan introduced me to some of the people she worked alongside, including a cousin of Father Nicolas Gorman, a fellow Pallottine, who was to become Superior General of the Society in 1971. He died seven years later, at the age of 48: a victim of alcohol abuse.

Even though I was now a priest, Joan and I never thought it unusual for the two of us to sit having supper in the Carlton grill that evening, or to travel on the bus back to the flat afterwards.

Two weeks later, I flew to Glasgow to do a fortnight's 'supply' in a parish next to the Gorbals, a district made internationally infamous by the novel, *"No Mean City"*. While there I took the time to visit my birthplace of Govan. It was a strange feeling to be walking again the streets I knew so well. Nothing seemed to have changed much. Most of the shops of my boyhood were still there; though some were under new owners, many of them Indian. Five Harmony Row where I was born,and 22 Langland's Road still stood where they had always been. But other parts of the district were already surrendering to the demolition squads.

I entered the close of number 22 Langland's Road and climbed the stairs to the top landing, where I found Mrs. Boyd standing at her open door. 'Hello, Mrs.Boyd,' I said quietly. She looked at me suspiciously for a few moments, as I continued to stand smiling before her. Then a look of recognition appeared on her face. 'Martin Gordon, is that really you?'

'Yes, it's me all right.'

'O my God! Margaret, look who's here,' she called in through the open door.

'Margaret,' I said, extending a hand to Mrs. Boyd's grand-daughter.

'Martin, what a surprise to see you again, after all this time,' she exclasimed, as she continued to hold my hand.

We stood talking about the old days and I enquired after various members of the family, before on an impulse, I asked both women if they would like to receive my blessing; explaining to them, the custom in the Catholic Church. Margaret knelt down, followed slowly by the older woman. 'If only your poor mother could see you now,' Mrs. Boyd said, with tears in her eyes, as I helped her to her feet.

I leaned on the banister and looked down as I had done those many years ago, when I had stood in the very same spot and watched my mother being carried away to die. As if from a distance, I heard a voice call my name. 'Are you all right, Martin?' I straightened up and turned a tear-stained face towards Margaret. 'Oh, Martin, you poor man,' she said, as she stepped forward and impulsively took me into her arms.

When I had recovered my composure, I said goodbye to my former neighbours, promising them that I would return at some future date to meet the rest of the family; especially Farquhar, my companion in the graveyard.

Upon my returning home, I waited anxiously for each day's post to bring my letter of appointment from the Provincial. But while I waited, hardly a day passed that I did not spend with Madeleine Conboy. When it was time for me to leave, if I were not staying overnight, we would stand at the front door, like two lovers unwilling to be separated for a moment more than was absolutely necessary.

One afternoon, we decided to visit Achill Island, but sadly a grey mist spoiled the outing. So we spent most of his time sitting in the car, where, at one stage, when I mentioned that I was feeling tired, Madeleine suggested that I stretch out on the back seat. But I decided to remain where I was.

During the returning journey back to Ballina, Madeleine told me about Father. Harrison, who had taught in the local college, but had left the priesthood for a local working-class woman. 'It wouldn't have been so bad, if she had been middle-class and attractive looking,' asserted Madeleine. Many years later, Ena Heffernan's husband Paddy Coen told me how he and a group of senior students had gone up to the railway station on the day of the priest's departure from Ballina to plead unsuccessfully for him not to leave. The family name is still to be seen today above a small public house in Ballina.

That evening, George Conboy enquired rather sharply, if his wife and I had gone on our own to Achill.

The letter that I had waited all that summer for eventually arrived on 9 September:

Dear Father Gordon,

I am pleased to inform you that the Provincial Council has decided to appoint you to the parish of St's Peter and Paul, Amwell Street, London. You are expected there on 23 September. I take this opportunity of wishing you every happiness and success in the Lord's vineyard. I remain,

Yours sincerely,
James Maher
Provincial.

23 September: Joan's birthday, I realised; what a coincidence. All connected with me were thrilled with an appointment so near home. Madeleine said that the Provincial must think a lot of me to send me to a parish in London. The next day, I wrote to Joan and told her of my appointment and the date of my departure.

The weather was warm and sunny for late September, when I arrived at Joan's flat. My flight was not until 8 P.M. During supper, Joan, and I talked about London, a city that neither of us had ever visited.

'Now that I'll be there, Joan, you will have to come over,' I told her.

'I'd love that very much, Martin.'

'Did you ever think all those years ago that we would be sitting here today, I a priest and you seeing me off from Dublin airport?'

Joan continued to pick the crumbs of Madeira cake from her plate. 'A lot of people thought that you had the vocation,' she answered, without looking up.

'But what about you, love?' I asked quietly.

Before she could answer the ring of the doorbell sounded shrilly.

'That must be your taxi,' Joan said, rising from the table.

Although it was late September, Dublin airport was crowded that Saturday evening, mostly with families and friends seeing honeymoon couples depart for, more than likely, Spanish destinations. I went to the bar and ordered two glasses of orange juice, and couldn't help overhearing the lewd remarks directed at one of the couples by two men who had clearly been drinking for most of the day.

Joan and I had just about finished our drinks when my flight was announced. At the departure gate, the two of us stood looking shyly at each other, not knowing what to say.

'I better go now, Joanie,' I said, as the P.A. system boomed out its message for the last time. A sad look came over her face. I bent down and kissed her tenderly on the cheek.

'Goodbye, Joan. God bless,' I said, and picked up my small suitcase.

'God bless, Martin,' she said, with a slight tremor in her voice.

I gave her a reassuring smile and walked quickly away, aware of the moistness in my eyes and heading for:

"A lonely and Loveless Life; Never knew kiss of Sweetheart. Never caress of Wife".

The Song of the Sourdough, 1907 by Robert Service.

THE NEW CURATE

On the journey by taxi from the West London Air Terminal, I recognized many of the city's well-known sights: Harrods; Hyde Park Corner; the Ritz hotel; Piccadilly Circus; the theatres of Shaftesbury avenue; Foyle's bookshop; they were all familiar to me from reading and films.

The door of number 5 Amwell Street remained closed after I had rung the bell and waited for at least a minute. I was about to press the bell again, when a voice from a doorway about twenty feet to my left called out 'Yes?' Lifting my suitcase, I walked to where a short, bespectacled priest stood waiting at the top of three steps for my arrival.

'I'm Father Gordon,' I told him.

'Come in. I'll tell the Provincial you're here. He's gone to bed.'

I groaned inwardly at the news. I recognised the priest as John Bergin, from his visits to the college during his term as Provincial.

'I expected you earlier in the day,' a sleepy looking Father Maher told me, rather crossly. 'You were expected to go down to Hastings, where they are a man short for tomorrow's masses.'

'I'm sorry, Father,' I mumbled in reply.

'There is no room for you here tonight. Let me see if I can get you in to a hotel.'

The Columba hotel in Gower Street was about ten minutes taxi ride away from Amwell Street, The noise from the traffic could still be heard through the closed windows of the room the receptionist had allocated me. Despite the stuffiness and warmth in the room, I decided to leave the windows shut.

Next morning, I felt confident enough to walk back to the church, but missed a turning along the way and had to ask man for directions, and within five minutes arrived at the church where I began my mass at the side altar of the Sacred Heart, while the ten o'clock mass was nearing its end at the main altar.While I was eating breakfast, the Provincial came into the dining room and informed me of the time of the train to Hastings. I could have my lunch first and then take a taxi to Waterloo station

On the train carrying me through the English countryside I recalled the little that I knew about the parish where I was going to spend the next two weeks. Star of the Sea church was the Pallottine's second oldest foundation in England and had been associated with the poet, Coventry Patmore, after he became a Roman Catholic in 1864. He contributed £5,000 towards the building costs. I knew all the priests currently in residence from the occasional sightings of them whenever they visited the college.

During my stay in Hastings I had very little to do apart from saying mass and dealing with the people who came to book masses or look for a priest who was on holiday. The rest of the time I went for walks and read a great deal. I particularly liked to go up into the hills above the town and gaze out to sea, thinking occasionally of Enniscrone. But after the first week I was beginning to feel bored with all the time I had on my hands, and wished that my stay would come to an end. Then came a letter from Madeleine Conboy to tell me that she was in London and gave me a telephone number at which I could contact her to arrange a day for a visit.

The weather on the day she spent with me was very warm for the first days of October. Madeleine wore a pink floral dress that I recalled her making herself, and whose loose, square neckline afforded one a rare glimpse of the top of her breasts whenever she bent down. She carried a light-blue cardigan over one arm and a white handbag in her hand. She looked happier than I had ever seen her in all the years we had known each other. Taking her by the arm I guided her to a nearby cafe where we sat outside with our coffees.

Afterwards, we wandered through some of Hastings narrow, old streets looking at the many antique shops situated in them. When we at last dragged ourselves away from the shops, we went to a seafront restaurant for lunch. After we had eaten, I suggested that we could go on the beach. Well 'beach' was probably a misnomer for the deep carpet of stones that served Hastings as a beach; but then coming from Enniscrone, I was spoiled when it came to beaches.

On our way we had to walk along an underpass. As we did so, linking arms as at home, Madeleine suddenly stopped, withdrew her arm from mine, and said 'Excuse me.' She then raised her skirt and began to adjust one of her stockings. I looked quickly away until I heard her say. 'That's better,' and felt her arm slip once more through mine.

The remainder of the day was spent visiting the church and having afternoon tea, before I took Madeleine to the station. As we stood at the barrier she opened her handbag and withdrew a ten pound note which she then pressed into my hand. As I protested, she said: 'That's for giving me such a lovely time, Martin. I've really enjoyed being with you. I hope that you won't be too lonely after me,' she said with a teasing smile.

'I will, Mam,' I told her; then laughed to make light of that reply. Madeleine looked at me, then leaned forward and kissed me tenderly on the cheek

During that walk to the Presbytery, I began to wonder about Madeleine's action in the underpass. There had been in her eyes, I recalled, a look that I had never seen before. As a seminarian I had read from time to time about women who looked on priests as a challenge, a prize to be won; and that very often these same women could be numbered amongst the most devout in the parish.

Upon returning to London at the end of my two weeks sojourn at the seaside, I was allocated a small room at the top of the Amwell Street Presbytery. Its furniture was nondescript, consisting of a single bed; a small, cheap wardrobe; an uncomfortable looking armchair; an antiquated wireless sitting on top of what appeared to be a chest of drawers hastily put together by an amateur carpenter; and a desk with a bookshelf.

The room had two large windows which afforded one a view of brick walls and windows of offices and small industrial units on the opposite side of the street. To the right across Rosebery Avenue stood Finsbury Town Hall, a lovely building of red brick and with an attractive, coloured glass canopy over its main entrance. A big clock hanging high above the porch was another welcome feature of the building. Rosebery Avenue was the main artery between much of North London and the West End, with the result that the decibel level was very high during the rush-hour periods, and even during the night, when huge lorries thundered past, or worse, used the street as a short-cut on their way to and from Smithfield and Covent Garden Markets. It was going to take me some time to get used to the noise, I realised after the first couple of days residence in my new home.

The Rector of Saints Peter and Paul's parish was Tom Hulhoven. A Gibraltarian by birth, he struck me as being a very serious type, even when he tried to tell a funny story. He was always moving his hands nervously when they were not occupied doing something else. Within the Society, and amongst the public, he was well known as the priest who had saved a convicted murderer from the gallows by organising a petition that persuaded the then Home Secretary to commute the man's sentence to one of life imprisonment for the murder of a soldier at the Angel.

Aidan McGuire, the priest I was replacing, was a Dubliner with a very cheerful disposition, five years ordained and now heading for a parish in Texas. But first he had to initiate me into my role as the 'New Curate.'

Within the presbytery the priests kept to a regular timetable as regards meals and Community Night Prayers. Outside of that one came and went as duty and free-time dictated. The hour one rose at in the morning was determined by what mass you were down to say. Father Hulhoven invariably had the 7am; John Bergin the mid-day – for which he was usually a couple of minutes late at least – the Provincial or myself took turns saying the 8am.

Behind the house and church was the parish primary school, with a small assembly hall that Father Bergin used for his twice weekly bingo sessions and Sunday dances. Most evenings of the week something was taking place either in the church or the hall; sometimes in both.

Amongst the parish organisations were the Legion of Mary; The St. Vincent de Paul Society; The Young Christian Workers – Fr. Hulhoven's main interest – the Youth Club; Brownies and Scouts and the Children of Mary. There used to be a Nurses Guild, but it had been dormant for the last couple of years.

The Royal Free Hospital on Gray's Inn Road stood just within the parish boundary, and therefore its Catholic patients were the responsibility of the priests of Saints Peter and Paul. My predecessor had been the hospital's chaplain, and now I was to succeed him in that duty. Further along the street, going towards Kings Cross, was the Ear, Nose and Throat Hospital. This establishment too was under our care; but was not as demanding on one's time as the larger general hospital.

The area of London in which the parish was situated had the typical mix of most inner city parishes – the people were mainly working class, with a sprinkling of middle class – who tended to be English. The majority of the parishioners were Irish or of Irish descent, but there was also a sizeable number of Italian families, among them some dear old ladies who dressed entirely in black and spoke little or no English.

The church itself had been built around 1835 as the Northampton Tabernacle for members of the Countess of Huntington's Connexions who had broken away from Spa Field's Chapel. This congregation did not last long, and a Roman Catholic Mission bought the building in 1847. The Pallottine Fathers took over the church in 1952

A short distance up Rosebery Avenue from the church was Sadler's Wells Theatre. I couldn't believe the coincidence, recalling that Christmas Eve in the farmhouse, when I listened to the radio as the Company staged the 'Merry Widow' But though the theatre was so near, it might well have been in Mongolia as far as my attendance was concerned. Canon Law forbade priests from being present at an opera. As I passed Sadler's Wells at least three or four times a week, the billboards advertising current and forthcoming productions of: 'La Bohéme,' 'Tosca,' or 'Madam Butterfly' would stare tantalisingly back at me.

From an historical perspective, I was now resident in a very interesting part of London. The monk, William Fitzstephen, Anglo-Norman chronicler of Thomas a Becket, wrote in the year 1180:

Round the city again towards the North arise certain excellent springs at a small distance, whose waters are sweet and salubrious and clear, and whose runnels murmur o'er the shining stones; among those shining stones, 'Fons Clericorum,' 'The Well of the Clerks,' may be esteemed as being much frequented, both by scholars from the school (Westminster) , and the youth from the city; when on a summer's evening they are disposed to take an airing.

Over the years, the 'Fons Clericorum' disappeared due to the extensive building work in the area. Fortunately, however, it was rediscovered in modern times and can be visited by applying to the local Borough office.

From even the most cursory glance through the registers of the parish church of St. James in Clerkenwell Green, it is clearly evident that this part of London was patronised by the nobility as a place of residence and the church as a place to have themselves married, their children baptised, and from which to proceed to their last resting place on this earth. Of interest to Irish people is the name, Richard de Burgh, Fourth Earl of Clanrickarde: it was he who led the Crown forces against the native Irish at the battle of Kinsale in 1619.

By the year 1661, the number of houses in the area totalled 418. Fifty years later, however, that figure had grown to 1,146. But it wasn't until the Great Fire of 1666 had ravaged the city that any extensive building took place in the district. With their homes lying in charred ruins, the citizens of London moved out to the suburbs seeking space upon which to build. The area around the 'Well of the Clerks' was an obvious choice for many of them.

In 1801 the population had reached 23,294. Thirty years later it had doubled. It was around this time that the district ceased to be purely residential. The industrialisation of England reached the area quickly and definitely. Its rural delights, gardens and springs were soon buried beneath the handmaids of 'progress:' noise and dirt.

The Census of 1861 records that there were in the area such diverse occupations as: goldsmith, jeweller, printer, shoemaker, to mention but a few. Many of these trades are still being carried on in Clerkenwell to this day. But extensive 'gentrification' of the area in recent years has considerably reduced their numbers. There also stood in the parish a school that was once a prison. The Fenian Society, in trying to release prisoners, placed a bomb against the prison wall which destroyed homes across the street and killed a number of their inhabitants.

'Amwell Street' gets its name from Amwell in Hertfordshire, where water from a spring there along with another at Chadwell, was the source of water supply to London in 1613.

This ingenious scheme was begun by a Hugh Myddleton-a visionary entrepreneur in the reign of Queen Elizabeth and King James 1. His idea was to cut an artificial channel from the springs to the metropolis, a distance of sixty-four kms. The project would have bankrupted him had not King James taken a half-share in the project.

re I am with Steve Chalmers and Bobby Lennox of the "Lisbon Lions" team, in a bar in Ballina, Co.Mayo.

Daughters Katherine and Victoria leaving our Ballina home for a local wedding.

I am so surprised at seeing the photograph of me playing my last game for the college, on top of my 75th. B'day cak

Louise and I attending a Masonic Dinner, Cork. 2009.

Pictured at a reception following a Mass of Dedication at St. Peter's and St. Paul's Church, Amwell Road, Finsbury, are stars from the world of show biz.

The occasion was to recognise St. Cecilia's Day — St. Cecilia being the Patron Saint of Music.

And attending the dedication service, led by Father Martin Gordon, the Catholic Stage Guild Chaplain, were people from various fields of music. Singing and reading during the service — c. Margaret Savage, from the Black and White Minstrel Show, actor Bruce Trent, and Diane Todd and Andy Cole both currently appearing at Sadlers Wells.

Eamon Andrews, Chairman of the Stage Guild, sent his apologies for not attending.

A very happy group of entertainers after a St. Celia Feat day mass in St.Peter and Pauls.

Joe Brady of " Z Cars" and soprano Diane Todd.

A very happy group of entertainers after a St. Celia Feat day mass in St.Peter and Pauls.

The pre-dance recption in the Green ford presbytery, 1966. L;R Fr.Gordon, George Graham of Chelsea F.C., Margaret Savage of the Black and White Minstrels, Terry Venables captain of Chelsea, Eddie McCreadie of Chelsea and Scotland, and Tony Hillier, who went on to write a Eurovision song contest winner.

Sir Alex Ferguson and I at Enniscrone. Circa 2005.

At Celtic Park, Glasgow with current manager Neil Lennon, my recently deceased brother William, the much-loved Henrick Larrson and self.

A chance meeting at Portadown, N. Ireland with former football manager Tommy Docherty and my friend Henry Coor...

Presenting a framed photograph of the "Busby Babes" to my old club Enniscrone United. L:R. Liam Tuffy, Club secretary Pat McKeon , self and club chairman Tony Connaughton.

In the Knights of Columba Club, Moodiesburn, Glasgow,admiring the Scottish League Cup won by Celtic. My niece Magaret's husband and former Celtic player, Pat McGinlay is second from the left.

In 1613, the New River, as it is still called, reached the New River Head in Clerkenwell. From there it was distributed to the city by wooden and lead pipes, to those who could afford to pay for it; and to others by water carriers - men with barrels carried on yokes across their shoulders.

I was going to like my parish, and hopefully my parish would like me. But there was still the little matter of hearing my first confessions. My 'box' was situated on the left hand side of the church, facing the Lady altar. In a Perspex panel over the door was my name: Fr. M. Gordon S.C.A. The panel lit up to indicate when a priest was inside.

"Bless me father for I have sinned.
It has been six weeks since my last confession".

The soft Irish accent filtered through the wire-mesh grille separating me from the penitent. It was the first of around twenty confessions I was to hear during the next hour and a half before supper. Men and women, young and old, children and teenagers, they all knelt before me and told how they had failed to keep one or more of the Commandments. I felt humble in the presence of so much innocence because, very often, there was no sin to confess, and at the realisation of the awful power given to me through the priesthood, as with right hand raised I pronounced the words of absolution over their bowed heads, 'I absolve you from your sins...' Not even the angels in heaven could say those words, our professors in the seminary had told us.

In college, one often came across in their spiritual reading reference to a holy person's 'odour of sanctity.' But the smell that pervaded the confessional after one woman left it was definitely not what the writers had in mind. She was to plague me for a long five years.

Returned to my room I thought about my experience of the last ninety minutes and was appalled at the lack of any formal training for the hearing of confessions. It bordered on sheer lunacy to call the six years in the seminary, training for the priesthood, when one of the most important aspects of the ministry was almost totally ignored. Learning the principles of moral theology and a few talks on the 'Dirt Tract' hardly prepared a seminarian for the problems he would be presented with in the confessional. Certainly a short, intensive course in psychiatry or psychology would not have been wasted.

In earlier times in Ireland, students for the priesthood at St. Patrick's in Maynooth, the national seminary, were issued with the 'Treatise on the Decalogue,' a textbook used to instruct them on the hearing of confessions. Let me quote a portion of it.

"Since the confessor acts the part of judge and physician he ought to become acquainted with the diseases and the offences of the penitent, in order that he may be able to apply suitable remedies and impose due penance, and lest a sin that is mortal should be accounted as venial or the foul viper lurking in the deep recesses of the heart should not venture to put itself forth to view, he ought to therefore sometimes to question the penitents on the subject of the 6th (7th) commandment, where he suspects that they are not altogether pure ... A prudent confessor will, as far as in his power, advance from more general statements to more particular: from the less shameful to those which are more so ... If the penitent shall answer that they had improper thoughts or irregular desires the confessor shall ask whether any improper actions followed. But if the penitent shall confess this, the confessor shall ask again, what were these actions. If the penitent be a girl she should be asked whether she has adorned herself in order to please men. Whether for this purpose she has used paint, or stripped her arms, shoulders or neck ... Whether she is not attached to somebody with a more peculiar affection; whether she has not allowed herself to be kissed".

The main topic of conversation at supper was who had won the big prize in the parish football pool. Some names were mentioned, but as yet they meant nothing to me. Fr. Bergin was in charge of this money-making scheme which, along with the bingo, brought in a sizeable sum each week. What he found most attractive in these activities was the fact that much of the money came from non-Catholics who bought tickets from parishioners and also attended the bingo sessions. If anyone criticised the priest's involvement in gambling, he would always point out that in the bingo hall he often made converts, and certainly brought lapsed Catholics back to the practice of their religion.

When Aidan McGuire took me on my first visit to the Royal Free Hospital, I was greatly amused to see the outrageous way he flirted with some of the very attractive nurses. On our rounds of the wards he introduced me to many of the sisters, staff nurses and nurses, and showed me how to fill out the small slips of paper that would tell the night staff which patients on their ward would be receiving Holy Communion at 6.30 in the morning.

In addition to my hospital work I had charge of the Legion of Mary's three Presidia which met on two nights of the week, and the Youth Club, which met on a Friday night in premises behind the library in Theobold's Road and provided by the borough of Holborn. Given my love of soccer, it wasn't long before I had a football team playing in one of the Sunday leagues. I named the team, Marian Rovers, and kitted it out in jerseys of blue with yellow 'V' neck, pants of the same yellow, and blue and yellow stockings. The most striking aspect of the ensemble was the large crest of the Madonna emblazoned on the jersey and encircled with the words 'Marian Rovers F.C.' The team trained one night a week, on a floodlit pitch close to the church and around the corner from Exmouth Market.

Vic Bird, the non-Catholic husband of Sheila, a parishioner, supervised the training. Vic had at one time played for the amateur team, Wimbledon: something I made certain all the players were aware of. In this way, I hoped to encourage them to work hard and pay attention to their trainer. Occasionally I donned a track suit and joined them; even managing to get on the team from time to time when it was short of players.

Apart from bringing Holy Communion to the hospital, I also took the sacrament to elderly or sick parishioners in their homes on the morning of a First Friday. One of my communicants was an old, Italian lady living on King's Cross Road, who with her husband had run a very successful restaurant, Peter Mario's, in Soho. A son and daughter were now in charge. Also working there had been a niece, Albina, who had arrived from Italy and was recently married to Henry Cooper, the country's favourite boxer. Henry had taken a course of instructions in the Catholic Faith at our church in advance of the wedding. Before leaving the flat, Mrs.Rizzi would press a pound note into my hand. Another dear old lady was the 'Duchess.' She lived in a block of flats at the bottom of Rosebery Avenue, and was able to remember the time when there was a stile at the junction of Rosebery Avenue and Farringdon Road, right where Mount Pleasant post office now stands today.

I soon became a familiar figure in the streets as I moved around either on foot or using the old bike that I had inherited from my predecessor. In the main, however, I restricted its use to urgent calls from the hospital; especially in the middle of the night.

Like all city parishes we had our daily quota of men, and sometimes women, knocking on the door looking for a 'handout.' According to John Bergin most of them were drawn to us by the presence of Father Hulhoven, and were in the main ex-convicts. This worried John a great deal because he feared for the football and bingo money stashed away in his bedroom.

One old Pallottine priest, when the Society was in charge of the Italian church on Clerkenwell Road, and the local Rowtan House was fully operational, used to ask those seeking alms to recite the Hail Mary. If anyone failed this test of their Catholicity, they were sent away empty handed. But it wasn't long before the men got wise to this and made sure that they learned the prayer from an Irishman before daring to approach the church for alms.

With the daily round of hospital visitations, meetings, house visits, preparing sermons and talks and all the other things that occupies a priest's waking hours, the time sped by at such an alarming rate that I received a shock when John Bergin announced at supper one evening: 'Sister Ann is bringing in some good stuff for the Christmas Bazaar.' Christmas, I realised, was only three weeks away.

That first Christmas Eve of my priesthood found me in the confessional from 10am until 11pm, with just breaks for meals and an hour of free time in between. Christmas is a traditional time for 'lapsed' Catholics to go to confession; hence the long, busy hours reconciling sinners with their God. I was deeply moved by the sincere remorse of men and women who, for one reason or another, had not been practising their religion for as long as ten or fifteen years. It took a lot of courage on their part to enter a confessional after such a lengthy absence. Their heartfelt, *"God bless you Father"*, reward enough for the long hours sitting within the confines of a dark, smelly and stuffy confessional box.

When the doors of the church opened at eleven fifteen, its interior was ablaze with lights and shining like the proverbial 'new pin:' the result of the hard work on the part of John Bergin's Children of Mary. Two tall, elegant trees decorated with dozens of electric lights stood one on either side of the altar. The altar itself was lavishly covered with vases of flowers: most of them gifts from local florists and traders in Covent Garden. If it had been the set of a West End play, the audience would no doubt have given it a generous round of applause. But for Sister Juliana, whose devoted work it was, there was no applause: just the satisfaction of honouring the Infant Jesus and of bringing a little bit of her German homeland's tradition into an English Christmas. She was just one of the many thousands of dedicated women who have given their lives to the church without hope of any earthly reward; despite sometimes being ridiculed and mistreated by the priests they so loyally served.

Exactly on the stroke of midnight, Fathers Hulhoven, Bergin and I, preceded by a pack of altar boys emerged from the sacristy, the Rector carrying the figure of the Child Jesus. With the choir, augmented by members of Sadler's Wells, singing *"Come, Come, Come to the Manger"*, we processed round the aisles to the crib built in front of the Lady altar, where Father Hulhoven gently placed the Infant Christ amongst the rustic gathering. *"Come, Come, Come to the manager, children come to the children's King"*, the choir and packed congregation sang, as we made our way to the High Altar to begin the first Mass of the Feast.

Christmas dinner was excellent. But whether it was from being over-tired or perhaps because my mind was thinking of Morrison Terrace, I didn't really enjoy the food. Another probable reason was the atmosphere of gloom around the table. Each of us four priests appeared to be present only in body; our thoughts, our memories were elsewhere. Maybe if I had broken my 'pledge' and had some of the excellent wine on the table, things might have been different. But I resisted the temptation and confined myself to drinking orange juice. Meanwhile, our housekeeper ate 'her' dinner alone in the kitchen basement.

Before I could escape to the seclusion of my room, I had to join the others in counting the collections from all the masses. By the time that was finished, I really was tired and my hands were filthy. I found it difficult to believe that we had actually counted money on Christmas Day. Surely, this task could, and should have been, postponed until at least the next day. While standing at my bedroom window looking down on the deserted streets, a feeling of deep sadness came over me. I placed my forehead against the cool glass and thought of the two women in Ballina. They would just about now be sitting down to their own Christmas dinner, after George, having sung with the cathedral choir at the last mass, had arrived home from his drinking session in the Moy Club, just in time to hear the Queen's speech.

As I undressed for a siesta I thought of my boyhood friend, Eddie Kelly, who within a week of beginning his ministry in a Glasgow parish, had found the loneliness of the presbytery very difficult to cope with. Now I understood what he meant.

After an hour's sleep, I walked to the hospital where I was expected to visit every Catholic patient. The windows of the flats I passed were all ablaze with light and the occasional small Christmas tree. Inside I could imagine families enjoying themselves. I walked across a deserted Kings Cross Road and passed by the empty Rowtan House that was, I had recently been informed, soon to become a hotel.

The wards of the Royal Free were beautifully decorated, and the nurses had obviously been having more than the turkey, judging by the gaiety I encountered as I made my way from ward to ward. Outside one of the wards I was cornered by a young nurse with a sprig of mistletoe in one hand, who chirped, 'Merry Christmas, Father,' before planting a kiss on my cheek, and running away in search of another victim. Although slightly embarrassed I didn't find the experience all that unpleasant.

I spent over two hours in the hospital that afternoon, giving at least five minutes to my patients, each of whom appreciated the visit from a priest. What did surprise me as I sat by one bedside was to observe the Anglican chaplain breeze in one door, and with a cheery *"Merry Christmas"* to everyone, exit through another door, without stopping by a single bed.

It was dark and damp as I made my way back to the Presbytery. As I passed the locked church a solitary taxi drove slowly along Rosebery Avenue. The light from the small tree standing on the dining room sideboard was the only sign that life existed within those walls. All else was darkness.

1961 was already three months old when Tom Hulhoven announced at supper one night that I was to lead the parish pilgrimage to Lourdes in September. Father Bergin, whose perk this had been since the pilgrimage began, stared down at his empty plate, his face turning red. Later on that night I happened to meet the Provincial in the downstairs passage. 'Be careful of Tom. He can be very dangerous,' he said mysteriously, before moving on. I stared after him, not knowing what to make of such a strange remark.

As the days lengthened and became warmer, I began to frequent the local swimming pool that was conveniently situated a mere fifty yards from my front door. From the first moment that I appeared at the pool side, a horde of excited boys and girls who attended the parish school surrounded me. 'Father, Father, watch me,' many of them would cry out as they demonstrated their diving ability. I was amused at the looks I was receiving from other users of the pool who were clearly puzzled by this man with so many children in tow. Delightful though these moments were, I was already looking forward to my holiday just four weeks away by then.

The day before I left for Ireland, Father Maher called me into his office to tell me that he was pleased with my first year in the parish and that my sermons were good and to the point. Big deal, I thought, as I went upstairs to finish my packing. I had taken an intense dislike to this man. I believed the cause of this antipathy towards the Provincial was a result of my observing how often he interfered in matters that were the responsibility of the parish priest. He was also clearly ambitious.

Pointing the nose of the hired car westward out of Dublin on a bright and warm Sunday morning, I had only the usual mass-going traffic to contend with, and judged that my arrival in Ballina would be around three-thirty in the afternoon.

Most days of the next three weeks I managed to spend some time, if not entire days with Madeleine; and when Joan came home, with her as well.

On our annual excursion to Bartra Island, Joan and I were again blessed with a glorious, hot day. George sat in the stern of the boat, one hand on the tiller; while Joan and I sat side-by-side on the middle seat. Wearing a sleeveless dress with light blue polka dots and a high rounded collar, stocking-less and in her bare feet, my heart ached every time she turned and smiled at me.

Once George had pushed off for a short spell of fishing before lunch, Joan and I decided to have a swim. The water in the narrow channel between shore and sandbank was colder than we expected, given how warm the day was. But as we swam up and down the channel's length, our bodies soon acclimatised to the water's temperature. Deciding to have a little fun, I suddenly dived beneath the surface. Above me I could see Joan's legs threshing about wildly as she tried to escape my grasping hands, but to no avail. When we surfaced together, spluttering and coughing, I took hold of her shoulders to steady her. A strap of her bathing suit had slipped allowing a breast to become partially exposed. When Joan stopped rubbing her eyes, she noticed the direction in which I was looking and saw the errant strap and her partial nakedness. Her face turned a deep crimson as she hurriedly turned away to adjust her costume.

'Martin, you're terrible,' she muttered, as she turned to face me again.

'I hope you are not angry with me?' I asked anxiously.

'I am,' she said crossly. Then she smiled.

I leaned forward as we stood chest high in the water and kissed her gently on the cheek. Then taking her by the hand we waded back on shore to dress and prepare the lunch.

The Royal Free Hospital had a deserted look about it on my first day back on the wards. I suspected that this was because it was high summer, and also that due to the fine weather, many of the patients were outside in the sunshine.

Jean McKay, a lovely young South African woman, greeted me with a big smile as I approached her bed. 'Father Gordon,' she said excitedly, at the same time extending her two hands to me. She looked so nice with her blonde hair cut short, blue eyes and small upturned nose – almost like Joan's – nice that was, except for the tell-tale yellowness of her skin. She was under the care of Sheila Sherlock.

I sat down on the edge of the bed, still holding her hands. 'Well, Jean, how have you been while I've been away?'

'Fine, Father, except for a couple of days when I was rather poorly.'

I gave her hands a reassuring squeeze.

'There's a young nun over there behind that screen,' Jean said. 'She came in two nights ago.'

I looked in the direction indicated, and made a mental note to speak to the staff nurse before I left the ward.

'Would you like Holy Communion in the morning, Jean?'

'Yes, please, Father; and I'd like to go to confession as well.'

I rose from the bed, releasing her hands at the same time. 'See you in the morning then. God bless you,' I said.

'God bless, Father.'

I smiled, and traced a small cross on her forehead, noticing as I did, a small teardrop roll down one of her cheeks.

When I enquired of the staff-nurse if I could see the nun, she told me that Professor Sheila Sherlock, one of the world's leading liver specialists, was with her.

'I'll do another ward or two then, and come back.'

The screen was still around the nun's bed when I returned. But one of the nurses told me that it was alright for me to see the patient. The nun's eyes were closed as I stood at the end of the bed and glanced at her chart. She was only twenty nine years of age and from a convent in South London. I clipped the chart back in its place at the end of the bed and approached the patient. She looked dreadfully pale.

'Sister,' I said quietly. There was no response. 'Sister,' I spoke louder this time. The nun's head moved and her eyes opened ever so slowly, trying to focus on the voice.

'Hello, Sister, I'm Father Gordon, the chaplain,' I explained to her.

The nun tried to smile, but it just wouldn't come. Then she withdrew an arm from underneath the bedclothes and offered me a hand, exposing one of her breasts in the process. As I took her hand, I casually pushed the bedclothes up higher round her shoulders.

'I would like to go to confession and receive Holy Communion, Father, she whispered in an almost inaudible voice.

I explained that I would be coming around in the morning at six thirty.

'Thank you, Father,' she said, as I blessed her.

'What's the prognosis on Sister Margaret, I asked the staff-nurse.

'She's not very good, I'm afraid, Father,' the tall, attractive red-haired told me, as we looked at the curtained-off bed.

I glanced at my watch. 'Time to be on my way or I'll be late for supper,' I said and handed the slip of paper to the staff-nurse.

At eleven forty-five that night the telephone by my bed rang out shrilly. 'Sister Margaret's condition has deteriorated, Father,' the voice of the night-sister told me.

'I'm on my way,' I said, as I swung my legs out from under the bedclothes.

Behind the screen round the dying nun I introduced myself to her Reverend Mother and another nun who had been alerted earlier to the sister's condition. The sick-call tray with its lighted candle was ready. I placed the stole over my shoulders, put the small bottle of holy water and the holy oil on the tray, then took the pyx from my inside jacket pocket and placed that next to the candle. I approached the young nun.

'Sister, it's Father Gordon. I'm going to anoint you now.'

'Father!' the nun's voice was barely audible. Her eyes remained shut.

With my thumb damp with the holy oil I traced the sign of the cross on the nun's external senses, while at the same time saying the prescribed prayers.

"Through this holy anointing and God's most tender mercy, may you be pardoned whatever sins you have done by seeing, hearing, by smell, by taste, by touch and by your steps".

Then I asked all the saints to pray for her. *"St. John; St. Paul; St. Peter; Mary Magdalen..."* I concluded by praying:

"May the Angels lead you into paradise, may the martyrs receive you at your coming, and may they lead you into the Holy City, Jerusalem. May the choirs of Angels receive you and may you have eternal rest".

A faint smile was now visible on the nun's face.

'Sister, I'm now going to give you Holy Viaticum.' There was a slight movement of her head. I opened the pyx, and taking the host between thumb and forefinger, said:

218

'May the Body of Our Lord Jesus Christ preserve your soul for everlasting life. Amen.'

'Amen,' the two kneeling nuns answered.

Sister Margaret's lips were still closed and very dry looking.

I asked the younger of the two nuns to moisten the patient's lips. It took the dying nun in the bed a few seconds to open her lips. Eventually they were wide enough for me to place the Host on her tongue. As I washed my fingers in the small bowl of water provided for that purpose the Reverend Mother called my name. I turned to look at Sister Margaret. On her face was the most beautiful expression I had ever seen on another human being. One had often heard the saying: *"She looked angelic"*. In the case of the dying nun it was the only way to describe the look on her face; only here it was no mere figure of speech.

The two nuns and I looked on as Sister Margaret's eyes gradually opened and fixed themselves on a spot above the end of her bed. She tried to raise herself off the bed but failed. Instead, she opened wide her arms. *"Lord, Jesus"*, she cried out before her outstretched limbs fell by her side and her eyes shut in death. The nun's companions blessed themselves as I went to fetch a nurse.

'I'm so sorry, Reverend Mother,' I told the elderly nun as I helped her to rise.

'She saw Our Lord, Father.'

I looked into her face. Yes, she was convinced that her young nun, lying lifeless on that bed, had indeed been granted sight of the Divine Lover to whom she had given her life.

'Yes, she did, Reverend Mother,' I answered, just as two doctors arrived. 'We'd better leave now,' I advised the nuns, the younger of whom was quietly weeping into a handkerchief.

Cycling back to the Presbytery I couldn't help thinking about what had taken place there in Annie Zunz Ward. A nun, so young and lovely, had died. The World would question the validity of the Christian claim that God was good: our assertion that *"God's ways are not our ways"*, rarely, if at all, satisfied such critics.

But what if Sister Margaret really had seen Christ, a vision that had brought such obvious joy to the dying nun? As I took a right turn out of Wilmington Square, the sharp blast of a car horn made me concentrate on my cycling. Anyway, in a few weeks time I would be in a place where miracles did happen.

The aircraft that was to take my Lourdes pilgrimage looked ancient I thought, as I led my little group across the tarmac of Southend Airport. It frightened me just to look at the thing. My fears were well founded when, as we sat ready for take-off the pilot announced that there would be a slight delay due to a minor fault. After about twenty nervous minutes, the plane eventually climbed slowly into the sky and out over the English Channel.

The small town of Lourdes had become famous when, on February the 11th 1858, a young girl, Bernadette Soubirous, claimed to have seen the Blessed Virgin Mary. During the next five months the Lady appeared on eighteen occasions to the girl, during one of which the vision revealed her identity: *"I am the Immaculate Conception"*, she told Bernadette: words that meant nothing to the girl. By the fifteenth appearance, a crowd of almost twenty thousand people had gathered to watch and pray, and in a few instances, to scoff. But it was during the eighteenth apparition that the real drama took place, when the Lady ordered the visionary to drink from the well and to bathe in its waters. This perplexed the girl for there was no such well in sight. But guided by the Lady, Bernadette dug and dug until finally water came bubbling out of the ground. Soon afterwards seven seriously ill people were cured of their illnesses while praying at the grotto. Lourdes began to attract ever increasing numbers of pilgrims, mostly Catholics but of other Faiths as well, and sometimes of none. Today, approximately four million people travel every year to that small French town in the Pyrenees. In the time since the apparitions the Church has recognised sixty four cures as miracles: but there have been thousands of others claimed as miracles.

Our group was booked into the Hotel Stella Matutina. Dinner, we were told, would be at six pm. in order for us to take part in the torchlight procession around the grounds of the domain.

The Saints Peter and Paul pilgrims, each with a lighted candle in their hand, joined the snake-like procession of thousands as it made its way around the domain singing the Lourdes' hymn: *"Immaculate Mary, our hearts are on fire"*.

Once the massive crowd had dispersed to fill the cafes and hotels with laughter and song, I sat with a number of other people in front of the grotto, and in the silence broken only by the sound of the river gurgling behind me, I looked at the large statue of the Virgin perched high in its niche on the rock face, and prayed for every person I could think of and for those whose names escaped me at that particular moment. The huge display of votive candles burned and spluttered in front of the shrine, illuminating the display of crutches left there over the years by their grateful owners who had found no further use for them. Heaven never felt so real or so near.

Early in the afternoon of the next day, the bell of the Basilica summoned the pilgrim population of Lourdes to the blessing of the sick. The amplified voice of a priest, leading those already assembled in prayer and hymn singing could be heard quite clearly, as I herded my little group through the gates leading to the esplanade in front of the Basilica. Wheelchairs and mobile stretchers went whizzing by pushed by cheerful young men and women who had come from all parts of the globe to help with the sick. The heat was intense. The singing grew louder and more fervent as more and more pilgrims joined their voices to the chorus of praise to the Virgin Mary.

The sick in their hundreds were assembled on the right hand side of the square. Members of the Lourdes Medical Bureau stood behind them. Although I had been a chaplain at the Royal Free for over a year now, nothing I had seen in its wards compared with what I now observed laid out in rows before me: the blind, the lame, the deformed with their contorted limbs; some barely recognisable as human beings, and most touching of all, the children. Representatives of human suffering were assembled in that small corner of the planet. The words of the gospel sprang to mind: *"Lord, they whom Thou love are sick"*.

Before the procession began, doctors and nurses dressed in white formed a guard of honour around the priest carrying the monstrance. As the cleric passed along the rows of sick pilgrims he held up the monstrance over them. Rosaries were raised; arms were outstretched to the sacramental Jesus. *"Lord, they whom Thou love are sick"*. The eyes of the sick were filled with expectancy. But there was to be no miracle that day.

On the way back to the hotel, I sat down outside a cafe and had a Dubonnet with ice, unaware that I had ordered an alcoholic drink.

One of the ritual acts of the Lourdes pilgrimage is the 'Baths,' recalling the episode in which the Virgin Mary commanded Bernadette to drink of the water she had miraculously provided, and to wash herself in it. Later on the visionary was to immerse a sick child in the

221

freezing water in an attempt to save the child's life. The infant was immediately cured. Now, each day, thousands of people queue up to bathe themselves in the water.

Wearing a long, blue smock, already wet from previous use, I approached the sunken bath in which two men were waiting my arrival. I stepped down gingerly into the water and straight away the two attendants, one of whom gave me a card from which to read the proscribed prayers, gripped me by the shoulders. When I had finished praying and the card handed back, the men unceremoniously immersed me in the water, which I was only too aware had been used already by countless other people suffering from a variety of diseases. Even the fact that the helpers from time to time drank this same water as an act of faith did nothing to assuage my fear.

That night there was a carnival atmosphere in the Stella Matutina Hotel as the various groups prepared to leave Lourdes the following morning. I'll be back, I promised myself, as I boarded the aircraft for the flight home. I kept that promise on three further occasions.

Some weeks after returning from France, I decided to go into show business when I came up with the idea of staging a variety concert to raise money for our missions. I'll never know what prompted me to do this; perhaps the proximity of Sadler's Wells and my acquaintance with some of the singers had a lot to do with the decision.

At first I thought of staging the show at the 'Wells' itself. But the fear of filling all the seats in a commercial theatre made me decide instead to choose the large auditorium in St. Pancras Town Hall. To help me assemble a cast that would fill all eight hundred seats, I approached the Catholic Stage Guild.

I was one of about fifty people who attended the next month's meeting of the Guild in the Spanish Club, Cavendish Square. The popular television and radio broadcaster, Eamonn Andrews, was there in his capacity as Chairman. He was the only one I recognised; although a pretty, dark-haired young woman did smile at me from across the room. When the formalities of the meeting were concluded, most of those present gathered at the bar, which is where I met Eamonn for the first time.

'Hello, Father, you are very welcome,' the broadcaster said in his rich, distinctive voice. After explaining who I was and why I was there, he smiled. 'So you would like me to appear as well?' he asked.

'Do you think that you could, Mr Andrews?'

A big grin was on his face by then. 'I'll see what I can do. Would you drop me a line giving me all the details, and I'll get back to you as soon as possible?' He then handed me his business card.

When I left the Spanish Club that night I had definite commitments from Victoria Sladen whom I had often listened to on the radio, while growing up in Glasgow, and Bruce Trent, a frequent broadcaster and a very popular singer on the musical stage. I had also the address of Michael O'Duffy, an Irish tenor.

By the night of the concert every seat was sold: Eamonn Andrews's name at the top of the bill had done the trick. As I stood at the back of the hall watching the audience file into their seats I marvelled at my audacity.

Supporting Eamonn I had the Jack Ruane Show Band from Ballina; Vicky Sladen; Bruce Trent; Gordon Traynor and Belfast-born mezzo soprano Mary Gilmore both from Sadler's Wells; Ronnie Uragalo, who ran a fish and chip shop at the top of Farringdon Road and who was a concert pianist in the making; Michael O'Duffy; a couple of musicians who worked at Mount Pleasant Post Office; and as compere, Jack Cunningham, an Irish actor, with Ballina connections.

When the curtain came down at the end of the show, I knew by the applause that the audience had enjoyed my first theatrical presentation.

As the people were leaving I found old Mrs. O'Malley, a blind parishioner whose confession I heard on the first Fridays, and brought her over to meet Henry Cooper who had sat alongside the Provincial during the evening. The boxer wore dark glasses to conceal the injuries he had sustained in a fight the previous week. Henry was visibly moved when Mrs. O'Malley told him how she had sat alongside her radio, rosary beads in her hands, praying that he would win the fight.

The Islington Gazette gave the concert a 'rave' review, and ended by saying how the reviewer was looking forward to Father Gordon's next show.

At the next meeting of the Catholic Stage Guild I was appointed chaplain to Sadler's Wells, and became a familiar figure around the canteen as I sat with a cup of coffee talking to singers. When I met with them on an individual basis, I was shocked to learn how naive the young Irish women were when it came to the matter of relationships with men. One of the older women amongst the chorus began calling on me at the presbytery on a regular basis.

'Father, I think I'm pregnant,' she told me on the first occasion.

I was shocked into silence for a few moments. I knew that she was not married and looked to be on the borderline of childbearing.

'You see I have had no period this month.'

I could feel my face burning. 'Perhaps it's late for some other reason,' I ventured at last, not daring to look her in the eyes.

'I don't think so.'

'Have you been to see your doctor yet?'

'No, Father.'

'Well, will you go and see what he has to say, and then come back to me?'

She took a few seconds to reply. 'Yes,' she murmured.

As she rose to leave, I asked if her friend was married.

'Yes, Father,' she whispered without looking at me.

From the world of opera I crossed over into the strange and wild world of 'pop' when I was introduced to Pat Sherlock, a 'song plugger' with Mills Music in Denmark Street: London's 'Tin Pan Alley.' The genial Irishman's office appeared to have a homing device that attracted every Scots and Irish singer, musician and footballer in London. People that I met there included the Chelsea players: Terry Venables, captain of Chelsea; John Hollins, an aggressive half-back on the pitch, but quiet and boyish off the playing field; George Graham, tall and good looking, who did some modelling from time to time. Inevitably, I soon started attending some of Chelsea's home games, courtesy of George Graham, whenever duty allowed. I enjoyed the matches, and afterwards climbed the stairs to the billiard room where I mixed with the players and their wives or girl-friends as they relaxed with cups of tea and cakes. Serving the refreshments was a friendly Irish woman who always took great delight in telling me: 'Here you are Father' I've kept the best cakes for you.'

It wasn't long before I noticed how the atmosphere changed when the manager, the abrasive Tommy Docherty, entered the room. He was a great favourite with the media on account of his quick wit and instant repartee. But in time I learned not to trust him, and secondly that he had a divisive effect on his young players.

With all these contacts in football, the idea of organising a charity game in aid of the Catholic Stage Guild became more and more an attractive proposition and I mentioned it to Pat Sherlock.

'What a good idea.' One of the teams could be the 'Top Ten Eleven' an outfit comprised of many of the then best known names in entertainment. Pat was its chairman. 'Have you given any thought to the other team?'

I hadn't really, but on the spur of the moment I suggested a team with the name 'Eamonn Andrews Sports Paraders,' after his popular Saturday afternoon sports programme on radio.

At the June meeting of the Guild I put forward my idea for the football match. Eamonn was instantly sold on the idea; especially when I told him who our opponents would be. He took out his pocket diary. 'Tell you what, Father, why don't we all meet for lunch and get the thing moving.' He flicked through the pages of the diary. 'What about next Thursday at Madame Prunniers?'

'That's fine with me, Eamonn. I'll check with Pat Sherlock and anyone else he wants to be involved.'

As well as Eamonn and I, the others who sat down in the restaurant to plan the fund raising event were; Bill Brown, the Tottenham Hotspur and Scotland goalkeeper; Pat Donnellan who owned a printing company in which the goalkeeper had some shares; Tony Hillier who worked alongside Pat at Mills Music, and Pat Sherlock .By the time we reached the coffee it had been decided to stage the game at the end of September or early October, and at a North London venue.

'You will have to play yourself, Father,' Eamonn said with a broad smile, before he began a careful scrutiny of the bill the waiter had placed in front of him. I made a half-hearted protest, inwardly, however, I was thrilled.

Despite my ever increasing involvement with the Stage Guild, Sadler's Wells and Tin Pan Alley, parochial duties were still my prime concern. I resurrected the Nurses' Guild, gathering around me an enthusiastic bunch of lovely young women who seemed to make me their own special property, from the very first moment we were introduced to one another over afternoon tea at their Highbury hostel. It was the Royal Free's way of ensuring that its

225

trainees would have someone to call upon if any of them needed help in the potentially, morally speaking, dangerous environment of a large hospital.

Outside of the confessional, the other place where I came across many human problems was in the 'Front Room' of the presbytery. More often than not the caller wanted nothing more than to book a mass for the anniversary of a loved one's death; or it might be a young couple coming to arrange their forthcoming marriage; or a mother wishing to have her new-born infant baptised. But occasionally, the callers and their needs were not so run of the mill.

One evening just as we finished night prayers upstairs in the community room, Annie, the housekeeper called out my name from the bottom of the stairs. I knocked at the door of the 'Front Room' before entering.

'Diane, what a pleasant surprise,' I exclaimed, when I saw that my visitor was the attractive, dark-haired woman who had smiled at me when I attended my first meeting of the Catholic Stage Guild.

'Hello, Father,' the young woman said as she stood up. 'I'm Diane Cowan' her accent identifying her birthplace as being Glasgow.

'Please sit down,' I motioned with my hand.

'Father, I'm no longer a virgin,' she blurted out. 'It happened in America,' she added.'

I didn't know what to say or where to look. Such an intimate revelation had taken me completely by surprise. I wasn't shocked – many months in the confessional had seen to that. But looking across the table at Diane Cowan's distressed face was a different matter. I was furiously trying to think of something to say to her.

'Why have you told me this, Diane; It's not as if you had to, you know; like in confession?' I said gently. 'Do you wish to go to confession?'

'No, Father, I just had to tell you about that night,' she paused and took a handkerchief out of her handbag,

'There, that's all right, Diane' I said quietly, as she began to cry. I wanted to take one of her hands but quickly pushed that idea out of my mind. The singer's tear-stained face looked at me.

'Now you won't think I'm so good, will you Father?'

'What you have told me about yourself, Diane, will not in the least alter my opinion of you,' I replied firmly.

A little smile flickered briefly on her face. She put the handkerchief back in her bag and stood up. 'I've taken up too much of your time, Father. But I feel so much better now.'

'Good. That's what I like to hear' I responded, as I saw her to the front door.

'Goodnight, Father.'

'Goodnight, Diane, God bless you.' 'Diane,' I called after her as she got to the bottom of the steps. She stopped and turned round to look back at me, 'Scotland the Brave, remember.'

The singer smiled and nodded her head affirmatively before walking quickly to her car parked up the street.

Back in my room I switched on the radio. Kathleen Ferrier was singing, 'Blow the Wind Southerly.' I sat down at my desk to continue preparing the Sunday sermon. I was going to preach on 'self-denial.' One of the quotations I was going to use, I saw amongst my notes, was from St. Thomas Aquinas: 'Man's heart adheres to one thing the more it withdraws from others.' Just as I sat back to think how I could develop this in the context of the sermon, the telephone rang shrilly. The Royal Free needed me to visit a suicide attempt.

Two weeks later, the housekeeper informed me that there was a lady downstairs to see me.

Seated inside waiting for me was one of the staff nurses from the hospital. Tall and slim, with auburn coloured hair, Susan was very attractive looking. We chatted about the weather, holidays and hospital life, while I waited for the reason why she was there.

'Father ...'

'Yes, Susan?'

The nurse hung her head. 'Father, I'm pregnant,' she said in what was almost a whisper.

'Do you have steady relationship with the man?' I asked her in as kind a tone of voice as I could manage.

'Yes, Father, he works in the hospital as a porter.'

The nurse's father was a Group Captain in the RAF; her mother from a landed family in Hampshire. Their daughter pregnant by a hospital porter!

'What's his name, Susan?'

'Billy Wallace, he's from Glasgow.'

'Do you love him enough to marry him?'

'Yes, I do,' she replied without a moment's hesitation.

'Will you ask Billy to come and see me?'

'I'll try, Father. But he's not a Catholic.'

'Don't worry about that, Susan,' I reassured her. 'As Glaswegians we can always argue about Celtic and Rangers.'

For the first time she smiled.

The Wedding making Susan and Billy husband and wife was a small affair; the parents and friends of the couple barely filling two rows of seats. Dressed in virginal white Susan had done a skilful job in concealing the bulge under her dress. At the end of the brief ceremony I wished the couple every happiness and reminded them that I wanted the honour of baptising their first-born.

As I stood at the presbytery door watching the newly-weds drive away, I thought of my own departure in a couple of weeks time for my usual holiday in Ireland: my second since coming to London in 1960. But for the first time I was beginning to have ambivalent feelings towards my life as a priest. I couldn't say for certain what caused those first stirrings of doubt. But the Provincial, Father Maher, I think had some part to play. Recently, he had passed one or two snide remarks about me that I felt were uncalled for. Analysing them afterwards, I could only conclude that they were motivated by jealousy on his part. Then there was that first Christmas dinner. Whatever the cause, I felt my commitment to the priesthood weakening. Added to that were my feelings for Joan. I loved her. But as a priest I repressed such a human emotion. No wonder I felt I was slowly but inexorably becoming a prime candidate for the psychiatrist's couch.

The highlight of that summer for me was the morning I drove to Ballina to collect Joan and bring her to Enniscrone to spend the whole day with me. Her mother wanted the two of us to wait until after lunch then she would come with us; but that was not what I had planned; and what amazed me, Joan as well. She flew up the stairs to collect a few things, with Madeleine still trying to persuade me to wait.

The weather was the most glorious that we were to experience that year. After lunch Joan and I accompanied Dad, my step-mother and their two friends from Glasgow, down to the strand, I had never seen Joan look as relaxed and happy as we all sat on rugs underneath the cliffs, laughing and talking and enjoying the sea air and balmy sunshine: in a photograph capturing that moment, Joan looked radiant and so, so happy.

After over an hour of the older people's company, Joan and I decided to walk the length of the beach as far as the 'Valley of Diamonds.' The tide was well out, so we decided to stroll along the water's edge in our bare feet. Occasionally as our hands or arms touched, I realised just how much I loved this woman; as much, if indeed not more than I had ever done since we first met that summer, all of seventeen years ago. But it was a love, I realised with a feeling of deep regret that would never be consummated.

After reaching the high sand dune which formed the 'Valley of Diamonds' I knelt on one knee and looked down into the valley whose floor, liberally sprinkled with thousands of brightly coloured shells, sparkled in the brilliant sunlight. Joan stood silent by my side, the hem of her dress flicking across my face from time to time, as the gentle breeze blowing from the direction of Bartra Island caught the fabric. Apart from the cries of a few sea birds, there was no sound of any consequence. With great difficulty I overcame the temptation to reach out for Joan's hand and lower her gently alongside me.

On the way back, as we walked along the fringe of the 'dunes,' with Joan on the inside, she suddenly cried out and bolted from my side, racing about twenty yards ahead before coming to a halt. I stopped and stared in amazement at her retreating figure.

Joan and I met with a frosty reception from her father when I took her home late that night. Madeleine had already gone to bed. But I knew that she must have stirred up things with George over Joan's refusal to comply with her wishes. I went upstairs to Madeleine's bedroom. At the time I never gave any thought to my doing so. But looking back on it now, I realise that it was the first time I had entered his wife's bedroom while her husband was in the house.

Downstairs, I found George in a more amiable frame of mind. Obviously Joan had set his mind at rest too. Joan looked up at me and smiled. 'How is Mam?' she asked, with a look that said: 'Is she in a bad mood as well?'

'She's fine,' I answered, and gave an almighty yawn.

Joan rose from her chair. 'I'm going to bed, Daddy.'

'Good-night, God bless,' George said, as Joan and I moved towards the hall.

'Thanks for a lovely day, Martin. It was wonderful,' she said.

'I had a wonderful time too, Joanie,' I responded, then leaned forward and kissed her.

Along the next few miles of deserted road I thought of the husband and wife whose home I had just left. What had gone wrong with their marriage? Madeleine had hinted at their being another woman at some time; but that was during their engagement; then of course money might have a problem. Was Joan also part of the problem? But whatever the reason for the breakdown, Madeleine remained imprisoned in a loveless marriage for the sake of the children and through a certain pride. As a substitute for love such women, and there were thousands of them in Ireland, became more and more devotees of every religious practise available to them within the church and haunted the confessional boxes, where they poured out their woes to the priest on the other side of the grille. However, there were some women who, unable to endure any more punishment from brutish, drink-sodden husbands, took the boat to England, or decided on the ultimate step and killed themselves in a final act of despair. One of Madeleine's neighbours had done just that.

No wonder Joan has problems, I thought, as I pulled up outside the cottage. As I walked up the path, I heard Mother Theresa's hard, dry cough through the open window of her room in the convent across the street, and wondered why the Order didn't send her to a warmer and drier climate.

The next day I returned to Ballina but finding no key in the lock, I made my own entry as usual on these occasions.

'I'm up here, Martin,' Madeleine called out.

I sat on her bed for about half-an-hour and answered her questions about the number of visitors in Enniscrone, about the Royal Free Hospital and so on. Eventually, I was able to put a question to her about Joan. 'Has she a steady boyfriend in Dublin,' I wanted to know.

'Not that I know of,' Madeleine answered tersely. 'Anyway, why do you ask?'

'No particular reason, Mam. I just feel that she is very unhappy looking at times, and wondered if it had anything to do with men.'

'I don't think Joan will ever marry. She is too modest. She doesn't even like to have straps showing through a blouse; and when she had her first period and I explained what it entailed, she burst out crying and ran upstairs,' Madeleine said. 'No, she won't marry because she is thinking of me,' she added almost defiantly.

'What do you mean, thinking of you?'

'After Daddy's gone, she'll retire and have her pension and look after me,' she said in a determined voice.

I was horrified. What mother worthy of the name would map out such a bleak future for a daughter, especially one as fragile as poor Joan, and how presumptuous of the woman to think that her husband would predecease her? I was unable to say anything, so shocked was I at what I had just heard. No wonder Joan was terrified of sex, as I believed. Madeleine had poisoned her daughter's mind with misrepresentations and exaggerations so that she might never marry. No wonder she was in such a confused state of mind.

Soon the holiday was once again a pleasant memory as I busied myself in my work as a priest. The 'big game' was a mere six weeks away, so there was a great deal of activity in preparing for the event. One of the things decided upon was that the *"Eamonn Andrews Sports Paraders"* would wear the 'famous' jerseys of the church team, Marian Rovers F.C.

In the intense training for the match I hurt the Achilles tendon in my right leg. The doctor told me that I had no hope of playing, even though the fixture was still three weeks away. But when I went to Stamford Bridge one Wednesday evening for a Chelsea-Manchester United game, I met up with Paddy Crerand, United's half-back and fellow Glaswegian, and asked him about the injury, explaining about my desire to play in the charity match. He called over the team's physiotherapist and had him inspect my damaged leg. Following his advice, I wore an elastic bandage and had daily treatments with a sun lamp at the local health clinic. By the eve of the game I felt fit to face the Top Ten Xl and confident that I would not disgrace myself.

On the Sunday of the fixture we had one of those balmy October days when summer seems reluctant to leave us at the mercy of approaching winter. The sun shone from an almost cloudless sky, and there was just a slight breeze from the West. I had plugged the game at all masses the previous Sunday and that morning as well; not forgetting to mention that a priest they all knew would be playing for Eamonn Andrews's team. From the many smiling faces in the pews it was clear that they all knew the identity of that priest.

The 'Top Ten Eleven,' our opponents, fielded many well-known names from the world of popular music and television. Actors Brian Blessed, Norman Rossington and comedian Stan Stennet were on the field, playing for the opposition.

But it was Eamonn's team that had the real footballers that day: Jimmy Logie of Arsenal and Scotland, and whom I used to meet for some years afterwards selling papers at Piccadilly Circus; Trevor Ford who played for Cardiff City and Wales, and boxing champion, Henry Cooper, who was marking the diminutive Norman Rossington.

As I pulled on the goalkeeper's jersey, I felt I had come a long way from the playing fields of Cork, Thurles and Enniscrone.

The game was hotly contested; something that surprised me until I realised that with so many former professionals on the field, it couldn't be but anything else. Tommy Docherty was the referee. Acting as linesmen were two of his Chelsea players, Terry Venables and Marvin Hinton. At the final whistle, Eamonn Andrews Sports Paraders were victors by five goals to two; it ought to have been only one for the Top Ten Eleven, but I 'gifted' a score to Brian Blessed, then appearing in 'Z Cars.'

'Thanks, Father,' he whispered, as he joyfully made his way past me back to the centre circle.

The following week's Catholic newspaper, The Universe, carried a report of the match and two photographs of me. None of my fellow priests made any mention of having seen the photographs.

Later that night as I was undressing for bed, the telephone rang. The call, naturally, was from the hospital. A dying patient wanted to see the 'football priest.' Puzzled, I asked the nurse how she knew that I was that priest. 'It was a patient in the next bed who told us,' she said. As I hurriedly dressed I could think of only one man who would call me the 'football priest.' He wasn't a Catholic but every so often I stopped by his bed on a Tuesday afternoon to discuss the previous Saturday's matches involving Chelsea, Arsenal and Spurs.

Behind the screens around his bed I found the man's wife, daughter and son-in-law. The patient smiled weakly at me.

'He took a great liking to you and always talked about you when we came to visit him on a Tuesday night,' the daughter said.

I proceeded to administer the sacrament of Extreme Unction, the 'Last Rites,' explaining what I was going to do to the patient's family before I began. As I said the Prayers for the Dying the two women were weeping quietly into their handkerchiefs.

"May the angels lead you into Paradise; may the martyrs receive you at your coming, and may they lead you into the Holy City, Jerusalem. May the choirs of Angels receive you and may you have eternal rest".

As I concluded my administrations the man in the bed opened his eyes and smiled. I bent down and whispered into his ear: 'My team won today. God bless you,' and squeezed his hand.

My legs felt stiff as I cycled back to the Presbytery. It had been a long and tiring day and was now well past midnight. Was it any wonder that I wanted to get to bed? Just before drifting into a deep sleep I thought about what had taken place in the hospital, and all through talking about football. But then what about the years of studying theology...? God sure moves in mysterious ways, I thought, as I gave a big yawn and switched off the light.

At first I thought that it must be my imagination. But from the day my photographs appeared in The Catholic Universe newspaper, relations between the Provincial and myself deteriorated rapidly. The situation became so bad that by Christmas I avoided being alone with him as much as possible.

That year I decided to send Joan something feminine for her Christmas present and made my way to Bourne and Hollingsworth's lingerie department, Oxford Street where I chose a pastel blue bed-jacket, explaining to the smiling assistant that it was for my sister who was just about her size.

During lunch on a day in February, John Bergin rose from the table to answer the telephone. 'It's for you, Fr. Gordon,' he said.

The caller was Father Moyles in Enniscrone. John McGowan was dead, and my aunt wanted to know if I were coming home to say the Requiem Mass.

'Just a moment, Father Willie.'

I told the priests at the table what the call was about and waited for a response. I looked at John Bergin who, after all, was my immediate Superior. But it was the Provincial who spoke.

We don't allow priests home for funerals other than for those of parents or aunts and uncles, he informed me rather coldly. I was tempted to explain that this case was an exception because of the years spent under John's roof. But the Provincial's whole attitude put me off. Instead, I told the priest in Ireland that I was unable to come and to please convey my sympathy to my aunt. I replaced the receiver and, leaving my lunch unfinished, left the dining room. Two years later, my classmate Christy Maher was allowed home for two weeks to attend an aunt's funeral in Dublin.

During sleep that night I had a massive 'wet dream.' Half awake, I didn't know what had happened until my hand touched the stickiness of my pyjama trousers. Then I cried, cried for the loss of my innocence. Next morning I had to decide whether I could say mass or go to confession first. But since the act was involuntary, no sin had been committed, I reasoned, and said my usual morning act of contrition.

Up until then women were attractive, pleasant creatures whose company I enjoyed; always mindful of course, that I was a priest with a vow of celibacy. On top of that, I recalled George Conboy's words: 'We don't mind a priest taking a drop from the bottle but we won't forgive a priest who takes up with a woman.'

But now in my ever increasing depressive state I began to desire the company of women more than ever and to admire their physical attributes. I became aware too that women were attracted to me as a man: at the head of that list was Diane Cowan.

On the 14th of February of that year, 1963, I somehow obtained the use of a box at the Royal Albert Hall for a Young People's Concert in which Leonard Bernstein was to conduct the New York Philharmonic Orchestra and discuss 'What is a Melody.' He would illustrate his points with passages from: Wagner's Prelude to Tristan and Isolde, Mozart's Symphony No. 40 in G minor; Hindemith's Concert Music for Strings and Brass and Symphony No. 4 in E minor by Brahms. The programme's final item was Mr.Bernstein's own work, Symphonic Dances from West Side Story. To further their musical education, I brought along two young parishioners, Vicki Bird and her cousin Mark Bird. It was a magical couple of hours for the three of us and the thousands of youngsters who packed the hall that afternoon, and whose cheering and sustained applause at the end brought tears to the eyes of the distinguished conductor and composer. When finally he could make himself heard, he said that he would love to stay and play longer for them, but he had to leave as the orchestra had an evening performance at the Royal Festival Hall in three hours time.

Three other musical memories remain with me: Isaac Stern playing Bruch's haunting violin concerto, and Yehudi Menuhin playing the viola in Berlioz's Chide Harold in Italy; both at the Royal Albert Hall. The third concert was Stravinsky conducting his own composition, The Rite of Spring at the Festival Hall. On this occasion I was the guest of Father Donald Logan, a priest of the diocese of Boston who was doing post graduate research at the British Library.

Before going away on my summer holiday that particular year, Diane Cowan invited me to dinner in her comfortable flat in Islington. After confirming that I liked fish, the singer prepared a meal of plaice, cauliflower and new potatoes with fresh strawberries and cream for the pudding. In the knowledge that the main course was to be fish, I arrived with a bottle of white wine labelled 'Chablis Grand Cru 1963.' Apart from Joan, it was my first experience of dining alone with a very attractive woman of around my own age, and I enjoyed it.

'Time to draw the curtains,' she said, standing up and walking over to the windows which looked out on the back garden.

'Let me help you,' I suggested, when I saw that she was having difficulty with one of the drapes. As I stood beside her a mere couple of inches between us, I could feel the warmth of her body and as I reached up to give a final tug to the curtain our fingers touched for the briefest of moments. I heard Diane give a sharp intake of breath and our eyes met as if drawn together by a magnet. How long we stood like that, I've no idea. But at the time it seemed like minutes.

Eventually I broke the spell when I stepped back from her side and said: 'There, now, Diane, a man comes in handy some times.'

Before leaving the singer told me that she was going up to Glasgow the following week. On an impulse I said that I was due to travel north as well. 'If I can get away next week, perhaps we could travel together,' I suggested.

'That would be lovely, Father,' she replied smilingly.

'I'll let you know tomorrow, Diane and if I can make the trip, will you book two sleepers; separate, of course,' I added quickly.

The woman's laugh made me realise what I had said, and I could feel my face going all hot. 'spoil sport,' the singer said, placing her hand on my arm.

At the front door of the house, I thanked her once again for a most pleasant evening and promised that I would take her out for a meal sometime in the autumn. Then I kissed her cheek, hurriedly whispered 'God bless,' and raced down the steps.

On the way back to the presbytery, the thought of Diane and I sharing the same sleeping compartment made me literally 'hot under the collar.'

During that night I thought I heard a bell ringing in the distance. Pulling the bedclothes up over my head I turned my back on the annoying sound. But still the bell continued to disturb my sleep. Slowly corning awake, I realised that it was my telephone that was causing the racket.

'Hello,' I murmured.

'Sorry for disturbing you, Father,' a man's voice told me. I glanced at my alarm clock: 3.40a.m. I gave an inward groan. 'I'm Ian Smith of the Daily Mirror,' the voice continued. 'Do you know the old lady who ran a little shop from her flat near the Italian church?'

My mind was gradually focusing on what the man at the other end of the line was saying.

'Oh, you mean Miss McCarthy.'

'That's right, Father. Well, I'm sorry to have to tell you that she has been murdered.'

'Murdered,' I exclaimed; wide awake by now.

'Battered to death in her flat,' the reporter informed me. 'Could I ask you a few questions, Father?'

I told the man to go ahead. My comments were duly reported in that day's Daily Mirror. The police were following a definite line of enquiry. Within a few days detectives from Kings Cross arrested a young male for the murder of the 'Holy Lady,' as the media were now calling her. The suspect lived in a block of flats near our church. But he wasn't a parishioner. Thank God for that, I thought. At least we'll be spared seeing some sub-editor's banner headline splashed across the front page. 'Devout Catholic murders Holy Lady.' The murder weapon was found alongside the railway line that carries the underground between Farringdon and Kings Cross.

The alleged murderer was duly brought to trial, but was acquitted due to lack of sufficient evidence. That night he and his family and friends celebrated his release in the Red Lion pub in Rosmon Street.

'We know he's our man Father,' one of my police friends told me after Mass the following Sunday.

Within a year the alleged killer was arrested as he raced out of an office building near the Angel, after committing a robbery. An off-duty policeman fly-tackled him as he fled the building.

Bishop George Craven came to Saints Peter and Paul to administer the sacrament of Confirmation the week before I left for Ireland. Among those to be confirmed was Henry Cooper, standing last in a long line of children moving slowly up the centre isle of the church. I couldn't help but admire the big man's humility. But obviously no one had bothered to tell the elderly bishop about Henry's presence. For when he looked up and saw the boxer's towering figure his mouth opened wide in astonishment. It took him about twenty seconds to recover his composure before giving the traditional gentle slap to the boxer's cheek. For a brief moment I fancifully waited for 'Henry's Ammer' to retaliate. But to my great disappointment, Henry allowed the bishop to bring down the Holy Spirit upon him, without doing the elderly cleric any damage.

My time at home that year followed the pattern of previous years: a few days in Dublin with Joan before she came down to Ballina. On one evening as we crossed from the G.P.O. after collecting her from work, on an impulse I bought a bunch of flowers and handed them to Joan. She blushed from her neck to the roots of her hair, but smiled gratefully up at me as she took my offering in her hands. I expect that it was the first flowers that she had ever been given by any man, let alone a priest.

One afternoon when I called to the house in Morrison Terrace I was disappointed to find that Madeleine and Joan had cycled out into the country to visit friends. George, on his half-day from Liptons, sat reading the Irish Independent, while I rummaged through a pile of religious magazines: The wide-eyed black babies still adorned the front covers,

'Making love to some women is like making love to that door there,' I heard George say grimly, at the same time indicating the door of the under-stairs cupboard. Was I expected to make some response, I wondered, startled by the suddenness of the outburst. I chose to remain silent and continued to turn the pages of The Far East, aware that George was staring challengingly at me.

When his wife and daughter arrived back from their excursion, Madeleine told me that Frances Heffernan wanted to see me. 'Why don't you go down now and find out what she wants, while Joan and I get the tea,' she suggested. Then as an afterthought: 'Ask Fran if she would like to come up for her supper.'

As was her custom, the young attractive doctor came straight to the point. She wanted to know if I could help a friend's daughter who was pregnant but didn't want to marry the father. To avoid any scandal in her home town of Galway, she was thinking of going to London. I told Frances that there was no problem of finding a job for her; I knew that Peter Norris's Keystone Employment Agency would help in that regard.

'Accommodation will be harder to find, Fran. But I'll see what I can do as soon as I get back to the parish,' I told her. Then I told her of Madeleine's invitation to tea.

'I'd love to. Just wait a minute and I'll change my skirt,' Frances replied.

After the meal was over and Joan and Frances were clearing the table, I heard Madeleine say to the young neighbour: 'That's a nice skirt, Frances.'

George Conboy, who was sitting in his usual armchair reading the evening paper, lowered it and interjected: 'It's not the skirt that matters, it's what's underneath that counts.'

Poor Frances, her face turned a bright crimson as she hurriedly went into the scullery. Madeleine Conboy gave her husband a look bordering on hatred.

Returned to Amwell Street, I read the back issues of the Catholic papers. All of then gave extensive coverage to the recent session of the Vatican Council. I loved, in particular, Patrick O'Donovan's words on the bishops processing into St. Peters:

"I saw executive faces and kindly faces and imperious faces and ascetic faces and faces that have known good tables".

Nothing as yet had emerged from the Council's deliberations to touch the lives of priests like myself. But changes were bound to come, I knew.

The 'front room' acquired a new visitor. Mary, I soon learned, was Irish, and 'worked' the streets around the nearby railway termini of King's Cross and St.Pancras She became a regular visitor, and if I were not at home she would go away again. Mary was a very sick woman when we first met; and on one occasion opened her voluminous bag from which she withdrew a plastic plunger contraption and some large, white, bullet-shaped tablets which, she told me, she had to insert into her vagina daily. Occasionally I caught a glimpse of Mary as she plied her trade around the stations. Eventually she ceased calling at the Presbytery, nor did I ever see her again on the streets.

The young, pregnant woman arrived from Galway with little sign of her condition showing as yet. I had been lucky in finding a family in Myddleton Square who had a spare room in their house and were more than happy to help the unfortunate girl. Peter Norris at Keystone Employment Agency got her a well-paid position as a secretary. So all that remained for me to do over the next few months was to call on her occasionally to ensure that she was well and was attending her pre-natal clinics.

One Friday evening I spotted her going into the church with a bouquet of flowers which I later found placed in front of the Lady altar. When I asked her about this she told me that this was something her mother did back home in Galway.

I was still very actively involved as Stage Guild chaplain to Sadler's Wells. On one occasion I was approached by Dennis Arundell, the producer, who requested that I join him for the dress rehearsal of Tosca. In addition, he asked me to supply altar boys for the production. I made no mention of any of this to my colleagues.

At the interval I had only one serious criticism to make to Mr.Arundell: the Archbishop processing down the length of the cathedral was blessing the floor, not the congregation. Attending the rehearsals at the 'Wells' was one of the perks attached to my position as chaplain; for, as I have already explained, a priest was forbidden to enter an opera house. Tosca; the Magic Flute; The Love of Three Oranges; La Boheme: I saw them all. Some months later, Mr. Arundell asked me to bless his house in Lloyd Square, because he and the man who shared the house with him were having serious problems with a poltergeist.

That Christmas I went down to Tin Pan Alley to wish Pat Sherlock and all at Mills Music a Happy Christmas. I could hardly get in the door of his office: half the Scots and Irish singers and musicians in London, not to mention the regulars from the Chelsea team: Terry Venables; George Graham, John Hollins and Eddie McCreadie were all crammed into the small office. Downstairs, young Reg Dwight, better known today as Elton John, was accompanying two young women from the Luton Girls' Choir on the piano. I did a quick head count, and of the fifteen people present at the party, only three were English.

Now in my fourth year as a priest, the Provincial surprised me one night when he appointed me Vocations Director for the United Kingdom. The next morning when I sat down at the breakfast table, there was a letter propped up against my cup and saucer confirming the appointment. As a first step in a recruiting drive for recruits to our Society, I placed adverts in the two main Catholic newspapers. Four weeks later I was on a train for Manchester to interview three boys who had responded to the adverts. After that I went north to my native city to meet four others. But before leaving London I had a visit from a man in his twenties who wanted to become a priest. He was just the type we were looking for: English,educated and refined. There was one problem, however: he was homosexual, but had not been an active one for the past year. Naturally I had to tell him gently that the Pallottines could not accept him for the priesthood.

When I emerged from Manchester's Piccadilly Station to begin the first of the interviews, the rain was pouring down. Given the weather, it took me ages to find a taxi to take me out to the Pallottine Sisters Convent at Rochdale, where I was to stay for a couple of days.

None of the Mancunian boys I met were seriously interested in becoming priests. They had filled in the coupons in the newspapers just for something to do, I expected. I fared much better in Glasgow, where three boys expressed a serious interest in becoming Pallottines. Lack of money I told their much relieved parents, was no barrier to their entering the college in September as First Year Postulants.

When the college year began the following September, two of the young men arrived in Thurles and went on to be ordained. Unfortunately, one of them became a victim of multiple sclerosis a few years after ordination and went home to Greenock to end his days. The only other child in the family, his brother, drowned in the Clyde after leaving a pub.

With my work completed I decided to fly to Dublin to spend a couple of days with Joan, who had been very much on my mind over the past forty eight hours. When I called at the Henry Street entrance of Dublin's G.P.O., the porter told me that 'Miss Conboy was not in that day.' I knew then why Joan had been on my mind so much during my stay in Glasgow. I caught the bus to Glasnevin and gave Joan one of the biggest surprises of her life when she opened the door and saw me standing there. She was dressed in the blue dressing gown that she often wore at home. Her fair hair was limp and bedraggled, and she was thin and deathly pale looking. My heart ached for her, and I wanted desperately to take her in my arms and tell her how much I loved her. Instead, I gave her my usual 'brotherly' kiss and walked through with her to the kitchen.

For the next two days I fussed over Joan, giving her breakfast in bed and making her stay there until mid-day, when I would have lunch prepared for the two of us. On the first morning that I served her breakfast, I smiled when I saw her glance down at her chest to see if her breasts were fully covered by her nightdress, as she sat up to take the tray from me.

On the morning of my departure, after I had cleared away the breakfast things and brought my suitcase out into the hall, then telephoned for a taxi to take me to the airport, I went into Joan's bedroom and sat on the edge of her bed. We talked about that summer's holiday and arranged that we both would be at home at the same time. She looked much better, I thought, after just two days of my tender, loving care.

'Thanks, Martin, for ...'

I placed a finger on her lips. I glanced at my watch. 'I better go now, love,' I told her. 'Good-bye, Joanie.' Then I bent down and kissed her tenderly on her lips.

Rising quickly from the bed before my emotions would overwhelm me, I had just gone half way towards the door when the sound of a loud sob from Joan stopped me. I looked back towards her. She was crying uncontrollably. I stood there, my hand reaching towards the doorknob, my heart breaking at the sight of my beloved Joan's tear-stained face and listening to the sound of her crying. Everything human in me, every fibre of my manhood urged me to rush to her side, gather her into my arms and with kisses tell her that I still loved her, always had loved her, and would continue to love her until the end of time. But I knew that if I did that there was no way that I would ever function as a priest again.

'Joan, I must go, was the only response I could make in a choked voice and closed the door behind me. But not before I heard another pitiful cry of anguish: a sound that has remained with me to this day. I hated myself then; and. still do.

On the way to the airport and on the flight to London I found it impossible to put out of my mind the thought of Joan lying alone in her bed in such a distressed state. Surely I ought to have done what any normal man would have done in that situation and to hell with the consequences. But then a priest is not a normal man, is he? To this day I still regret not having stayed with Joan on that morning, whatever the outcome might have been for the two of us. When I came home the following July, Joan told me shyly that she had got out of bed and stood at the French window, to watch my plane fly over the city towards Wicklow.

'Father Gordon, you have been a long time away,' was the Provincial's greeting when we met later that afternoon.

'You gave me a job to do, Father, and I did it,' I replied coldly. 'If you like I'll give you a full written report by to-night,' I added, and stormed out of the room before I said something that I might later regret. Of course I realised that it was the thought of Joan that had triggered my angry response. But I had come to loathe Father

Maher. If one were to ask me why, I would find it difficult to give a reason for my feelings. There was just something about his bearing, and certainly in his attitude towards me that I found repugnant.

As I crossed the street to board a bus for Victoria the next afternoon, on my way to Westminster Cathedral for confession, I felt a tingling sensation on my lips as the memory of the previous day's kiss resurfaced. It left a warm feeling within me and a desire to be alongside Joan again in Dublin.

Once I had made my confession and was about to leave the confessional, I was startled to hear the priest ask me to hear 'his' confession, and was greatly disturbed to hear him declare how he 'cruised' London's Turkish baths. Up until that moment I never thought about priests and homosexuality. Then I remembered how the appearance, mannerisms and speech of one student in Thurles had always puzzled me.

Soon I was once again immersed in the work of a priest. The opera singer called on me once again to announce that she was pregnant. But like the other times it was a case of 'wishful thinking.' I really felt sorry for the poor woman; she was a lovely person and so obviously wanted to have a child. But why she continued in her relationship with a married man I'll never know. But no matter what advice I gave her, she would not give him up.

One of the urgent calls from the Royal Free around that time was to administer the Last Rites to a young boy of seven or eight years of age, who had been badly burned when climbing a transformer somewhere around Highbury. He was lying naked and unconscious and with a tube inserted into his little penis. I looked questioningly at the nurse, who shook her head. Because of his burns I could only anoint the poor child on his forehead.

Another patient I saw that same week was a lady dying of cancer. One of her breasts had been removed the previous year, but the disease had spread to other parts of the body. Before administering the sacrament, we talked for a while. She told me that she was offering up her life for a priest friend, and then went on to relate the whole story.

'Father Michael has left the priesthood and no one knows where he is or what he is doing. If only he would get in touch with me before I..' she began to cry softly. I reached towards the box of tissues on her bedside locker and handed one to her.

'Please God he will hear of your illness and come to see you,' I suggested.

The woman dabbed her eyes with a tissue. 'Do you really think so, Father?'

I took one of her hands in mine and gave it a reassuring squeeze. 'I'm certain,' I assured her.

'You are so kind, Father, and remind me a lot of Michael.'
After I had given her the sacrament of Extreme Unction, I advised her to rest and told her that I would be around in the morning to give her holy communion. On an impulse I bent down and kissed her tenderly on the forehead.

'That's from Michael,' I whispered.

She was obviously very much in love with the priest, probably from their childhood. Michael, I only hope that you are worthy of such love, I murmured to myself as I walked to the lift.

On a visit to the Eye Ear and Nose Hospital, I met Tony Hancock's wife Freddie Ross, who was having surgery for a broken noise, after the comedian had given her a bad beating. His violent mood swings and his alcoholism eventually drove her away.

On a Sunday afternoon shortly afterwards I had a wedding to perform. The bride was of Italian descent from Farringdon Road, the groom was English, from Kensington. With about ten minutes to go before the bride was due to arrive, the Registrar from Finsbury Town Hall and I were talking in the sacristy when he asked me to bring in the groom who was already seated in the church. After the usual social courtesies the Registrar asked the man for his certificate from the Borough of Kensington. To the Registrar's consternation the man told him that he had forgotten to collect it.

'In that case the marriage cannot go ahead,' the official said.

The poor unfortunate man turned to me. 'What am I going to do, Father?' he wailed. Just at that moment word came that the bride was waiting in the church porch to make her grand entrance.

'Isn't there anything that you can do?' I asked the Registrar.

He shook his head.

'Marcella will kill me. She'll never marry me now,' the groom muttered disconsolately, and buried his head in his hands.

I placed a reassuring hand on his shoulder. 'I better go down to the door and break the news to the bride,' I said quietly.

'I'll never marry him, never,' the bride screamed when I broke the news to her, as diplomatically as I could. She threw the bouquet of flowers on the ground, and for a moment I thought that she would stamp on them, such was her anger. The two young bridesmaids were in tears by now. Stirred by the commotion in the porch, the bride's mother arrived to find out what was delaying the wedding ceremony. Soon her wailing was added to that of her daughter and the bridesmaids. I mumbled a few unintelligible platitudes and retreated to the relative safety of the sacristy, where I persuaded the groom to go and face his bride, not to mention the mother-in-law. After arguing for a couple of minutes the entire wedding party left the church and made their way to the hall where the wedding reception went ahead as planned. The marriage eventually took place three weeks later.

Writing about weddings reminds me of the saddest one that I was called upon to perform. A parishioner called on me one morning. She was from Dublin and had a boy and girl attending the parish school. Her husband came to mass occasionally with her; but I suspected he wasn't a Catholic. The reason for her coming to see me, she quickly explained, was to find out if her marriage outside the church could be rectified.

'You see, Father, I have cancer,' she said quietly. After questioning her for a few minutes I was happy to tell her that there was nothing to stop her marriage being regularised within the church.

'Oh, I am so happy, Father, I could cry,' the poor woman exclaimed, as she dabbed at her eyes with a tissue. Two weeks later I cycled up to the Liverpool Road annex of the Royal Free to marry the woman and her husband according to the Rites of the Catholic Church.

Propped up in bed by numerous pillows, Mrs.Garwood looked awfully frail, as I greeted her and her family. The nursing staff had prepared a small vase of flowers and two candles by the bedside, and had tied a blue ribbon in the bride's hair. With two nurses acting as witnesses, and the couples' children looking on, I 'married' their father and mother. When they came to promise that they would love each other *"Until Death do us part"*, I had to close my eyes and fight to control my emotions. Within a week the bride was dead.

Despite my busy life, and I should add, the knowledge that I was helping my people in many small ways, and indeed in some very important matters, something was missing. An aridness began to creep into my spiritual life. Was this the 'Dark Night of the Soul' that one read so much about in the lives of the saints? I was lonely and sad. How much my love for Joan played in this, I have no idea. But I struggled through each day until it was time to climb those stairs to my lonely room at the top of the house.

I decided to stage another concert that year at the same venue as my first one. Again the demand for tickets ensured another packed Assembly Hall. With Pat Sherlock's help I put together a cast of: Joe Brady – then appearing in the popular T.V. series, 'Z Cars;' Dermot Kelly, the Irish comedy actor, also currently on television; the Irish actor, Tony Doyle, who would go on to be in great demand for stage and T.V. drama; Soprano, Diane Todd, from Sadler's Wells, and later to sing at Drury Lane; and The London Scottish Junior Choir; all supported by a number of other talented singers, musicians and actors. Anna Cowie from Glasgow, who had accompanied many of the world's top singers, was the pianist on the night.

An imaginative feature of the night was having song writer Tommie Connor lead the audience in the singing of some of his well-known songs such as: *"I saw Mammy Kissing Santa Claus"*; *"It's My Mother's Birthday Today"*; *"Lily Marlene"* and *"The Little Boy That Santa Claus Forgot"*.

Diane Todd sang *"My Ain Folk"* and, while dabbing her eyes with a handkerchief after she finished, looked down to where I was sitting and said: 'That was for you, Father Gordon.'

In an attempt to attract more vocations to the religious life, the religious orders the diocesan bishops had conceived the idea of holding an exhibition at Earl's Court at which many religious orders and societies, the Pallottines included, would have stands. The title given to the event was 'Challenge 65.' As Vocations Director for Great Britain, I had to organise our exhibit. To help me with the Pallottine stand I called upon the expertise of Matt McCarthy who was involved in the world of the cinema and was also a parishioner. On his advice we formed a small committee of professional people who set to work with great enthusiasm to design the stand first of all and then to produce a four minute slide show with full sound effects. Eamonn Andrews agreed to record the commentary. To this epic we gave the title *"The Man on Hand"*. I was its star.

In 1965, a new parishioner came to S.S. Peter and Pauls. Sir Arnold Lunn had been a renowned skier and had invented the slalom in 1922. His father had founded Lunn's travel agency that would later become Lunn Polly. He followed his father's Methodism. But after an epistolary debate with Monsignor Ronald Knox, the priest received him into the Catholic Church in 1933. The new convert became a prolific and effective writer of Catholic tracts for many years of his life.

When Challenge '65' opened, I invited many of my show business and sporting friends to visit our stand, and to be interviewed by me on the closed circuit television shown on monitors throughout the vast hall Amongst those interviewed were: Sir Arnond Lunn; Margaret Savage and three other attractive ladies from their highly popular Black and White Minstrel show; and Bill Brown, the Spurs and Scotland goalkeeper, who attracted a huge crowd around the interviewing area.

The Pallottine stand, which took the form of a small cinema, was manned by me and a couple of other priests, along with a nun and the three girls from the parish who had entered the convent in Rochdale the previous September. Their smiling, attractive faces drew many young girls to the stand; not to mention many an admiring glance from passing males. I don't recall the Society gaining one lasting vocation to the priesthood from all our efforts. The sisters fared a little better, I believe. Father Bill Hanley, who had come to Amwell Street as the Provincial's secretary, was quite adamant that the three young women would be better of married than wasting their lives in a convent. A strange comment, I thought, from a man who was tipped to succeed Father Maher as Provincial. The Pallottine display was voted the second-best of 'Challenge '65.' Some weeks after it had closed, a man stopped me near Victoria Station and said: 'Aren't you The Man on Hand?'

On the front cover of the following month's magazine from the Catholic T.V. Centre at Hatch End was a photograph of me interviewing Margaret Savage and her three attractive colleagues at 'Challenge '65.' Again, none of my colleagues referred to the picture.

Sir Arnold and Lady Lunn invited me to dinner one evening a week later. Before leaving, he presented me with a signed copy of his book, *"The Cult of Softness"*. I made no mention of this event to my colleagues.

One morning shortly afterwards, I was called down to the front room. Inside was a tall well-dressed Irish man of about thirty five years old. Without wasting any time he explained that he and his wife were on their honeymoon, but that they were experiencing a problem. I asked him to wait while I telephoned the marriage guidance people at Westminster Cathedral for an appointment.

The person I spoke to wanted the couple to call in two days' time. But once I explained that they were on their honeymoon, I was told to send them down right away. The husband was delighted at the offer of immediate help and invited me out to the church where his wife was waiting. She blushed and hung her head as I was introduced to her. I took them both outside and pointed to the bus stop over at Finsbury Town Hall, and told them to get the 38 bus to Victoria. Over the years I have often wondered about them and how their lives have been ever since. If by any chance they read this, perhaps they would contact me through the web site.

Before I left for the annual trip to Ireland, my first group of Catholic nurses invited me to join them for a celebratory dinner: they had done their final exams and had all passed them. It was the first time that we had met as a group since that introductory meeting at their Highbury hostel four years previously. Their freshness and femininity that night was just the tonic I needed, as my commitment to the priesthood was at its lowest since ordination. Looking at photographs taken around that time, I am shocked at the depth of sadness clearly evident on my face, as I stare unsmilingly into the distance. Even my holiday that year only served to increase the tension building up within me.

If any of my nurses read this book, I hope at least one of them will make contact with me through facebook or the web site:

www.authormartingordon.com

During that year's holiday Joan and I drove out to Gortnor Abbey to visit her nun friend, Mother Loyola. Parked in front of the convent of Jesus and Mary I stood by the car admiring the glorious view of lake and mountains while Joan went to fetch the nun, who, when after we had shook hands said: 'I was at my window when I saw the two of you get out of the car. I thought you were a honeymoon couple.'

Joan's face turned a deep crimson. I smiled with pleasure at the thought of what might have been.

After Mother Loyola had shown us the interior of the new chapel, Joan went into the convent to meet some other sisters that she knew while the nun and I went outside into the brilliant sunshine. As we walked in the grounds Mother Loyola suddenly stopped and looking at me said: 'Martin, take care of Joan; you're the only one she's got.'

If her words surprised me it was the seriousness with which she said that impressed me most. All I could say in reply was something to the effect that I knew Joan needed looking after.

It was a very depressed and troubled priest who returned to Amwell Street. I could barely bring myself to perform the most basic duties of a priest: even saying mass became a chore; especially if I were on the 7a.m. and had not even a congregation of one or an altar server to give the responses. I seethed with anger as I raced through what was becoming for me an empty ritual. Fortunately help was near at hand, or so I thought, when the Provincial informed me that I was being transferred to the Pallottine parish at Greenford, Middlesex, and was to take up my appointment after our annual retreat.

So after five years at Saints Peter and Pauls I was moving on. I had seen the film: *"Going My Way"*. But I doubted very much if my departure would be anything like that of Bing Crosby, when his time came to say 'Goodbye' to Barry Fitzgerald. I asked the Provincial if might say farewell to the parishioners at each mass on my last Sunday. But he turned down my request. I could only announce my departure my own mass. Then what about a little informal party one night that week, I suggested. Again, the answer was in the negative. No reasons were given.

The venue for our annual retreat was Southall House, the Jesuit residence on Fitzjohn's Avenue, Hampstead. The previous year it had been held at Alington Castle in Kent, where I slept in a room allegedly once occupied by King Henry VIII. That year's retreat was conducted by the Provincial of one of the German Provinces who startled the retreatants on the very first evening by declaring forcibly that *"Many priests are driven into the arms of a woman by fellow priests"*. Was he a mind reader, I wondered.

Encouraged by this, I had no hesitation the following day in having a counselling session with the Retreat Master, during which I poured out all my doubts and frustrations. He listened sympathetically, interrupting only a couple of times to ask a question or make a suggestion during the lengthy period of my anguished soul-searching. When he realised what was at the root of my problem he said:

'But Father, you took a vow.'

'I know that,' I interrupted. 'But when I took that vow of celibacy I really didn't know what it would mean in terms of human relationships. Forbidden to have sex, that I realised. But not the loneliness of the celibate life, that was something I didn't expect; that was something new; especially when one is feeling low and depressed. There's no one to turn to, is there? No shoulder to cry on, so to speak.'

'Go on Father,' the priest told me kindly, when I stopped and looked at him.

'I doubt very much if there is a priest who really knew what the vow entailed when they took it. We all got dragged along by the consoling idea that once we were priests, somehow we wouldn't need any human companionship; especially of a woman. After all, we had Christ. That, we were told, would be enough to see us through any crisis in our celibate lives. Somehow we were expected to discard our manhood and become as angels. But it's not like that, is it Father?'

'There is a certain amount of truth in what you say,' the priest replied. 'But even you must admit that during his seminary years a priest receives instruction and advice to prepare him for his life in the ministry.'

'That's just my point,' I interjected. 'We had very little advice and instructions; certainly not of a professional nature, and certainly no experience of the opposite sex.'

'Some priests do,' the Retreat Director said quietly.

'Then they are the exception,' I retorted. 'How many seminarians have ever walked a girl home after a dance and kissed her good-night? How many, Father?'

The priest opposite me was shaking his head. 'If all students for the priesthood were to experience such moments, how many would continue on to ordination?' I asked angrily.

The German priest put up his hand to make a reply but I resumed my diatribe.

'Father, don't you understand that what we priests are asked to do – to be celibate – has nothing to do with loving God; it is a man-made rule. God didn't say: 'Martin Gordon, you cannot be a priest unless you give up the natural love for a woman. It is man who has made this decision; and at what a price, as is evidenced by the untold numbers of priests addicted to drink and illicit sex.'

I bowed my head and thought of one of my classmates in America who had run off with the parish secretary within twelve months of ordination; and what was really bizarre, another St. Pat's man who had dressed up as a woman and entered a woman's toilet in America. His bishop gave him 24 hours to leave the diocese. Later, another St.Patrick's man left the priesthood and became manager of an abortion clinic; another one on the eve of his becoming a bishop left his parish with the secretary

After the end of mass my on that final Sunday at Saints Peter and Paul, I waited in the sacristy, believing that some of the parishioners would come to wish me God-speed. But after waiting about ten minutes, and not a single soul had come to the sacristy, I emerged into an empty church and a deserted street. Five years of my life given to the people of Saints Peter and Paul and there I was alone and crying out for someone just to say even a simple few words of regret or gratitude. At another time I might have shed a few tears. But at that moment, anger was my predominant mood. Was this what I had given up my youth and early manhood for; not to mention the love and companionship of a woman? I wanted to scream out in anger and frustration. But who would hear my anguished plea for love and understanding.

"Tonight, Lord. I am alone.
Little by little the sounds
died down in the church,
The people went away,
And I came home,
Alone".

The Priest: A prayer on a Sunday Night. Michael Quoist

I glanced up and down the empty street before joining my colleagues for lunch. During the five days left to me at Amwell Street, a number of cards and presents arrived. Among them one I shall always treasure. It was from two Irish girls who worked as maids in the Royal Free Hospital. The message was very simple: *"We will miss your smile"*. Enclosed was a five pound note. Sheila and her husband, Vic Bird, my football trainer, gave me a Parker pen. Sheila's eyes were misty as she handed me the package. I thanked her, kissed her cheek and hurried out of the close before she could see my own emotion at our parting. The O'Callaghan sisters, who so kindly put Joan up, gave me a ten pound note to say a mass for them. But what really saddened me at my departure from Saints Peter and Paul was the comment made by a member of the parish Saint Vincent de Paul Society, which was holding its weekly meeting in the 'front room.' I knocked on the door and poked my head in. 'You probably know I'm leaving on Friday, so 1 just wanted to say good-bye,' I told the brothers.

'Does that mean we'll have to put our hands in our pockets,' one of them responded.

No words could describe the shock I felt at that moment. That after five years of giving myself to the people of the parish, all one of the 'pillars' of that same parish was concerned about was would he have to contribute to a 'going-away' present. I stood for a few seconds unable to reply, noticing at the same time that the man's colleagues were all looking down at the table. When I had partially recovered my composure, I slowly backed out of the room and without speaking closed the door behind me.

When the actual moment of my departure arrived I found that I was pleased to be leaving Amwell Street. But like a lover who has found that his partner has been unfaithful, I too felt betrayed by those to whom I had given, not only my love, but five years of twenty four hours a day unpaid service. Then to be asked:

"Does that mean we'll have to put our hands in our pockets?"

Thirty six years on, the memory still hurts.

'You're very welcome,' said Father Sean Noone as he ushered me into my new home. 'Come upstairs and I'll show you your room.'

The Greenford Presbytery was relatively modern and provided each priest with a sitting-room and a bedroom; luxury compared to Amwell Street. On the same floor were the toilet and separate bathroom and the community room equipped with television and comfortable armchairs. On the ground floor were the reception rooms, dining room, kitchen and housekeepers flat. A door at one end of the corridor led into the church: a concrete hangar-like edifice that one would pass by without realising that it was a church. When I told Eamonn Andrews where I was now based, he expressed surprise that there was a church there; as he passed that way many times. I took an instant dislike to it from the first moment I stood within its cavernous, cold interior.

My guide was the only member of the community I met that night. The other three priests I didn't see until we all met for lunch the next day. Michael Martin, a close friend of the Provincial, mumbled grace then hardly spoke again until he prayed at the end of the meal. Most of the conversation at the table came from old Harry Treacy, who took great pride in boasting that he was the only Cockney in the Society, and Harry Madden, from County Tyrone, a boisterous character with a raucous laugh and an embarrassing habit of grabbing the knee or the thigh of the person he was conversing with at the time; even in public. Sean Noone, I soon discovered, had a problem.

During the months leading up to Christmas I just about managed to survive and keep my sanity. I had been unhappy enough and unsettled when I arrived in Greenford, but by December I was morose and uncommunicative with my colleagues: not that they seemed to notice or indeed care.

The hours between supper and bedtime were the worse; especially if I was in the house and had no meeting to attend or callers to see. By 10p.m., no sound disturbed the silence. It's like the tomb; I thought grimly, as I stood one night outside my door for a few seconds and listened. Yes, that's what the place resembled; a tomb, but without the promise of an Easter Sunday. I decided at that moment that I had to get away from Greenford. Like Brian Moore's fictional character, Mary Dunne, I could well have remarked:

"This life I live isn't believable, not even to me".

Before lent began I organised a dance in the school hall and persuaded Ray McVay to bring along his orchestra for a very nominal fee. I also invited my Chelsea football friends, Terry Venables, George Graham and Eddie McCreadie to come along with the women in their lives. Also gracing the occasion were Tony Hillier from Mills Music and Margaret Savage from the Black and White Minstrel Show. The evening was a tremendous success: helped no doubt by the fact that there was a bar, despite the objections of the Headmaster, and wonderful food prepared by a bunch of marvellous ladies for the Orchestra and my special guests. So it was no surprise to me when Ray's musicians wanted to know when they could come back again.

Late that night I came to the conclusion that I was more ill than I had at first realised. Obviously being in the same house as priests like the rector and poor Sean Noone hadn't helped. I felt a deep anger towards Father Maher. How could he, knowing Sean's drink problem, leave him in a parish where he was a scandal to the people. His condition demanded urgent treatment. I too was in urgent need of help, I realised. But my sickness was one of the soul, and therefore probably more difficult to cure. So far I hadn't found either the person to treat me or a palliative to effect a cure.

'Oh Joan,' I groaned quietly, as tears began to trickle down my cheeks.

It was not long afterwards, when Michael Martin and Harry Treacy and I were having afternoon tea, that the door to the dining room burst open and a dishevelled and bleary-eyed Sean Noone stood in the doorway peering at us through half-opened eyes. 'Am I late for breakfast?' he wanted to know, as he swayed unsteadily on his feet. There was an embarrassed silence round the table. I told the poor man the time. He looked at me in total surprise. Then a sly look came over his face and without any comment he closed the door and returned to his room, not to appear again until three days later.

By the time that June arrived that year of 1966, I had decided that I was not going to return to Greenford. In fact, I had decided to leave the priesthood. It was not a decision that I took lightly. I had gone to Farm Street and spoken to a Jesuit. I tried the Benedictines at Eating Abbey to see if either of them could offer me some advice.

But I got the impression that neither man wanted to get involved in helping me to make a decision. I was on my own, I realised, and it was awfully lonely.

Things had come to a head a few months earlier on the occasion of a concert I had staged at the brand new entertainment centre that the Borough of Ealing had built in Greenford, and which my concert was to be the Grand Opening. The Mayor of Ealing and many of her councillors attended. Father Martin had invited the Provincial to attend. I can't recall if he said anything to me when we met briefly in the foyer.

As usual I assembled an attractive line-up of singers and musicians, and heading the bill Thora Hird and Freddie Frinton, at the time currently popular in a T.V. comedy series. This time, I did include Margaret Savage and had her close the first half of the show. She walked off the stage to loud applause that continued while she stood alongside me in the wing. 'Shall I go on again?'

'No, Margaret, leave them looking for more,' I told her. Then I kissed her. 'Thanks,' I said.

Next morning I counted the previous night's takings. £480 pounds was a nice tidy sum to hand over to the rector. Michael Martin called out, 'Come in,' when I knocked on his door. He was seated at his desk, enveloped in a haze of tobacco smoke.

'Here's the money from the concert, Father,' I told him placing the small canvas bag in front of him.

He remained silent and never even acknowledged my presence.

I stood there for some seconds waiting for the man to say something about the show; about anything. But I might as well have been invisible. Feeling foolish and humiliated, I left the room. That evening I bought the Evening Standard to look for somewhere to stay when I returned from my holiday.

During my remaining days in the parish I shed many bitter tears. My worse moment was when I had to decide what I was going to take with me and what was to be left behind. There were so many items that had been part of my life for sixteen years; and now I had to part with most of them. The football boots and track suit caused me great distress as I held them in my hands and recalled the many happy moments with Marian Rovers. But I knew that I would have no need of them in my future life – whatever that was going to be.

My sermon notes I decided to take with me as well as the beautiful statue of the Virgin Mary given to me as a present by a Saints Peter and Paul parishioner.

When all the packing was done, I sat in the armchair for a few moments and tried to imagine what life for me outside of the priesthood was going to be like. During my sixteen years as a student and priest my every need had been catered for: well, almost every need: now, all that was about to change. I would have to fend for myself in a life for which I had no training.

"The world will train you", Aunt Nellie had often told me. I'm sure it will, I'm sure it will, I thought, with some degree of apprehension.

Two days before my departure, I moved my worldly goods from the Presbytery to the flat of a woman I had met while she was a patient in the Royal Free. A widow, she was still seriously ill from cancer and really ought to have been dead months before; but sheer will-power kept her struggling on day after day through unspeakable pain, for the sake of her thirteen year old daughter. No wonder the hospital consultant called her his *"miracle woman"*. Before I left the flat, I asked Mrs Fennell if she would allow me to stay with her for a week when I returned to London, until I found a place of my own. She was visibly upset when I explained that I was leaving the priesthood, but agreed to my request, saying that I could use the sofa that doubled up as a bed, if that were all right by me.

Having said the first mass on Monday morning and had breakfast I went up to my room for the last time. Making certain that I wasn't leaving anything behind of any value, I picked up my suitcase and walked out the door and downstairs and into the church. As I passed the small room to one side of the sanctuary that served as a storage place for cleaning materials and the collection of flower vases, I smiled at two women who were working there.

'Have a nice holiday, Father,' one said.

'Come back to us,' her companion added.

I smiled and kept on walking through the cool, dark building into which not even the strong July sun could infuse any light or warmth, and emerged into the brilliance of that morning. As the taxi taking me to Heathrow passed the Presbytery, I looked to the opposite side of the road.

With just one week left of the holiday – the most miserable one I had ever spent at home – Madeleine Conboy complained at how painful her arthritis in the shoulders was. I immediately offered to massage her and suggested that she go upstairs while I searched downstairs for some oil or cream. When I entered her bedroom, having been unsuccessful in my search, she was sitting at the dressing table, her dress lowered down around her waist. 'Don't come in, I'm half undressed,' she called out. I stopped just inside the bedroom door puzzled by this. But thinking this was really only a half-hearted female ploy, nothing more than a token gesture of protest to remove from her mind any self-reproach for what she might do with a priest on her marriage bed, I ignored her plea and walked the length of the room until I stood behind Madeleine, looking at both our reflections in the mirror and conscious of the statue of the Virgin staring at us from two feet away.

Later downstairs as the two of us stood no more than a few inches apart, I was startled when Madeleine suddenly cried out: 'Why does he have to come into me in the daylight; why can't he do it in the darkness?'

That night I slept for the last time in Joan's room and during sleep had a 'wet dream.' The following afternoon, I watched Madeleine angrily wash the tell-tale stain on the sheet.

The next day I found Madeleine in bed as usual and, and as was my custom, I sat down alongside her. To my surprise she suddenly threw off the bedclothes and started to rise from the bed to look out of the window behind the bed, saying excitedly: 'Did you bring the car with you; where have you parked it?' I stared at her semi-nakedness in disbelief. She knew I had the car with me and where it was parked. Was she trying to seduce me by displaying more of her body than I had ever seen before; and in her bedroom? I can think of no other reason.

No more intimacy took place during the last remaining days of my life as a priest. However, a disturbing incident with George Conboy did take place when I called in to Lipton's to say goodbye. He was pleasant enough to begin with as we stood at the bacon counter talking about the fishing, the weather and Joan's arrival the following day, suddenly his whole demeanour changed and his face took on an angry look. 'The tinkers give a good beating to a man who comes between a husband and wife,' he said sternly and with a look that left me under no illusion as to whom he was referring.

I mumbled some words of farewell and hurriedly left the shop.

Leaving Enniscrone had always been a wrench. But this year was going to be the hardest departure of all my years of coming and going. The secret abandonment of my priesthood and the incident with George Conboy both added to my burden. And as I closed the suitcase and looked out from the bedroom window at the view of the bay and dunes – a scene still ingrained in my memory – a sob of despair fought to explode from deep within my body. I could feel tears welling up in my eyes as I picked up the suitcase and made my way down the narrow stairs to say a hurried goodbye to my father and his wife.

Instead of taking my usual route through Ballina, stopping for a few moments with Madeleine, I decided to cut across the Ox Mountains and join the Dublin Road at Charlestown. At the top of Attychree Hill – 'Place of my Heart' – up and down which I had travelled so often when saving the turf, I stopped the car and got out. I stood for a while savouring the wonderful view of Enniscrone and the bay lying in the sunlight far below, while a fresh North West breeze blew in my face. The words of H. W. Longfellow came to mind as I quote:

> *"Often I think of the beautiful town*
> *That is seated by the sea*
> *Often in thought go up and down*
> *The pleasant streets of that dear old town*
> *And my youth comes back to me".*
> **Henry Wadsworth Longfellow**

No longer able to control my anguish, I burst in to tears. *"O God, why is this happening to me"*, I moaned, and laid my head against the car roof. How long I would have stayed there I do not know. But the sound of an approaching vehicle forced me to get into the car and resume my journey to London and to ... ? Only God knew that, I thought, as I struggled to see the road ahead.

Shepherd In The Mist

For two weeks after returning to London, I stayed with Mrs Fennell and her daughter, Maureen, while I looked for a job and found myself a flat. With barely one hundred twenty pounds to my name, the search to find employment was a priority. However, after scanning the situations vacant pages of that week's Sunday Times, I realised that despite ten years in seminaries and six years as a priest, I had not acquired even the most basic of commercial skills and was therefore totally unprepared for the job market. With a sigh, I put aside the newspaper and decided the best course of action for me was to call on Peter Norris at his Keystone Employment Agency.

When I emerged into Rosebery Avenue the next day, I had obtained an interview for a clerical position with Keymarkets, a supermarket chain whose office was situated close to London Bridge. I knew nothing about Keymarkets. The first time I had heard of them was when Peter Norris gave me the name and address of their office.

After a few minutes questioning by the general manager, he took me out into the main office to meet a Mr.Smith, who would be my immediate boss. I liked the look of the man and his kindly smile. It took him about twenty minutes to explain what was required of me in his section of the office. I felt I could do the job, despite the frightening prospect of being in such close proximity to so many women on a daily basis.

Just as Mr.Smith and I turned to walk away, I heard an unmistakable Irish accent say: 'I was going to leave, but I think I'll stay now.' I glanced in the direction of the voice and saw a young Irish-looking woman in her mid-twenties who began to blush furiously when our eyes met.

Within a week of commencing work, I found myself a rear flat on the second floor of a large gloomy-looking house in Carleton Road, Tuffnell Park. The accommodation was very basic comprising of a kitchen and a bed-sitting room, the furnishings of which were an armchair, a table, two chairs and a divan. The floor was covered with a thin carpet which appeared to have been there since the house was first occupied. A heavy green, velvet curtain hid a double door leading into the room to the front of the house which was occupied by another tenant. During the time I lived there, I often heard my neighbour cough and move about, but never once did we meet. In the kitchen, there were the usual domestic items. The refrigerator, however, had seen better days. The two redeeming features of my new home were: it was about ten minutes walk from the Northern Line and my windows looked out onto the back garden with a majestic tree standing at the far end.

Two weeks into the job I was depressed and appalled at the sheer drudgery and boredom the work entailed. Could this be the reason, I wondered, why so many of my fellow travellers on the tube each morning looked tired and unhappy. The lines of a poem by Carol Houselander came to mind.

"Poor little birds in a cage;
Sitting behind the bars!
It isn't life:
It's the living wage
And the night without the stars".

As the days dragged on into November, my depression worsened by the hour, especially in the evenings when I returned to my lonely, companionless lodgings where, after cooking a light meal – usually of tinned or frozen food – I would sit in front of the gas fire reading the Daily Telegraph and feeling sorry for myself. Occasionally to break the monotony of my life, I would take a bus down to the bottom of the Caledonian Road and walk to Amwell Street, either by way of Pentonville Road or Kings Cross Road. Upon arriving there, I usually stood at the corner of Hardwick Street, opposite the swimming pool, and stare down at the Presbytery, a mere fifty yards away. Many a time, on these excursions, tears flowed freely. How long my lonely vigil lasted would depend on whether any parishioner or one of the priests emerged from the church or presbytery. When that happened, I would turn and slink away up Amwell Street like a thief in the night.

Shortly before Christmas I decided to visit Peter and Bernie Norris at their flat two floors above Peter's Employment Agency:

'Father, how nice to see you, Bernie exclaimed when she opened the door. Then she became flustered when she realised how she had addressed me. 'Oh, I'm sorry,' she said, blushing with embarrassment. She looks lovelier than ever, I thought, as I took her hand and gave it a reassuring squeeze.

Divested of my overcoat and settled in a deep armchair, I was already beginning to feel my depression lifting a little. Behind me the heavy, red velvet curtains helped to shut out the mid-evening's traffic heading towards the Angel

'Now, what would you like to drink...,' Bernie hesitated. 'Martin,' I interjected.

She smiled down at me. 'Martin.'

'I'd love a Scotch and soda, please.'

Pouring our drinks, Bernie called out. 'Peter is at his Boy Scouts meeting.'

She must have noticed the puzzled look on my face when she handed me the Waterford tumbler. 'It's really his Masonic meeting that he's gone to; I had to invent that story as a cover-up when my parents came over from Dublin,' she explained, as she lowered herself into the armchair opposite me, arranging her shapely legs under her before pulling down her skirt to cover her knees.

'Sláinte,' we both said simultaneously, raising our glasses to each other.

The two hours that I spent there that night were the happiest of my new life as a layman. As we sat and talked and laughed and Bernie replenished our glasses, she told me that my former colleagues at St. Peter and Pauls had not spoken about my leaving the priesthood. To all intents and purposes I was still ministering in Greenford. Some people in the Amwell Street parish still talked fondly of me, Bernie told me. 'Even my hairdresser, who isn't even a Catholic, still asks about you.'

This puzzled me as I didn't know who she was talking about. Bernie cleared up the mystery. 'She often met you on Rosebery Avenue and you would smile at her. She thinks you are lovely.'

Relaxed by the whisky and the warmth of the room, not to mention my delightful hostess, I began to dread the moment of leaving to return to my solitary, bare existence in Tuffnel Park

As Bernie helped me on with my coat at around eleven o'clock, she made me promise to call again, soon. At the door, encouraged by her smiling eyes and emboldened by the whisky, I leaned forward and kissed her on the cheek. 'Thank you for a lovely evening, Bernie,' I said.

The alarm clock woke me at the usual weekday time of 7.30. I switched it off and went back to sleep. It was the sound of voices that eventually woke me. I glanced at the clock: quarter to ten. The woman's voice I recognised as belonging to the married woman from the top flat. But the man's voice was definitely not that of her husband. As the couple began to climb the stairs, the woman laughed. Seconds later, the door to the flat above closed. Footsteps and more laughter sounded faintly through the ceiling. Then there was silence.

I lay there picturing exactly what was taking place a few feet above my head. The silence was broken by footsteps and more laughter then the sound of bedsprings. There was more talk and what sounded like a nervous laugh from the woman, before the bedsprings began to creak rhythmically.

I saw the woman's male companion a few days later as they left the house and got into an expensive looking car. The man was years older-looking than my neighbour; small and plump and almost bald, he looked to be of Mediterranean extraction, a Cypriot perhaps, who worked in the 'rag trade.'

Although I had ceased to be active in the priesthood, I had not given up on religion. Each Sunday saw me present at mass in either the French church off Leicester Square or the church in Warwick Street; sometimes, I even travelled as far as Westminster Cathedral. I still prayed a great deal. Did I miss the priesthood? The honest answer at that time was no. I did miss the people and serving them in some capacity, but not as a celibate. I could never envisage myself living again in an all-male environment where most of the men were ill with what Fr. Bernard Haring has given the name, *"Ecclesiagenic pathology"*.

As Christmas approached, my emotional state worsened so that by Christmas Eve it took a mighty effort of will to persuade me to go to work. A wrong word from anyone, and I would have burst into uncontrollable weeping. Christmas Eve at Keymarkets had ended with the traditional office party. I had read newspaper articles about the 'goings on' at these annual events, but if anything out of the ordinary was taking place, I certainly was not aware of it. By four o'clock, as people began leaving for home, I had not been kissed by any woman or I kissed any woman under the many sprigs of mistletoe decorating the office. The nearest I had come to any involvement with a woman that afternoon was when Mr. Smith said that I was the only man that he would trust to take home Rose, the most attractive young woman in the office.

When I let myself into the house, there was an envelope addressed to me lying on the hall table. It had been delivered by hand. I waited until I arrived upstairs before opening it. The small sheet of paper contained an invitation from Mrs Fennell to spend Christmas Day with herself and her daughter.

Late that Christmas Eve night, I sat alone in front of the gas fire with a tumbler of whisky in my hand and thought of all those Christmases spent with Joan and her mother, recalling in particular that night I had met Joan at the railway station, but before allowing her to enter the house, I had rushed inside and switched on my portable record player, before placing my arm round her shoulder and ushering her indoors to be greeted by orchestra and choir performing Adeste Fideles.

'Mam, Joan,' I cried out. Startled by the sound of my own voice, I glanced anxiously at the curtained doorway and hoped that the man on the other side was out.

Despite the warmth from the fire and the temporary solace the whisky provided, a deep melancholy took hold of me and deepened even as I consumed the second tumbler of whisky. I wondered if any of my parishioners would remember Father Gordon that night as they knelt at Midnight Mass in Amwell Street or in Greenford. Surely some of them would recall me in their prayers. I would have hoped that Diane Cowan certainly would remember me. Joan and her mother would not be at mass until 9 o'clock the following morning. I could guarantee a prayer from them. 'Happy Christmas everybody,' I whispered, as the first tear trickled down my cheek.

Christmas morning I attended the 11am mass in Westminster Cathedral, then taking a 38 bus to the Fennell home, alighting at the Angel and cutting through Chapel Market to Copenhagen Street. With me I had a large box of chocolates as a present for mother and daughter.

As we sat down at the table for dinner I noticed that it had been set for four people. But as the three of us rose from the table at the end of a delightful meal, the extra setting remained unused. After her daughter had gone to her bedroom to listen to some music, Esther Fennell and I sat talking in the semi-darkness of the sitting-room. It was then I learned how she had become a widow.

Her husband, Peter, a Dubliner like herself, worked as a railway guard out of Euston Station. One evening he left the flat to take a train to the North of England, saying that he would return the following day. As usual he kissed his wife and daughter goodbye. Before departing, his wife had told him that she and her friend, Mary, would be going that evening to a social at University College Hospital, where they both worked in the canteen. She promised him that she would take a taxi home.

The party had been most enjoyable and she had hardly left the dance floor all evening. But when it was time for her and the friend to go home, instead of them sharing a taxi, Esther accepted a lift from a man she had danced with more than once.

Parked outside the block of flats, she and the man sat talking. Just as he put an arm around her shoulder, Peter Fennell appeared at the passenger door, threw it open, pulled his wife from the vehicle and almost dragged her towards the flats.

In the lift on the way up to the third floor he punched her couple of times on the face and body. Once indoors, he hit her repeatedly and finally kicked her in the ribs as she lay cowering in a corner of the hallway, all the time accusing her of being unfaithful and yelling that he had been suspicious of her conduct for a long time. 'I never forgave him for what he did to me. We never lived together again as man and wife,' the woman said quietly, as she looked at me with eyes brimful with tears. 'He will be dead three years next month.'

How did he die, I was about to ask, when the young girl came into the room to watch a Christmas Special on television.

At the urging of mother and daughter I stayed overnight, sleeping on the comfortable pull-out bed in the living-room. I was glad to accept the hospitality as there were no buses running.

Before returning to Tuffnel Park the following afternoon, I found an opportunity to ask Mrs. Fennell the question I was about to articulate the previous night: how did her husband die.

One Sunday about three weeks after the horrific attack on her, Mrs. Fennell sent her daughter into the bedroom to tell her dad that his dinner was ready. The girl came running back to the kitchen to say that she couldn't waken up her daddy. Her mother rushed immediately from the kitchen. One glance at the empty aspirin bottle made her flee from the bedroom out onto the landing screaming for someone to help her. Her husband died the next day in the Royal Free Hospital, without regaining consciousness.

The most harrowing part of the tragedy was that as the ambulance men manoeuvred the stretcher carrying her father's inert body from the flat, his daughter called out: *"My daddy will be all right, he's taken aspirin"*. Ever since, the young girl had set a place for her dad at their table.

When I left the Fennell's, I was in no frame of mind to face the loneliness and drabness of my own flat during those festive days, so I decided to pay another visit to Bernie Norris in the hope, if the truth were to be told, that she would once again be alone.

'Peter at his boy scouts again?' I said with a smile when I found my prayer had been answered.

'No,' she said grimly. 'He's at his mother's and won't be home until tomorrow.'

As on my previous visit, glasses in hand, we sat and chatted about her husband's business, the latest news from the parish and about her parents in Dublin. There was still no sign of her becoming pregnant, I noticed, despite many consultations with specialists.

When she rose up from her armchair to replenish our glasses for the third time, Bernie turned off the more direct lighting in the room before sitting down close to me on the sofa. How, I wondered, could a husband leave such a gorgeous creature like her at any time, let alone at Christmas?

As I went to kiss her goodnight on the cheek, as on the previous occasion, Bernie offered me her lips instead. I found them deliciously moist and welcoming.

Upon returning to work after the Christmas break, I knew that I just had to get out of the job, in fact get out of London as well. An avenue of escape appeared when the accountants arrived for the annual audit and found a paper deficit of almost a million pounds in my section. My incompetence would be the excuse I needed to hand in my notice, which I duly did at the end of that week.

Out of a job and with no idea what I was going to do next, I now understood why so many unhappy priests are reluctant, frightened even, to leave the security of the priesthood; the prospect of having to fend for themselves for the first time in their lives is too daunting a prospect. In desperation I telephoned Eamonn Andrews at his home, 'Parknasilla' in Chiswick. During our brief conversation he told me that the members of the Stage Guild had been wondering what had become of me. I then asked him if he would consent to meet me. To this he readily agreed, and we arranged to meet outside Imhofs in New Oxford Street the following afternoon, and then proceed to the Norris's flat. I knew that there would be no problem in obtaining the use of their home as a venue for the meeting.

Seated in the deep armchairs, a full bottle of Dimple Whisky and thick, cut-glass tumblers on a small table near us, Eamonn and I chatted amiably on a variety of subjects until I felt it was time to come to the reason for his being there. Could he help me find a job in Ireland? But first I told him that I would not make a final decision regarding the priesthood until I had spent a few days in an Irish Monastery.

'Whatever decision you come to let me know, Father, and I'll help you in any way I can. Grainne sends you her best wishes,' he added.

With my mind made up to leave London, I wrote the following day to Dr.Frances Fox, as she now was, telling her that I would be arriving in Galway in three days time and asking if I could stay with her and her husband. I was sorry to say goodbye to the Fennells. Mother and daughter had provided me with warm friendship and a refuge when I needed them most. I promised to keep in touch as I headed for Euston Station and the train to Holyhead.

Frances and Eddie Fox were most supportive and kind during my brief stay with them in Galway. They asked no questions, except on one occasion when Frances surprised me by asking: 'Is it Joan?' I told her that I did not believe my love for Joan had anything to do with my current position viz-a-viz the priesthood. I loved her, always had done and probably always would, but I was not 'in' love with her. The young doctor looked into my eyes and smiled. Did I really believe what I had just said? Somehow, I don't think that I did.

While I was staying with Frances and Eddie, she arranged for me to see a psychiatrist, who gave me a dosage of pills to take;

their effect on me was to make me want to sleep at odd times of the day.

I kept the promise made back in London to Eamonn Andrews and stayed at the Cistercian Abbey of St. Joseph, Roscrea, County Tipperary. Frances drove me there and promised to collect me two days later. Originally the Abbey was the estate of 250 acres belonging to Richard Heaton, a clergyman of the Established Church, who had come to Ireland with the army of King Charles the First. Heaton was Ireland's first botanist and did much to identify and catalogue the flora of the country. The original house, now the monastery guesthouse, was built by Heaton's son near the end of the 17th century. Eventually the estate was acquired by a Count Arthur Moore of Moorsfort, and given by him to the Cistercian Monastery of Mount Mellery in County Waterford: it was from there that Mount St. Joseph's was founded. The Tipperary Monastery is unique among the Foundations of the Cistercian Order, in that it is the only one to which a boy's school is attached.

There were three other residents of the guesthouse, I discovered, when we gathered for supper that February evening. One of them looked like another priest with a problem. It wasn't alcohol; of that I was certain. If it were he would be resident in the already mentioned Mount Mellery, which had acquired a certain reputation for rehabilitating unfortunate priests who had succumbed to the 'drink.'

The four of us said little during the meal. We sat down as strangers, and when we rose some twenty minutes later we were still strangers. As Charlotte Bronte put it in one of her earliest poems:

"The human heart has hidden treasures
In secret kept, in silence sealed".

During the night the sound of a large bell tolling woke me up briefly. Even in my drowsy state I knew that somewhere in that monastery the monks were silently making their way to begin their long arduous day by chanting the first hours of the Divine Office: and it was still only 2a.m. During the time I spent with the Cistercians, I sat for many an hour in the Abbey Church praying about my future. Did I return to the priesthood or not? It was as simple as that. On the morning of my departure, I decided that there was no going back, no matter how difficult the road ahead might be. I liked the company of the opposite sex, and having tasted the moist warmth of two women's lips I felt no urge to return to the barren, celibate life that had been mine for 16 years.

"Marriage has many pains, but celibacy has no pleasures", wrote Samuel Johnson. That about summed up my attitude.

> *Two roads converged in a yellow wood*
> *And sorry I could not travel both*
> *And be one traveller, long I stood*
> *And looked down one as far as I could*
> *To where it bent in the undergrowth*
> *Then took the other.*
> *I took the one less travelled by,*
> *And that has made all the difference.*
>
> **The Road Not Taken by Robert Frost.**

At the appointed time for Frances to collect me, I dipped a finger into the holy water font inside the front door of the guesthouse, blessed myself and went out into the grey February day, closing the heavy wooden door behind me. I can't recall if I put any money in the box left conveniently for departing guests to make a donation towards their stay. At the bottom of the steps Frances stood beside her car smiling up at me.

The following day I wrote to Eamonn Andrews informing him of my decision and included the telephone number of my hosts in Galway. On the Monday morning following, I received a telephone call from Fred O'Donovan, the Managing Director of Eamonn's entertainment business in Ireland. After introducing himself he said that Eamonn had just been on the telephone from London and then went on ask me if I were free to come up to Dublin on the Wednesday afternoon for an interview at 3p.m. in the Gaiety Theatre.

The meeting between me and the smiling but brusque mannered Fred O'Donovan was brief. I could commence work for Eamonn Andrews Productions whenever I was ready to do so. The salary would be £18 a week.

'We don't accept clock watchers,' he warned me.

The meeting over, I descended the magnificent staircase to the theatre foyer just as a wave of laughter filtered through from the matinee audience enjoying the pantomime in which, a large poster told me, Ireland's much-loved comedienne Maureen Potter was the star attraction.

Within two days I had found digs in the Rialto district of the city by virtue of telephoning friends in London who put me in touch with an elderly relative, whose lodger I was to become the following Saturday. Biddy and Barney Cahill welcomed me warmly and during my stay with them never asked me any questions of a personal nature. Instead, they regaled me with interesting and sometimes humorous stories about their own lives.

On the eve of my starting work in Eamonn's company, I went for a long walk through the Phoenix Park, passing close to the spot where Joan and I had lain in the grass two years previously. I gave a sigh and turned homeward to prepare for my new career, recalling the words of a Mayor of Finsbury that I would end up in show business.

The building where Eamonn Andrews's Studios was the sole tenant stood at the far end of Henry Street and opposite one of the city's major stores. An unimpressive door admitted me to a narrow flight of stairs when I arrived that first Monday morning, shortly before 9 o'clock. I gave my name to the three young women who sat talking in the cramped office on the first floor. The eldest of them rose from her chair. 'I'm Nuala, Mr. O'Donovan's secretary.' He told me to look after you. If you follow me, I'll show you to your office.'

On reaching the top floor, my guide ushered me into a small, dusty room where the only furniture was a desk and a chair. Some files lay scattered on the floor and on the shelves that stood along one wall. A threadbare carpet was but a token gesture for a floor covering, and the single window looking out on to Henry Street was without curtains and needed cleaning. The room was cold and had a musty smell.

Before leaving, Nuala told me to expect Ursula Doyle to look in on me when she arrived later on in the morning. 'She works with Mr. O'Donovan on the production side of the business,' the secretary informed me.

Approaching eleven o'clock there was a light knock on my door, and before I could say anything it opened to reveal a small, blonde-haired woman, smiling as she advanced across the room. I stood up as she extended a hand across the desk.

'I'm Ursula Doyle. You're very welcome,' she said as we shook hands. Then she glanced at her watch.

'Look, I have an idea, why don't we get acquainted over a cup of coffee across the road.'

My face must have registered some sign of the surprise I felt at her suggestion.

Ursula Laughed. 'I expect Fred told you that no tea-breaks were allowed?'

I nodded affirmatively.

That rule doesn't apply to me,' she said, almost defiantly. When she thought I still hesitated about accompanying her, she gave my shoulder a reassuring pat. 'Trust me,' she advised. The morning excursion to Roche's Store became a regular event for the two of us whenever Ursula was in the office.

From my colleagues I learned that my companion was the widow of the man who had long been regarded as Ireland's most popular comedian, Jimmy O'Dea.

At the end of that first week as an employee of Eamonn Andrews's Studios I was just as bored as I had been at Keymarkets. There was just nothing for me to do all day and I felt very guilty when handed my wage packet on Friday. It was obvious to me that Eamonn had created a job where none existed. However, as the weeks passed, I became more and more involved in the work of the Studios; even acting as office manager for two weeks, when the elderly Tom Walsh fell ill. During that period, I offered tea and biscuits to any of the performers who called at the office to discuss their work with the Studios; something that had never been done before.

One actor, Ray McAnally, when he heard me speaking, told me 'With that voice, you ought to be down in Galway with John Huston.'

Most of my work involved meeting the artists who were being booked to appear in the many special functions that the Studios produced and which took place mainly in Dublin hotels and occasionally down the country as well. One I recall was for a visiting Trade Delegation from the Soviet Union at which a group called 'WE FOUR' appeared. The female singer in the group is now the well-known operatic star with Welsh National Opera, Suzanne Murphy.

The major event produced by the studios was 'Jury's Irish Cabaret' in the hotel of the same name. The show, as the name would suggest, had a cast of traditional musicians, dancers, harpists, a very funny pint-sized comedian and the ubiquitous Irish tenor, without whom no Irish show would be complete.

A novel feature of the night's entertainment occurred at the interval when a line-up of the country's most beautiful models displayed a wide range of Irish clothes for the mainly American audience. Fred O'Donovan handed me the task of supervising this nightly entertainment for the whole of the summer. The job was straightforward: ensure that everything went smoothly, to speak with any important overseas visitors, especially if they were from Broadway or Hollywood, and most importantly, ensure that the cast did not stray from the rehearsed script. To compensate for my working evenings, I left the office at lunchtime.

On the opening night of the 1967 season, I stood backstage with a typed running-order on the clipboard I held in my hands. Out front a packed audience appeared to be enjoying the show. Patrick O'Hagan, the tenor, was a great favourite with his combination of Irish melodies and delightful banter as he sauntered amongst the tables. The comedian raised howls of laughter from his listeners. But I had heard that if the little man felt his audience's response to his jokes was not good enough, he would berate them for their lack of appreciation.

During the interval, the gorgeous models began the fashion show. I was surprised to observe that they had no changing facility; instead they stood in panties and bra while they changed swiftly from one outfit to another. To my amusement I saw two young men from the traditional musicians staring goggle-eyed at the alluring display of female nudity standing just a few feet from them. I was more interested in looking at the reaction of the men than taking any delight in the shapely young women. But I did catch the eye of one very lovely blond-haired model, who flashed me a most heart-stopping smile just before she pulled a dress over her head.

For the second-half of the show I took a seat on the narrow balcony that ran down the side of the room. I was soon joined by the model whose smile had so dazzled me backstage. Close up and even under the subdued lighting, I recognised her as Ann Marie Berkley, one of Ireland's top models, whose face I had seen many times in the pages of the Sunday papers. I asked her in a whisper if she would care for something to drink. She declined saying that she would soon be going home to have her hot milk and biscuits. Before departing, she asked if I would be in the same spot the next night. I assured her that I would. This seemed to please Ann Marie.

The next night and from then on, Ann Marie and I sat side-by side and talked between acts about a variety of subjects, I learned that she was an accomplished violinist and had won medals at Dublin's famous music and singing competition held each spring at the Royal Dublin Society in Ballsbridge. She wouldn't mind, she informed me, trying to break into show business.

I liked the girl, finding her refreshingly natural as well as being stunningly beautiful. But I was under no allusion as to the outcome of our current relationship. Ann Marie had the pick of Dublin, indeed of the entire country, where male companions were concerned. Furthermore, most models, I knew from reading about their weddings, usually married men of position and with lots of money.

A few weeks into the cabaret season, the manager of the Gaiety Theatre, Joe Kerins, telephoned to tell me that he had arranged for me to meet a person connected with Dublin Tourism. The problem was that he had fixed the time of the meeting for 3p.m. I explained to him that I finished work at 1p.m, to enable me to get home and then return for the evening session in Jury's Hotel. I asked him politely if he would please reschedule the meeting for another day and at a suitable time. When I entered the office Studios the following morning, Fred O'Donovan called me into his office and promptly sacked me. 'But you can stay on until you find something else,' he said.

Shocked and angry, I climbed the stairs to my garret and promptly gathered my few personal affects. I had decided to leave immediately. To continue working there after being so casually and unfairly sacked was unthinkable. I slipped out of the office without saying goodbye to any of the staff.

That afternoon, I wrote to Eamonn Andrews in London giving the explanation for my dismissal and thanking him for his help.

At that night's cabaret my place was taken by Tom Walsh, the general manager who, when asked by John McNally, the singer, where Martin was, replied that 'I was no longer with the organisation as I couldn't do the job.' 'Well, he was the only one who treated us as human beings,' the singer answered curtly. It was Patrick O'Hagan, the tenor, who told me of this exchange when we met the following day. He also informed me that Fred O'Donovan was trying to trace where I lived; he had even asked Patrick. But the singer refused to divulge my address unless I gave him permission to do so.

As I packed my suitcase that night for the return to London, having decided that there was no future for me in Dublin, I thought of what Patrick O'Hagan's wife had said to me when I spent a delightful Sunday afternoon with the family in their Howth home. She cursed Fred O'Donovan and hoped that he would burn in hell. I never found out the reason for the woman's deeply felt hatred for her husband's employer.

I left Ireland deeply disillusioned and fearful for my future. Added to that was the regret I felt at not having used the weeks in Dublin to see Joan from time to time. Although we worked at opposite ends of the same street, only once did our paths cross when I met her and her flatmate, Maureen Hannifan, as we all returned to work after the lunchtime break. It was Maureen who invited me to come and have supper with them some evening. I never took up the invitation. If Joan had done the inviting, then more than likely I would have accepted.

Once again I availed of the Fennell's hospitality on my return to London and began the search for a job. This time, however, there was no Peter Norris to turn to for help, as I expected him to be very annoyed with the way I walked out on one of his clients. To be honest, I had no idea what kind of job to look for; added to that was my precarious financial situation. Therefore, to alleviate the situation while I looked for work, I signed on at the local unemployment exchange on Barnsbury Road.

Over the next couple of weeks in glorious sunny weather, I did a variety of part-time jobs such as cleaning offices in the evenings, pushing leaflets through letterboxes and even spending a week as a barman in a pub near the Angel, until I got the sack. All the while

I kept on searching the newspapers in the hope of finding suitable employment. But what was suitable employment for an ex-priest?

One afternoon as I was returning to Islington on the tube - from hours delivering promotional leaflets for a 24 hour repair service for household emergencies to homes in the Clapham Common area, I saw an advert for an 'art buyer' in the Evening Standard. I liked the sound of it, but had not the faintest idea what the job involved. By the time I reached King's Cross, I had decided to telephone my printer friend Pat Donnellan and ask him. When Pat realised who the caller was he sounded surprised and happy at the same time. Eamonn Andrews, he informed me, had called him and asked Pat to help me if I got in touch with him. I asked the printer about the job of 'art buyer.' Could I do it I wanted to know. His answer was short and uncompromising, 'No you can't.' Then he wanted to know if I really needed a job. I assured him I did. 'Why don't you come down and see us at 5 o'clock tomorrow evening. You know where we are.'

The first time I had visited Donbro Printers was when I had some photographs taken for the vocations exhibition, 'Challenge '65.' So as I climbed the stairs to the printers' first floor office on that Friday evening, I wondered if any of the staff would remember me.

When Pat Donnellan brought me into his office be introduced me to a swarthy-looking man with a beard. 'This is Alf Freedman he owns the company now. I'm the Sales Director,' he said. After a few minutes of polite conversation Pat suggested that we retire to the 'boardroom' which I discovered, was the pub on the corner of Paul Street and Scrutton Street. Alf Freedman would join us later after he made a couple of telephone calls.

Being a Friday, the pub was packed. 'Nearly everyone in here is connected in some way with printing,' Pat informed me before pushing his way through the crowd to get our drinks. While we waited the arrival of Alf Freedman, Pat explained how he had come to lose his company. Donbro had a silk screen subsidiary based in Surbiton that had run into financial difficulty, and as a result had put the parent company into liquidation. Another contributory factor was the conduct of two of his managers at Donbro who were doing private printing work at night, using the company's machines and materials. Once he had discovered what was going on, he sacked both men on the spot. 'Where are they now? 'They set up their own company a few yards down the road from here,' he replied.

Just then, Alf Freedman joined us. A short time after Pat returned with a drink for his managing director, my friend wanted to know if I were looking for job. I told him I was.

'How do you feel about selling print?' The question took me by surprise.

'To be honest, I never thought about it. As you know I have never done it before.'

'Well, if you can't sell print, nobody else can,' Pat said. With a vote of confidence like that I had no hesitation in accepting the job.

The compositor was already at work when I arrived on the first floor office the following Monday morning. The production manager arrived soon after. The introductions over, he advised me to sit at one of three desks while he discussed work schedules with the different departmental managers. From the floor above came the faint hum of the printing presses. When eventually the last manager had gone and he had sorted out his post, the production manager waved me over and motioned for me to sit alongside him. 'Your first job, I've been told, is to be my assistant while you learn the basics of the printing trade.' I nodded my assent though I thought I was going to be a sales representative. 'Then in January, if it all works out, you are going into sales,' he added.

For almost the whole of the next hour, interrupted only by a few telephone calls from clients, the manager explained how the firm's docket system worked as a means of costing and keeping track of the work flowing through the factory at any given time. His explanations were clear and I felt confident that I could handle this aspect of my new position. Furthermore, the work seemed interesting.

When I returned to my desk, I found the firm's three sales representatives had arrived at their desks. Last to breeze in was Pat Donnellan, who shook hands with me and invited me into his office. 'Let's have a cup of tea,' he suggested and went out again. While waiting his return I examined a large framed photograph on the wall of Jimmy Greaves scoring a goal against Scotland at Wembley. I was at that game and watched England put nine goals past the hapless Frank Haffey. There was also a painting of the famous Spurs team that included Danny Blanchflower, Dave McKay, John White and Bill Brown.

'That was some team,' said Pat when he saw the object of my interest. 'The day we opened for business the entire Spurs team was here in the office. Danny Blanchflower stood up on the big desk outside there and made a speech. They came because Bill Brown was my partner in the business.'

That would account for the 'bro' in Donbro, I thought. I was impressed. It was while we sipped our teas that Pat finished the full story of how he had come to lose his business.

The financial situation and become so desperate that one Thursday morning he had no money to pay the worker's wages. Sick with worry Pat had taken to his bed rather than face an angry workforce. Vera, his wife, took the decision to telephone Eamonn Andrews and tell him of her husband's problem. I said nothing upon hearing this, but was surprised that Pat had possession of Eamonn's number. After asking a few questions, the T.V. presenter told Vera Donnellan to keep Pat at home and that he would telephone her again around 11 o'clock. A few minutes after the pre-arranged time, Eamonn called to say that the money to meet the wage bill was even then waiting to be collected at a bank near Donbro. I was amazed, Pat and Eamonn hardly knew each other and, as far as I was aware, had met on only a couple of occasions after I introduced them. To finish the story, Pat went on to tell me how the following week the Freedman brothers, Alf and Charles, arrived to inspect the factory on behalf of friends of Eamonn's, who had expressed an interest in buying the company. Whatever report the Freedmans gave, the other party pulled out of the deal. The Freedmans bought it instead and retained Pat as Sales Director.

The new owners already had a large letterpress factory in Golders Green that did a lot of work for the 'rag' trade and brochures for many of the big charity events in London.

By Christmas I had acquired enough knowledge of the print trade for Pat Donnellan to inform me that come January I would begin my new career as a sales Representative. I was also by then on first name terms with most of the company's clients when they came to the office to have a few drinks and then depart with their individual rewards from a grateful Sales Director.

On Christmas morning after attending mass in the French church,

I walked through the almost deserted streets all the way back to Islington, arriving just as Mrs.Fennell was placing a large chicken on the kitchen worktop. The table, as the previous Christmas, was placed in the living-room and had four places set.

As I sat pulling contentedly on a small cigar later that afternoon, a glass of Cointreau in the other hand, I thought back to the barren, lonely Christmas days of my priesthood and realised how unattractive an existence such a life was for those thousands of men, who, like me, had made no deliberate choice of celibacy when choosing to become priests: which explained why so many of them abandon their vocation when the reality of living without a loving relationship with a woman becomes an intolerable burden. Taking a sip of the liqueur, I let my eyes shut and tried to imagine what my new life as a sales representative was going to be like?

Up until early January of 1968, relations between young Maureen Fennell and I had been very good. However, one Sunday at the end of January, while mother and daughter were attending a party for widows and children of deceased railwaymen, I rearranged the position of the standard lamp and one of the chairs to provide myself with better light for reading. I had moved back in with the Fennell's when Mrs.Fennell had to go into the Royal Free hospital for at least three weeks treatment, and she asked me if I would look after Maureen. When mother and daughter arrived home and the girl saw what I had done, she uttered a terrifying shriek and burst into tears. She then raced round the room putting the two items of furniture back in their original positions, all the while sobbing uncontrollably. Satisfied that the room now looked the same as before, she shouted angrily at me: 'Everything must be left the same as when my daddy lived here.' She then fled to her bedroom, slamming the glass-panelled door behind her.

As Pat Donnellan promised, I became Donbro's fourth sales representative in January, 1968. But first I had to take the Northern Line to Golders Green to collect my car, a small, blue-coloured Austin that had belonged to Charles Freedman's wife, Ruth.

To kick-start my career, Pat took me to the offices of the advertising agency, Benton & Bowles at 197 Knightsbridge, where he introduced me to Terry Walker, a print buyer. He was a small, lightly-built man in his early thirties and with a hook-shaped nose and a beard. He told me that his wife, Patsy, was from Tuam in Co. Galway and they had been married there. That's a good start, I thought to myself.

Up until my taking over the account, it had been generating a mere £300 a month for Donbro: a pittance when one considered the huge sums of money the print buyer was spending on an almost daily basis. My task was to increase substantially that figure by calling regularly to the agency. One of the accounts handled by Benton & Bowles was that of the Irish Dairy Board. So it was no surprise that very soon a substantial amount of work from that source was flowing into Donbro.

An important part of my new calling was to socialise each Friday at lunchtime with the print buyer and other members of the Benton & Bowles production department and an assortment of other print representatives and block-makers. The gathering usually took place in a pub situated in a side street directly across from Harrods. I have to confess that I found the two hours spent there was the worst aspect of the job. The conversation was boring and at times embarrassing, as pint after pint was drunk and the topics discussed were limited to D.I.Y, cars and naturally, sex. No crudity was left unsaid if any attractive young woman was unlucky enough to come under the group's scrutiny.

On the 6th February, I received a telegram from aunt Nellie informing me that my father had died the previous morning in Glasgow. Heartbroken, I went into Mrs.Fennell's bedroom and cried for that gentle man who, I regret to say, I never really got close to. The picture of him that comes to mind is of him kneeling down in the kitchen saying his bedtime prayers.

"Father forsaken, forgive thy son feeling a deep sense of having failed that quiet, pious man who had asked so little of life".

Those words of James Joyce sum up my feelings even thirty years later. I decided not to attend the funeral out of feelings of shame at having abandoned the priesthood.

On the last Friday in February, Pat Donnellan called me into his office. 'Close the door,' he told me. He then opened a drawer in his desk and withdrew a brown envelope which he then proceeded to hand to me. 'This is for Terry Walker. He's on two and half percent commission of all the work he gives us,' the Sales Director informed. me. 'Mum's the word now.'

Back at my desk I did a quick reckoning. Terry Walker had earned himself £37 free of tax since I took over the account. I never knew such a practice existed and wondered how widespread it was. Did all those other representatives who gathered in the pub also hand over brown envelopes?

When I made that first payment to the Benton & Bowles print buyer no words were exchanged between us as he slipped it into the briefcase propped up against the side of his desk. Afterwards I decided that it was much too risky to continue doing this in a busy advertising agency, where anyone could walk in just as the envelope was being passed over the desk. From then on, the transaction took place in the pub next to the Caledonia Road police station.

I got my colleague, Jerry Moore, on his own a few weeks later, and asked him about the 'backhanders' given to print buyers.

'I can assure you old boy that everyone's at it. I have a client who has a villa in Spain and a yacht on the Solent. How do you think he got those?' The practice of 'backhanders' in the business was not the only thing out of the ordinary I learned as the months passed. Not only was Jerry Moore having an affair, but so were Pat Donnellan, both Freedman brothers, Alf and Charles and Lionel Silver, their fellow director at the Golders Green factory. Jerry Moore was quite open about the 'other woman' in his life. It was difficult for him not to be when she telephoned almost every day, sometimes twice or three times. The girls in the office told me that the two 'lovers' met regularly at the Ritz for afternoon tea.

The three Freedman directors and Pat Donnellan were more discreet. There was a flat somewhere in the Bloomsbury area that was used as a 'love nest' by them. The Freedman's mistresses were women who worked in the Golders Green office, one of whom was eventually to give birth to a child fathered by her lover.

Pat Donnellan, on the other hand had no regular companion. He did try to start a relationship with a woman who looked after the accounts at Donbro, but it never got past the first lunchtime date. The attractive, married woman gave me all the details one morning when I enquired as to how she had incurred her discoloured face. It happened, she told me, when after lunching with Pat, the two of them had gone to the flat near the British Museum. As she climbed the stairs ahead of him she suddenly realised what was expected of her and balked at the prospect of giving her body to an inebriated, overweight, middle-aged man. When she turned to explain to her boss that she had some personal business to attend to, the sexually frustrated man lashed out her with a clenched fist, knocking her off her feet. It was only with great difficulty that she hung on to the banister to prevent herself tumbling headlong down the stairs. Before the enraged man could inflict further damage on her, she stumbled past his raised fists and fled the scene. I could scarcely believe what I was hearing. That the woman was telling the truth I had no doubt. Pat had the face of a boxer; his nose, for one thing, had all the appearance of having been broken in the past. But to attack a woman in the manner just described because she declined to have sexual intercourse with him?

Despite being successful in increasing Benton & Bowles turnover, as the months of winter gave way to early summer, I was finding it increasingly difficult to open up any new accounts. Then quite unexpectedly I received a call from the Public Relations Office at the Hilton Hotel requesting me to go and see its manager.

'Be careful, Martin, she's a man-eater' Jerry Moore told me when he learned of where I was going. But I emerged from the Hilton with an order to reprint the hotel's postcard and my virtue intact, having dealt with an assistant rather than the great lady herself. I also had the added bonus of acquiring my first new client when the Public Relations assistant directed me downstairs to meet the manager of Trader Vics' restaurant who wanted to talk about printing all of its menus.

Jackie Laugenie was a small, chunky, volatile Frenchman who had started out working for the family catering business in France before arriving in London to work as a chef. He was now Managing Director of Trader Vics' European operations.

'I want you to print all my menus,' the manager informed me, as we sat in his cubby-hole of an office at the bottom of the stairs that led down from Park Lane. Coffee soon arrived, brought to us by one of the loveliest young women I had so far encountered. She was tall and slim with coffee-coloured skin, and in her long black hair hanging almost down to her waist perched a flower over one ear. She wore a dress of coloured silk material, high to the neck but with liberal splits up each side to reveal a generous amount of thigh.

'Have you got the positives?' I asked.

Jackie frowned.

I explained what the term meant. But as I expected they were with the previous printer of the menus who, for some reason, had now lost the business.

'It's going to be very expensive to start again from scratch,' I warned.

Jackie looked thoughtful for a few seconds. 'Give me a quote for doing all the work, but showing the separate cost for the...' he hesitated.

'The positives,' I prompted.

'The positives,' he repeated. 'Now, would you like to join me for lunch?'

Once introduced to the delights of Trader Vics' extensive menu, it was not long before I began using it as a luncheon venue for Terry Walker and myself.

As that year of 1968 was drawing to a close, I was pleased with the manner in which I had settled into my new career. Of my previous life, I thought very little; except when I occasionally drove up or down Amwell Street and saw Sheila Bird or any other parishioner walking along. But I was acutely aware that the long years in the seminary and the years as a priest had left their mark on me. More than once, the people I now mixed with would often look at me in a puzzled manner and say: 'You're different. There's something about you...' I would just smile and change the subject of conversation.

Late in the spring of 1969, I waited at the stage door of the theatre where Margaret Savage was appearing in the Black and White Minstrel Show. A girl friend of the singer was also waiting. When Margaret emerged she seemed genuinely pleased to see me, and invited me to join her and her friend for a late supper in a nearby restaurant. But since I had only a few pounds in my pocket, I reluctantly declined and sadly bade them both goodnight. Would anything of a romantic nature have developed between Margaret and me if I had gone with them? I doubt it.

Some of the Pallottine Fathers to this day continue to believe that I abandoned the priesthood because of an infatuation with Margaret. Then again, the rumour was that a red-haired staff nurse at the Royal Free Hospital was the 'femme fatale.' I did know such a one; but we never met outside of my duties on her ward; except on one occasion when she came to the Presbytery to purchase a 'missal.'

I began again the search for new clients. But the many 'cold calls' I made proved unfruitful. Then one Friday morning while enjoying my toasted bacon sandwich and strong cup of tea in a cafe close to the office, I spotted in the pages of Campaign, which I had begun to buy religiously each week, a notice that a Pat O'Driscoll had been appointed Promotions Manager of AEG-Telefunken. I can't explain why, but at that moment I felt my luck was about to change. Back at my desk, I cut out the details and filed it for another day. It was a full three weeks before I got around to telephoning the offices of the German company, which I discovered were conveniently situated at the top of the Caledonian Road. 'O'Driscoll here,' a cheerful voice announced when I was put through. I introduced myself and then said: 'You must be from Ireland.'

'I am.'

'And with a name like yours you must be from Cork or Kerry,' I ventured.

'From the County Kerry; to be exact, from Valentia Island, the home of the mighty Mick O'Connell,' he boasted, mentioning one of Ireland's famous Gaelic footballers. After a short exchange of such pleasantries I had no problem in arranging a meeting for the following day.

Within a couple of weeks I had forged such a close, friendly relationship with the genial Irishman, that hardly a day passed that I did not emerge from his office without a couple of orders in my briefcase. Admittedly they were only in one, or at the most two colours, but Pat O'Driscoll was already discussing the need to produce a range of four colour promotional material for forthcoming Trade Shows.

After five weeks of doing business with AEG-Telefunken, I was able to hand Pat a brown envelope, and but for the slight rise in colour in his cheeks he gave no indication that he guessed what largesse was being given to him.

One afternoon walking along Bond Street on a hot sunny, afternoon, I noticed a small crowd gathered outside Ireland House. As I stood on the fringe of the gathering looking on,who should appear in the window but Ann Marie Berkley, the model from my days in Dublin. Instinctively I pointed at her and mouthed her name. Ann Marie must have read my lips for she smiled and nodded, before turning around and disappearing from view. I immediately hurried to the building's Bruton Street entrance and waited.

When Ann Marie emerged some five minutes later, she greeted me warmly. As we stood talking, I filled her in on my sudden departure from Dublin and a few details concerning my new career in London.

'All the cast were sorry that you went,' she told me.

'Including you?' I brazenly asked.

The model blushed. 'Including me.'

'Where are you staying?'

'I'm at the Irish Club until next Tuesday' she replied.

'Would you like to go out on Saturday night? I asked, not believing I had the temerity to ask this adorable creature such a question.

'I would love to,' she answered promptly.

Standing in the foyer of the Irish Club waiting for Ann Marie to come downstairs, I realised that this was my first time to enter the premises; even though I had noticed it on numerous occasions when driving pass on business. The sound of footsteps turned my eyes upwards in time to see the model come skipping lightly down the wide staircase. She was wearing a light, floral dress of sufficient shortness to display her shapely long legs to the best advantage. While we shook hands, I noticed the admiring looks a few men standing near the reception desk were given my delectable companion.

Outside in Lyall Street, I suggested that we go to the open air symphony concert at Kenwood House.

'It sounds wonderful,' Ann Marie responded, linking an arm through mine.

The overture to the Barber of Seville had just started as we took our seats and I handed Ann Marie a programme. After a few seconds perusing its contents, she leaned towards me and pointed at an item that was to be played as the final piece. It was Dvorak's New World Symphony: the first L.P. I had purchased in Thurles.

'You like it?' I whispered.

She nodded, with a smile that made me catch my breath. My God, she's beautiful, I thought.

Midway through the second-half of the entertainment I saw Ann Marie give a slight shiver. 'You're cold,' I said with concern, as I removed my jacket and placed it around her shoulders. She smiled her thanks as I took one of her hands between my own two hands and began to gently massage it.

Making our way back to Compton Avenue where I had parked the car, I suggested to Ann Marie that we go and have something to eat; having already decided that Casa Pepe in Dean Street would be an ideal place to bring her. We were in luck. Senor Pepe himself was there and greeted us most warmly, kissing Ann Marie's hand and presenting her with the flower from his buttonhole. The distinguished looking Spaniard doesn't recognise me, I realised with some relief, even though we had met on a number of occasions when I had dined there as a priest.

As we ate our Paella Valenciana and sipped the crisp, white wine recommended by the restaurateur, Ann Marie regaled me with many amusing stories and jokes garnered from the many hours she spent travelling with other models around Ireland. She then asked me a number of questions the answers to which would reveal my personality.

While we waited for the coffee to arrive, Ann Marie became a little more serious. 'I have these two boy-friends, one is a doctor, the other a builder,' she confided. 'Which one do you think I ought to stick with, Martin?'

Why was she asking me this most difficult question, when not many minutes ago she had told me I was 70% sex and 30% intellect? I took a sip of my cognac before replying.

'It's difficult for me to give you an answer, Ann Marie, since I have never met either of the two men concerned. But if you were to push me for an answer I'd say the doctor.'

'Why?' she asked quickly.

I explained that I based my answer on what it was that motivated both men. I knew that it was a fairly simplistic answer, but it was the best I could come up with at that moment. Ann Marie looked thoughtful as she gazed into the distance.

Finally, she asked if I thought it correct and proper for her to go on holiday to Yugoslavia as a member of a foursome. She's treating me like her confessor, I thought wryly. I assured her it was.

Ann Marie and I met just once more before she returned to Dublin, when we attended a Charity performance of Handel's Messiah at the Royal Albert Hall in the presence of Her Royal Highness, Princes Alexandra and organised by Roy Strong. The purpose of the evening was to raise money to keep a painting of Handel with the score of the Messiah in England. Joan Sutherland was one of the soloists. My companion was thrilled to see that the princess was seated directly above us. The following day I drove her to Heathrow and kissed her goodbye. Some years later, Ann Marie married the builder and has three children.

Once that summer had passed, a steady stream of orders began pour in from my three clients. Pat O'Driscoll continued to perform like a conjurer pulling a continuous stream of coloured handkerchiefs from his pocket as day after day, he handed me print orders which, I began to suspect, were not strictly necessary perhaps until many months hence.

It was round that time that I began to frequent the Irish Club, after being inside it for the first time when collecting Ann Marie, and soon became a regular in the spacious bar on a Saturday night. Mrs. Fennell was always enquiring of me why I had not found an attractive woman. There were plenty of women huddling together in small groups around the bar or sitting down; most of them I judged to be between 30 years old and into their middle 50s. None, I recall, were at first glance attractive-looking, or for that matter well-dressed. Career wise I imagined them to be in the civil service or in banking.

There were a number of occasions between my joining the Irish Club and that Christmas when I took women home; but usually there were at least two of them sharing the same flat or mews house. I was always invited indoors and given a late supper of ham and eggs by my grateful companions of that particular night. However there was one occasion when I did find myself alone with a young South African woman, whom I met at the folk club attached to the Carmelite Church in Kensington. When we reached the block of flats close to the Albert Hall where she lived, she invited me to come upstairs with her and listen to some Frank Sinatra records. It was a tempting offer especially when I deduced that the flat belonged to her parents, who must have been quite wealthy to own such a property. Once again my years as a priest left me unprepared to cope with such a situation. As I drove toward Knightsbridge corner I felt sorry for the woman. What must she think of me?

It was February before I returned to the Irish Club. In the intervening weeks I learned one more trick that print-buyers used to ensure that their commission kept on growing.

On a couple of occasions I noticed that Terry Walker offered quotes to me that I knew Donbro had no earthly chance of winning, either because the print run was too big or the sheet size was too large to fit our machines. Puzzled by this, I eventually asked Pat Donnellan to explain. 'Well, it's like this Martin. When a really big job comes along, the print¬ buyer will want one of his friends to get the order. Since he has to obtain at least three quotes, he chooses a small firm like us to be one of the printers, knowing that our price will be so high that we won't have a hope in hell of getting the order. Against our price his friend's quote will look good and the order will go to him; and very often, added Pat, 'the print buyer will add a little extra to share with the printer.'

As I stood at the far end of the bar in the Irish Club that February Saturday night, I noticed an attractive looking dark-haired woman in the company of two men, one of whom looked Irish; the other was small and dark with a pencil thin moustache.

'Who is that woman?' I enquired of a man standing beside me. He looked in the direction I indicated.

'Oh, that's Louise,' he told me in what I considered a rather dismissive tone of voice. The woman in question must have sensed our interest in her, for she turned away from her companions and looked directly at us and gave a slight smile before resuming a conversation with the men. For the rest of the evening, 'Louise' gave up all pretence of being interested in the two men she was with, and instead kept glancing in my direction.

When I decided it was time to leave the bar, I walked nonchalantly past 'Louise' on my way out to the foyer, where I sat down on a chair usually occupied by Miss Conroy, when she was on security duty. Above my head was a poster advertising the club's St. Patrick's Night Ball at the Hilton. I would like to attend that, I thought, but as yet I had no partner. The bar door opened and 'Louise' emerged. She stopped and smiled down at me. 'Do I know you?' she asked.

'I'm not sure,' I answered, rising to my feet.

She began to fire questions at me: Did I work in Mayfair? Did I go into the Bon Appétit in Albemarle Street? I told her I had on a couple of occasions. 'Then perhaps that is where we saw each other,' she concluded.

'Are you going to the St. Patrick's Night Ball?' I wanted to know.

'Are you?'

'I would like to but I'm looking for a partner.'

'So am I,' Louise said quickly.

'Would you like to go with me then?' I asked shyly.

'I'd love to.'

This was the first time she had attended a St. Patrick's Night Ball, she told me weeks later.

On our first date the following Saturday night, we ended up having dinner at the Spaghetti House, Knightsbridge, after failing to obtain a table at the Royal Garden Hotel, Kensington. Afterwards, I drove Louise home.

While we chatted about the forthcoming Ball, I confessed that I wasn't a very good dancer. On hearing this, Louise said that she would teach me some basic steps over the next few weeks.

One night the following week, I arrived with a record of the Joe Loss Orchestra. Louise took me through all the dance routines, even trying out the tango. 'You dance very well and have a good sense of rhythm,' she told me.

'Do you think so?' I enquired, with a grin.

Louise nodded her head. 'I think you are teasing me. You know full well how to dance.'

At the end of three weeks together, we had not even exchanged so much as a 'peck on the cheek' in the way of a kiss. As this was my first serious involvement with a woman I was unsure as to how one proceeded in such matters. Naturally, courting did not figure on the seminary curriculum. What I didn't know at the time was that my lack of ardour was the subject of much speculation amongst the staff of the Elizabeth Arden Salon in Old Bond Street, where Louise worked as a beautician. Doubts were raised as to my masculinity. But they need not have worried. On what was to be the last dancing lesson before the Ball, Louise stumbled backwards and fell on the bed pulling me down on top of her. She has consistently maintained over the years that her stumble was an accident. I maintain that it was deliberate act of seduction on her part.

It was shortly afterwards that Louise said to me that she thought I was too good to be true. I believe it was then I hinted that there was something in my background I would tell her about in due course. 'What were you, in jail or something?' she wanted to know, with just a hint of anxiety in her voice. 'Are you one of the Great Train Robbers? Obviously, she found me totally different in some way from other men she had been out with. But to think of me as a criminal...!

When I collected Louise for the Ball, I was disappointed with her hair: she had chosen to tie it back in the form of a bun which didn't suit her. The make-up was perfect and the salmon-pink dress was lovely on her.

As we drove towards the Hilton she explained that she had to do a rush job on her hair because one of the hairdressers in the salon had let her down at the last minute. As was only to be expected on the night that was in it, the London Irish waxed lyrical about their homeland as they danced to the music of the Joe Loss Orchestra. Men and women sang nostalgically of *"The Dear Little Shamrock"*; *"Killarney"*; *"Mother Macree"* and *"Danny Boy"*, as they swirled round the dance floor.

From that moment, my relationship with Louise deepened and intensified to such a degree that, within a few months, she invited me to her home in Cork for a holiday

The Kinmonth family lived in a spacious Victorian house near the docks. Louise's parents, Bill and Ettie, her brother, Paul, and an aunt, were its only occupants. With Bill Kinmonth, Louise's father, I formed a strong attachment, and most nights found the pair of us in the Port Bar across the Street. Occasionally his daughter joined us; but more often than not she stayed behind with her mother to drink innumerable cups of tea, smoke a couple of cigarettes and talk about Martin Gordon.

Walking and driving around Cork, I found it difficult not to smile as Louise pointed out some of the city's better-known landmarks. One afternoon, on the pretext of visiting the western suburbs, we drove out to Wilton and I expressed surprise at the sight of the African Missions church, suggesting that we pull in off the main road to have a look at it.

Nothing had changed, I noticed, as we walked up the aisle to the sanctuary. Standing at the altar rails, I decided to visit the side chapel where I had sat for two years trying to meditate, all the while fighting to stay awake.

Outside again, we walked round the side of the church and unexpectedly, as it were, we came across the community cemetery. There were many new headstones, among them that of dear Father Harmon. May their souls rest in peace, I whispered within myself.

'Are you alright, Martin?' Louise asked anxiously.

I blinked a couple of times, 'Yes, I'm fine; just a speck of dust in my eye.'

Back in London again, Pat O'Driscoll had thrilling news for me. 'Are you sitting comfortably,' he wanted to know as he smiled across his desk at me.

'Pat, have you been drinking?' I asked.

'No, I haven't, but both us will be after you hear what I have to tell you..'

'5 tons of flat sheets have arrived from Germany and are lying at King's Cross waiting for you to collect for overprinting and folding into an eight page broadsheet. How about that for an order,' Pat exclaimed exultantly.

I emitted a low whistle. Just wait until I give the news to Alf Freedman, I thought.

As I drove back down the Caledonian Road, I estimated that AEG's Sales Promotion Manager would be at least 200 pounds the richer. It would do wonders for my own commission too, I thought delightedly.

With all accounts performing well and my future at looking secure, I decided that the moment was opportune to ask Louise to marry me.

When I put the question, she tried to speak but couldn't. Instead, she nodded her head and opened her arms to embrace me. 'I love you, Martin,' she whispered shyly into my ear.

'Louise, there's something I must tell you,' I said solemnly, releasing myself from her arms and taking hold of one of her hands.

A worried look appeared on her face.

'I am a priest.'

She made no reply for seconds while she assimilated this startling news.

'Is that all you have to tell me?' she asked happily. 'I thought you were going to tell me that you were married, or as I said before had been in prison.'

'I'll tell you everything then you can make your mind up,' I told her.

'I've already made it up,' she said, as she reached out and pulled me down beside her on the bed.

An hour later, we freshened up and went round to the Irish Club for a celebratory dinner. After we ordered from the menu, Louise went to telephone her parents in Cork.

'Well, were they surprised?' I asked upon her return.

'Mammy said she expected the news any day. In fact we looked so much in love while we were in Cork that she thought that we would announce our engagement there.'

I pulled a face.

'Don't be like that, mammy and daddy would have thrown a big party for us.'

Yes, I thought grimly, and your mother would have invited some of your ex-boyfriends to try and make me jealous.

For an engagement ring Louise chose a lovely small Victorian piece from a stall in Portobello Market. That night we again had dinner at the Irish Club and were congratulated by many of the members, some of whom had known my fiancée, for a number of years.

Our next big decision was to fix a date for the wedding. After consulting the calendar, Louise suggested August the 21st of the following year, 1971. But first I had to try and obtain my laicisation. I had no idea how long this process would take, but knowing how slowly the Vatican works. I had read, however, that Pope Paul VI was granting dispensations to priests in their thousands who, like me, had become disillusioned with celibate lives. I hoped, therefore, that once I had sent my application to the Pallottine Provincial, who was my former colleague at Saints Peter & Pauls, Bill Hanley, my dispensation would arrive in time for the marriage to take place on the date we had chosen.

Louise suggested that she would speak to Mrs.Orson Welles, one of her clients at Elizabeth Arden, who, she thought, being an Italian Countess, must have some influential contacts within the Vatican.

It took until May of the following year, 1971, for my dispensation to be granted. Quickly scanning the two pages of Latin I was relieved to see that I had been dispensed from my vow of celibacy and was now 'reduced' to the lay state. Louise and I could now proceed with our plan to marry on the 21st of August. But first we had to collect all the various documents the church required of those wishing to marry.

Since it was customary for a wedding to take place in the bride's parish, in our case Westminster Cathedral, we decided to delay approaching its Administrator until it was absolutely necessary. My reason for doing so was that I didn't like the idea of the wedding ceremony taking place in the crypt with the minimum of liturgy lf we were lucky there might be two candles on the altar. Louise deserved better than that, I decided.

Within a few weeks, a small miracle took place. Louise was offered a basement flat in Linhope Street, off Dorset Square. It belonged to a colleague in the salon who was returning to Australia. It was compact with its own kitchen and bathroom. An elderly couple occupied the ground and first floors, while Nadine, Countess of Shrewsbury lived at the top of the house. The Countess had ambitions to become a professional singer and had studied with the highly regarded teacher, Maggie Teyte, who had once had a very successful career as an opera singer. To further his wife's career, the Earl inaugurated a new festival at his palatial home *"Ingestre"*, in the West Country. This was supposed to launch Nadine's career. But the conductor, John Pritchard, objected to her singing in Purcell's Dido and Aenaes. To save face, the Countess recited a poem especially written for the occasion.

Apart from the improved accommodation, the new address meant that we could now choose either the church of Lisson Grove Parish, which was situated near Lord's cricket ground, or St. James's, Spanish Place; even though Linhope Street was not in its parish. However, once we began attending Mass there, we decided that was where we would like to get married.

With the marriage just three months away, I began reading the 'house for sale' page of the Evening Standard in the hope of finding a suitable property. One morning, as I sat eating my bacon sandwich in a cafe near the office, I came across the following:

HIGH BARNET.
Edge of green belt, owner returning to Switzerland in August. Semi-detached, 3 bedrooms (two with fitted wardrobes), through lounge with stone fireplace, kitchen etc; large rear garden with shed. Near schools, market, good shops and transport. £7,500 Freehold.

On my return to the office, I telephoned the vendor and made an appointment to view the property at eight o'clock that same evening. After a quick look round the cottage-style house and the garden, where the shed turned out to be a brick, world war two air-raid shelter, Louise and I decided to make an offer near to the asking price. But we had to wait until later on that night before finalising the deal over the telephone.

Our next major task was to approach the parish priest of St. James's, Spanish Place for permission to marry in his church. When we left after about fifteen minutes, our marriage was fixed for 3p.m. on Saturday, the 21st of August. We booked the organist, but turned down the offer of the red carpet. I told the priest that we would supply our own singer. Reluctantly, I thought, the priest agreed to a Nuptial Mass but politely requested me to avoid any publicity.

After we had taken care of all the necessary documentation, the last exercise I had to perform was the printing and despatch of the wedding invitations. I put the order for the cards through Freedman's and was delighted when I was told that there would be no charge. My only regret was that my employers, Alf and Charles Freedman and Lionel Silver would not be able to be present at the wedding, since it was being held on a Saturday.

In the hectic weeks of preparation, there was only one real moment of tension between Louise and I. That was when she suggested that we invite a man she had gone out with three or four times in Cork and London. Her reason, she explained, was to provide a partner for Elfie, one of her bridesmaids I vetoed the idea. By the beginning of August, 81 acceptances had been received to attend the wedding and the reception in the Presidential Room of the Irish Club. Amongst those who were unable to attend were my two Scot's friends, singer Margaret Savage and the Arsenal player, George Graham, who sent us a pair of nylon sheets.

Wedding gifts began arriving, most from our wedding list at the John Lewis store in Oxford Street. But many of Louise's clients at Elizabeth Arden were especially generous. One woman gave her a cheque for 100 pounds; another purchased a pouffe from the original salon in old Bond Street – Louise bought a second one so as to have a pair – A Mrs. Brondsberg, whose son Andrew worked with filmmaker Roman Polanski, was a dear old lady and a great favourite with us both, gave enough red velvet to make almost all the curtains for our new home. The Freedman's gave me 100 pounds in cash.

Louise had selected two of her closest friends at the salon to be bridesmaids: both striking-looking young women. Ann Fairbairn was blonde and English, Elfie Kleminjac was dark and from Austria. For my Best-Man I chose Pat Donnellan and Terry Walker as chief usher.

The night before the wedding Louise and Elfie stayed in the Irish Club, while I slept at the Linhope Street flat. But I would leave for the church from the Highbury home of Peter and Bernie Norris, who did not want to see me set out on my own for such an important and emotional occasion.

Although the morning had been damp and slightly overcast when I left Linhope Street, by the time I reached Highbury corner around mid-day the cloud had broken up and there were patches of blue sky beginning to appear, allowing the sun to shine through. Within minutes of arriving at my friends home, Peter and Bernie escorted me round to their local pub for a few drinks prior to us having a light lunch. Without considering the fact that I had eaten nothing substantial all morning, I drank three gin and tonics: one less than Bernie, I noticed.

After tea and ham sandwiches back in the house, I went upstairs to change into my morning suit hired from a shop next to Baker Street Station and the shirt and shoes bought at Austin Reed. When I eventually came downstairs, top-hat in hand, Bernie's eyes became moist as she appraised my appearance.

'Well, will I do?' I asked her.

'Oh, Martin,' she exclaimed. 'Here, let me fix that tie.'

After making the necessary adjustment, she stood back. 'Now, that's better.' Then she kissed me tenderly on the lips.

'All ready now,' Peter Norris called out as he emerged from the kitchen.

Most of the guests were already in their places when I walked down the aisle of the church escorted by Terry Walker. The organ began to play softly as I knelt down. As I finished my prayers, Pat Donnellan arrived at my side. Just then the opening chords of the traditional wedding music told me that Louise had arrived.

When Louise reached my side, I turned towards her and whispered: 'You look lovely.' She smiled her appreciation, and together we went forward into the sanctuary where the celebrant was waiting to greet us. During the Nuptial Mass, the soprano, a member of the D'Oyly Carte sang 'Gounod's' *"Ave Maria"*, *"O.Sanctissima"* and *"Panis Angelicus"*.

After signing the registers in the sacristy, Louise and I walked arm-in-arm down the aisle smiling at our guests, amongst whom were two Pallottine nuns. Their presence, despite their reassuring smiles, made me lose my composure for a few seconds, and I almost dragged Louise off her feet as I hurried her away outside. It had been a strange experience for a former priest to be walking down the aisle of a church, with a woman on his arm, when for ten years other priests in the seminary had been warning him of the dangers such creatures were to one's vocation.

By now the warm sun was shining brightly as we had the traditional photographs taken and were greeted by our guests who, I had to admit, looked as if they had been assembled for their part in a film; especially the Elizabeth Arden contingent, amongst whom was Mrs. Wonnacott, the Manageress of the London Salon and a personal friend of Elizabeth Arden herself. This was the only time she had attended the wedding of a member of her staff. The many non-Catholics present were full of praise for the ceremony. One even went so far as to say that she would become a Catholic just to be married with a Nuptial Mass.

Upon arrival at the Irish Club, I had just time to kiss my wife before we stood inside the door of the Arran Bar to greet our friends. It was many kisses and handshakes later before we were able to join everyone for our own glass of sherry. Looking at the invoice in front of me, I see that the wedding party of eighty four downed 144 glasses of sherry prior to going upstairs to the Presidential Room for the five course dinner. The same document states that we consumed 36 bottles of red and white wine and numerous bottles of champagne. For the record, the bill came to 203 pounds, thirty five pence, including 5 pounds for flowers.

A soft summer breeze was blowing in through the open windows which opened on to the balconies overlooking Lyall Street, as the assembled guests stood while I said grace and felt the first sign of a headache. Half-way through the meal, Father Bill Hanley, the Pallottine Provincial arrived, and was promptly seated a few places to my right.

When Pat Donnellan read out a telegram from the Arsenal team, there was much laughter when he finished. I was delighted that George Graham had remembered my wedding day, but acutely embarrassed at the message: *"Best wishes to you and your helpmate. Want any help, mate"?*

When it came the moment for me to say a few words, the headache that had been threatening for the past hour worsened. I had prepared my short speech in advance and got a few laughs when I recited a Russian proverb:

"When you go to war you should pray once;
when you go to sea you ought to pray twice;
but when you marry one should pray three times".

I concluded by saying that Louise and I had actually thought of eloping, and would have done so were it not for all the gifts that we would have missed out on.

Once the meal was over, a five piece band soon had the room filled with couples dancing to many of the standard numbers of earlier years. The vocals were professionally rendered by Danny McNamara, husband of my wife's cousin, Maura. Danny, who sadly dropped dead some years later in the car park of a London pub, where he had just finished a singing engagement, had been the vocalist with one of Ireland's top dance bands and had come second in a national competition organised by the Irish television station, R.T.E. He ought to have won it, but the judges were swayed by youth and female beauty. Even in summertime, when he sang in Ireland, Danny would receive innumerable requests to sing Silent Night.

All too soon it was time for my wife and I to bid farewell to our guests. But first we had to change into our going - away clothes. When we came downstairs, we were made to stand in the middle of a circle they formed and then, as they sang to the playing of 'Now is the Hour,' Louise and I moved around kissing and hugging them one by one. A few of the women were crying; two widows in particular shedding copious tears.

As we drove away, we could just make out the cheers from the balconies. I sounded the car horn twice in response.

Within Louise's Linhope Street flat, where we were going to spend our wedding night, I took off my shoes and jacket, loosened my tie and stretched out on the bed. I was really ill with the headache and feeling a strong feeling of nausea. Suddenly I needed to reach the bathroom and made it just in time to disgorge the entire wedding feast into the toilet.

'Are you alright, Martin?' Louise called anxiously from the hallway.

What a bloody stupid thing to happen on my wedding night, I thought, as I rinsed out my mouth and splashed water on my face. When I emerged from the bathroom, my wife was removing her suit.

'What made you sick, Love?' she asked, as she stepped out of her skirt.

I explained about the drinks with Peter and Bernie Norris.

'That was very silly of you, knowing that you can't drink like them,' she chided.

'I realise that now,' I replied weakly.

'Get ready for bed, darling, and I'll get a cup of tea for us both,' Louise said.

Lying in her arms after we drank the tea, I apologised to my wife of eight hours for spoiling her wedding night.

'Don't worry, Love,' she whispered, and switched off the light.

THE WORLD, THE FLESH
& THE DEVIL

We consummated our marriage early the following morning and I was bitterly disappointed. There were no bells ringing; no fireworks exploding and no cannons roared. It was not what I expected; but then perhaps my expectations were too high.

Having decided to delay the honeymoon, we spent the first few days of married life doing work on the house and having the carpets fitted and curtains hung. Apart from our new king-size bed, our only other furniture was the coffee table, the record player, a small display cabinet and a portable picnic table, all from my wife's flat. But within a few days, we purchased a lovely Edwardian, walnut display cabinet from Harrods Antique Furniture Department, in which to display Louise's extensive collection of Waterford Glass. At the same time, Harrods also supplied us with a large comfortable sofa and two armchairs in wine red to match the velvet curtains in the living room. The total bill at the store came to just over 500 pounds. Our final item was a Victorian breakfast table from Maples at a cost of 240 pounds.

Satisfied that we had the basics of a home in place, we drove down to Devon for a four-day stay at the Cockington House Hotel outside Torquay.

During our brief but enjoyable honeymoon, we went one night to a variety show in a nearby village. Imagine my surprise when Alex de Gabriel of the Shannon Players appeared on stage; who you will recall, appeared in Enniscrone during the summer.

The cost for our half-board four-day stay in Devon, including extras at the bar, came to the princely sum of 32 pounds and 78 pence.

Returned to work, I was saddened to learn that my colleague, Jerry Moore, had lost another client and was now in grave danger of losing his job as well; and Pat Donnellan had made his intentions known of leaving to set up as a 'Print-Farmer;' a recent phenomenon in the industry. I had heard the term mentioned recently, but had yet to meet one of the species. 'Print Farmers,' I was to discover, had neither premises nor machinery.

The reason for 'Print Farmers' existence was graft. Print buyers tried to justify dealing with them by claiming that these men knew where to get a job done in time and at a good price. Rubbish! Every print buyer had hundreds of printers knocking on their door begging for a chance to do work for them. 'Dropsy' to use a slang term, 'a drink' or just the good old basic 'back-hander' was the only reason for the existence of 'Print-Farmers.' They now, I believe, go under the name of 'Print Broker.' Has the reason for their existence changed?

Two months into the marriage, Louise became pregnant but decided to continue working at Elizabeth Arden, at least until after Christmas. Naturally, we were thrilled at the prospect of becoming parents.

At first, the pregnancy went well. But early in the New Year, she began to have problems with her blood-pressure and had to spend a few days in Barnet General. We debated whether she ought to give up work. But Louise thought she could continue for another couple of months to help with our hire purchase payments and mortgage.

Meanwhile, the furnishing of the house continued. From Cork came a Sheraton-style, small armchair and four dining-table chairs that originally belonged to her grandmother. From a client of Louise's, a Mrs. Leftman, I purchased a large antique Georgian-style armchair for 20 pounds; she offered me another matching one, but slightly larger. I was tempted, but the pair would have been too large for the living room. From a shop in Hadley Green I bought an elegant console table with marble top and a matching desk set to go with it for 300 pounds.

Pat Donnellan eventually left to set up at as 'Print-Farmer.' Within twenty-four hours of his departure, I acquired one of his accounts: an American travel company with an office in Bruton Street. There I met your archetypal Irishman, Kelvin Houchin. He loved the company of women and was great companion to have a few drinks with in the 'Jaws of Death' pub near his office.

One of his amorous experiences that failed to live up to his expectations was the occasion when he and a woman in the travel industry travelled to Cork to attend a weekend conference: He had booked a double room for them both at the Vienna Woods Hotel and was greatly excited at the thought of the two of them in bed on that first night. But as Robbie Burns so well put it:

"The best laid schemes of mice and men gang aft agley".
The woman was a lesbian.

One of Freedman Brothers' clients was Ron Shapiro, brother of the singer, Helen Shapiro. Ron, was print-buyer at a small advertising agency at the Kings Cross end of Pentonville Road. Although placing substantial amounts of print orders, Ron gave our Golders Green factory little more than a couple of hundred pounds worth of letterpress business a year. I asked Alf Freedman if I could call on Ron, he readily agreed.

'You will find him difficult,' he advised.

Undeterred, I telephoned the print-buyer and made an appointment to call on him the next day. Ron Shapiro was a sad-looking young man. But after the usual introductory small-talk between us had ended, I casually asked him what team he supported. Immediately, the weight of the world seemed lifted from his shoulders, and he became alive. 'The Gunners, of course,' he answered enthusiastically.

With a flash of inspiration, I asked him if he would like a seat for the season at Highbury.

'Can you get me one?'

I didn't know whether I could or not, but it was worth a try. I knew a ticket agency in St. John Street, close to Sadler's Wells, whose coaches I used for transporting my parish football team and for parish outings; with a bit of luck it might still have a few seats unsold.

The Patron Saint of sales representatives must have been watching over me that day, for when I emerged from the agency I had two seats in the front row of Highbury's West stand. So for the next two seasons, Ron and I became regular supporters at most of Arsenal's games. When on a couple of occasions the print-buyer was unable to be present, Louise came along instead and thoroughly enjoyed the experience. At the end of my second year of doing business with Ron Shapiro, my turnover with the buyer was in the region of 12,000 pounds.

About six weeks before the expected birth of our child, my wife's voice woke me up in the early hours of the morning. 'Martin something has happened to the baby,' she said anxiously. I switched on the bedside light and pulled back the bedclothes to see a large, dark stain on the under-sheet.

'I better telephone the hospital,' I said quietly, trying to disguise the concern I felt for the baby's well-being. I was told to drive Louise there as quickly as possible.

Early the following evening, after I had eaten my supper and was preparing to visit Louise in the Barnet General, the telephone shrilled loudly. I hesitated for a few seconds and prayed that it would not be bad news. When I replaced the receiver, tears were already streaming down my cheeks. 'Oh, Andrew, Andrew,' I called out to the empty house, as I stumbled upstairs and stood outside the small, front room we had designated as the nursery. 'My son is dead, my son is dead,' I wailed, as I pushed open the door and entered. Through tear-filled eyes I looked down on the empty cot and slowly let my glance take in all the usual objects associated with the arrival of a new baby. How long I stood there I can't say. But eventually I fell to my knees and pressed my forehead against the cot, calling out my son's name, over and over again. Then looking up at a ceiling I could scarcely see, I almost shrieked in anger, 'Why God, why?' I demanded to know, before a new paroxysm of grief overwhelmed me. My howl of despair could have been that of Joseph Conrad's fictional character, Almayer, after he had lost his wife and two young sons cried out:

"What's the sense of all this? Where's your providence? Where's the good for anybody in all this? The world's a swindle! A swindle! Why should I suffer? What I have done to be treated so?"

When I had sufficiently recovered my composure, I went downstairs to telephone my wife's parents. Fortunately, my father-in-law answered the telephone, but his wife soon arrived beside him and, on discovering the reason for the call, cried out, 'No.'

I buried Andrew three days later in Hendon Cemetery. Father Anthony Canning, an elderly Pallottine priest from the Provincial House in Golders Green, conducted the graveside service. Alf Freedman, who had insisted on being present, stood by my side. When the small, white coffin was lowered into the grave and as the first sods of damp, dark earth showered down on the casket, I whispered a silent farewell to the son I'd never know, with whom I would never kick a football or take to Highbury to watch Arsenal in action.

On Sunday the 3rd of June of that year, 1972, as Louise and I walked home from mass, I glanced at the front page of the Irish Sunday Press, and saw a small heading about a drowning tragedy at Enniscrone. On reading the piece, I discovered that my friend

Tommy Forde, his nine year old son, Aidan and two other local men, the Fitzgerald brothers, Christy and Noel, both of whom I knew, had died when their small boat capsized early on the previous Saturday morning while hauling in a salmon net. Once in home, I immediately telephoned Sean Gannon, whose father, Tom, was also a fisherman. I was certain that he would have all the details of this terrible tragedy.

'I've been on the phone all night,' Sean told me. 'When I heard the news from home, I knew the accident had to have happened off the little river. And you know, Martin, the awful thing is, Daddy was just coming back into the pier as the other boat was going out, and he advised them to put back in again, as the sea was becoming treacherous.'

According to an eyewitness to the tragedy, the victims were over at the yellow marker picking up their nets and had got inside the breakers. He saw them getting over a couple of the breakers and then the boat seemed to be swamped. He and a couple of men raced over to the strand, but when they arrived all they could see was the upturned boat, the 'Naomh Antoine;' a 24 foot craft driven by a nine horse power engine. It was Tommy's first time out fishing that season, and it was his little son's first outing ever with his dad. Tommy left a wife and four other children. I recalled the words of my Aunt Nellie concerning Tommy: *"He won't have a long life"*. But in prophesying his short life, never for a moment had she in mind the manner of his dying.

In October, Louise announced that she was pregnant again. This time, we decided, there would be no more working at the salon for her during this pregnancy. In the months that followed, Louise experienced no problems other than those of any normal pregnancy. My career continued to flourish, when I became Sales Manager and took possession of a brand new Triumph 2000 automatic. The corresponding increase in salary and commission, made the loss of my wife's income less noticeable in our budget. Life was good; but I still thought often of Andrew.

On the 28th of July 1973, Louise and I became the proud parents of a lovely daughter whom we named, Katherine. We decided not have her baptised in High Barnet, because by then, despite my previous bad experience of working in Ireland, I had obtained a job with the Cork printing firm, Guys, and so decided to have the ceremony performed when we arrived in the Southern capital.

On the baby's first night at home, we stood the cot at my side of the bed. I hardly got any sleep, as the smallest sound or movement from the infant two feet away, immediately catapulted me out of bed to check on her welfare. I lost count the number of times this happened, so that by the morning I was a nervous wreck and suffering from stomach pains. Obviously unfit for work, I visited our doctor who had the greatest of sympathy for me, but was able to see the funny side of my complaint.

Unwilling to experience a second night of similar trauma, I scanned the yellow pages and was lucky enough to find an excellent nurse who looked after Katherine for the next two weeks, while Louise and I enjoyed the sleep of the blest.

Despite my continuing success in opening new accounts, the death of our first child had turned us against living and bringing up a family in London. It was irrational, I know, but how else explain my giving up a career which promised to provide us with a lifestyle that could never be matched in Ireland. The clients thought that I was crazy. The only person glad to see me go was Alf Freedman: look at all the money he was going to save on wages and commission.

But as the day of our departure drew nearer, little nagging doubts began to trouble me. However, it was only when Louise and the baby were in a neighbour's home waiting for the taxi to take us to Heathrow airport, and I stood alone in the empty house surveying the walls bereft of their pictures and plates, looking down at the bare floorboards and letting my eyes rest on the uncurtained windows, that I knew for certain that I had made a terrible mistake. A tear trickled down my cheek.

In Cork our new home of four bedrooms was of modem design and situated in a development called 'Richmond;' but locally referred to as 'Snob's Row.' Interestingly, it was a mere hundred yards from the Provincial House and church of the Society of African Missions on the Blackrock Road.

My main task as a salesman at Guys was to service the already existing clients of my predecessor, Willie Bateman, who was leaving to set-up his own packaging business, and wherever possible to open up new accounts. But I was aware from the start that given the size of Cork and the 'clanish' reputation of its people, to be as successful there as I had been in London was going to be very difficult. My only hope lay with the steady stream of foreign companies establishing themselves in the area.

One of the first of Guy's clients I met was a Mr Musgrave, who, as I was about to leave his office, said: 'I expect we'll see you at the meeting on Wednesday night.' My look of incomprehension made him aware that I didn't have a clue as to what he was referring. But by the time I reached my car, I realised that he being a Protestant assumed that I too subscribed to his faith and was therefore a Freemason, because of my employment at Guys. Had John and Gerry Guy made the same mistake based on the fact that they knew my wife's cousin, Professor John Kinmonth, a well-known London professor of medicine, who they got to know each summer at Baltimore, in West Cork?

Within a couple of weeks, I knew that the tears shed that evening in our empty home in High Barnet presaged the disillusionment which now afflicted me. Instead of dealing with clients who placed orders worth thousands of pounds, I was being asked the price for a couple of hundred letter-headings and envelopes or a couple of balls of string and a few sheets of brown paper. If that were not enough, the weather itself seemed to share my sorrow by raining almost continuously through those first early months. The Cork of those days was very provincial. Since then the city has been transformed and is reckoned to be a better place to live in now than Dublin.

Joan telephoned before the autumn Bank Holiday and 1 invited her, after a brief word with Louise, to come and stay with us over the coming holiday weekend. The three mornings she was with us, I served her tea and toast in bed. But it was the joy on her face as she wheeled Katherine in her pram through the streets of the city, which gave me the greatest pleasure. As her train pulled out of Cork Station on the Monday night, I can still see her standing up in the carriage and blowing a kiss to me.

One interesting fellow sales representative I encountered as we serviced Dunnes Stores for our respective companies was Tomas MacCurtain whose father was murdered by the British during the 'Troubles.' Elected the first Republican Lord Mayor of Cork, he was murdered at home in front of his children by members of the Royal Irish Constabulary at 1.15a.m.on Saturday the 20th March, 1920. It was revealed that a couple of days before his death, he had received a death threat in the form of a letter saying:

"Prepare for death. You are doomed".

An Irish Court, I learned, had passed the death sentence on his son, Tomas, for the murder of a detective. It seems that MacCurtain became exasperated at the continuous surveillance he was being subjected to as a member of the I.R.A., and finally turned on his 'shadow' and shot him dead. Tried and convicted, he was saved from hanging by the intervention of Eamonn de Valera and served a lengthy term in prison instead. Some years later Tomas MacCurtain's only son died while still a teenager.

Louise became pregnant again. Naturally, we both hoped for a brother for Katherine, but when the baby arrived on the 26th of August 1974, it was another girl, whom we named Victoria Louise; soon shortened to Vicky.

We had our first visitors come to stay with the arrival of actress Adrienne Corri's son and daughter, who were on a visit to relatives in nearby Kinsale. When they left they took with them an old print showing the wives of King Henry VIII that I had picked up at a house auction outside Limerick. I wanted their mother to have it valued for me, since I knew she was a friend of Dr Roy Strong at the Tate Gallery. I never saw the item again or heard from Adrienne Corri as to its value.

By the following year, 1975, I was so depressed by life in Cork, that to relieve the boredom I assumed the mantle of Impresario, while continuing my day job at Guys. To launch my new career I brought over the Syd Lawrence Orchestra from England to do a short tour of Ireland, with the final concert taking place in Cork's fine city hall. Sitting alongside me on the night were music-loving Donal Crosbie and his wife Norma. Donal was a member of the family that owned the Cork Examiner newspaper, and had been impressed with the quality of the acts I hoped to of bring to his city. The large audience gave the orchestra a standing ovation.

As Syd Lawrence sailed back to England, international cabaret and recording star Matt Munro began a week's engagement at the Cork Opera House, at a fee of £2,000. I also paid successful lyricist Don Black a 'finders' fee of £500. I was confident that I was going to recoup my investment, given the singers popularity.

With two days to go before opening night, Pat Fleming, the recently appointed manager of the theatre informed me that ticket sales were very poor for Matt Munro. I couldn't understand this: if Matt Munro was not an attraction in Cork, then who was?

When the post of manager of the Opera House had become vacant, Joe Lynch, who had starred in *"Coronation street"* and *"Never Mind the Quality Feel the Width"*, telephoned me from London to tell me that I was on the short list of three for the job. But I hadn't applied for it, I told Joe. It must have been Donal Crosbie, I deduced, who had put my name forward.

The Directors appointed Pat Fleming as the new manager. *"After all, he is one of our own"*, the theatre's secretary was to tell me afterwards, even though he had no experience or contacts in show business.

On the show's opening night, there were barely three hundred people in the audience. I felt very sorry for the singer. The attendance figures see-sawed up and down for the remainder of the week, but never reached anything like the number one would expect for Matt Munro. Those who did attend loved the performance.

Late in August, our Austrian bridesmaid Elfie came to visit us. On the eve of her departure, Louise and I took her to Blackrock castle for dinner and invited Ted O'Connor from Swissco, whose account I had won, despite heavy opposition from Smurfits, and his fiancée, Margaret, to join us. Near the end of the meal, I heard Louise say:

'Margaret, tell Martin what you have just told me.'

What I learned shocked me. It emerged that not only Ted and Margaret failed to obtain tickets for Matt Munro, but also dozens of staff at the hospital where she worked had the same experience. It was then I recalled the set designer telephoning me to say that his grandmother could not get a ticket for the show either. At the time, I thought he was looking for a 'freebie.'

Elfie said that she would be a witness to what she had heard and would happily fly from Rome, at her own expense, to appear in court.

Following my letter to Pat Fleming alleging wrong-doing on the part of his front of house staff, including the young man who sold the ice cream, a letter came to me from Barry M O'Meara, solicitor for the Opera House, denying my allegations and commanding me to refrain from making any further untruthful allegations against the Opera House staff.

Legal proceeding dragged on into the following year. It was a case I could not win; given that some of the city's most prominent business men were on the Opera House Board of Directors, and a few of them, close friends of my employers

In the meantime, I discovered more people who had failed to gain admittance to Matt Munro: a plastic surgeon and friends; the Secretary of the North Infirmary and an employee of the Cork County Council. Obviously, there were hundreds more who had suffered the same fate.

Some years ago, I read the following:

"It can also happen that a theatre owner is guilty of sleight of hand. If he is being offered a production which seems likely to earn big profit and wants to get rid of another which is doing badly, he can instruct his box office manager to sell LESS TICKETS. People who ring up can then be misinformed about what seats are available and business rapidly declines".

THE SET UP by Ronald Hayman.

Although the sabotaging of the Matt Munro Show by the employees of the Cork Opera House was not inspired by anything like the above, it indicates that such a practice exists.

When Cameron Macintosh came to visit me in Cork and I told him the story, he said that he would have sued the Opera House for £10,000.

For my first promotion of 1976, Syd Lawrence returned to play in three new venues: two nights at the RDS in Dublin; Leisureland in Galway and the 1400 seat Savoy in Limerick.

It was on the first night of the Dublin shows that a Garda detective attached himself to me on the pretext that he was a big-band fan, and invited me to visit him at Garda H.Q. in the Phoenix Park. But I began to have suspicions about him when he casually asked:

'What are the Russian doing in Dublin?' Some months previously I had visited the Russian embassy in Dublin.

When we arrived in Limerick, the Savoy's assistant manager assured me that up to 1200 seats had already been sold, thanks to the 'plug' Ireland's favourite broadcaster, Gay Byrne, had given the show; and judging by the long line of people still purchasing tickets, it appeared to me that we were going to have an almost sell-out performance. Bob Marr the orchestra manager agreed with my assessment. During the interval, he tried to persuade me to go and collect my cheque from the manager of the Savoy and that he would accompany me. But I told him to wait until the show was over.

When the manager, Paddy Ryan, handed me the cheque, I could barely contain my anger. Instead of a sum of money equalling an almost full house, the figure on the cheque represented no more than about 900 patrons. Yet, as you will recall, the assistant manager had informed me before the concert that 1200 seats had already been sold. 'I want my unsold tickets,' I demanded, only for Ryan to say that Mrs.O'Mara, a director's wife, had taken them home with her.

After attending Sunday mass at the city's Augustinian church, I walked to the Savoy in the hope that someone other than Ryan would be on duty. A young lad was brushing the foyer and went to tell the assistant manager of my presence. 'You've come for your things, have you? I'll go and get them for you.' While he was away, O'Mara, one of the directors arrived.

'Successful night last night,' he said.

'That remains to be seen,' I replied, and could have cursed myself for my indiscretion. For O'Mara, upon hearing my words immediately walked towards the office. I padded softly behind him and was just in time to hear him tell the assistant manager to leave everything there and let Paddy deal with it.

Accompanied by Syd Lawrence, we arrived at the Savoy at the appointed time of 2p.m., to be told by Ryan that Mrs.O'Mara had my tickets and refused to come in with them. I did manage to get the case against the Savoy into the Cork court, but my solicitor,despite the defendant's non-appearance, allowed them more time to appear. Meanwhile the case against the Cork Operas house was going nowhere; and never would.

On the 21st of June of that year, 1976, a son was born to us to whom we gave the name Martin James. But by the Autumn, Louise and I had decided that there was no future for us in Cork. As a priest, I was totally unprepared for the criminal mind and evil intent on the part of the 'good Catholics' I had encountered in Limerick and Cork. I had shed a few tears upon leaving London, but no such emotion disturbed me as we sold our home and headed for Dublin. Perhaps there was ring of truth, after all in the words of Sean O'Faolain:

"To succeed in Cork you have to have the skin of a rhinoceros, the dissimulation of a crocodile, the agility of a hare, the speed of a hawk. Otherwise the word is 'Get out of Cork and Get out quickly".

Upon returning to London, I managed to find employment with the family printing firm of Richard Madley & Co. situated near the Archway. But the job soon ended when the firm closed down, due, the two elderly owners maintained, to restrictive union practices.

We were living then in a large family room in the Irish club. It used to give me a lot of amusement when people asked me where we lived to tell them: *"Eaton square"*. Fortunately, through my having recently become a member of the Catenians, I met Bill Coffey, the Managing Director of W. H. Smith's printing subsidiary at Huntington, who offered me a job on the strength of the only two accounts I had at the time, Trader Vies and Her Majesty's Stationery Office on Holborn Viaduct.

The Catenians is an organisation of Catholic men, akin to the Masons but without their ritual or influence. The word, Catenian, comes from the Latin word for 'chain:' hence, each branch is called a 'circle.' The Belgravia Circle, to which I now belonged, met once a month in the Irish Club. Its members came from a wide range of professions and occupations, including a high-ranking officer based at Scotland Yard, the producer of a popular television crime series on ITV, Inspector Morse, and a former bodyguard of Sir Winston Churchill.

I was finding it very difficult to open new accounts. Fortunately, I soon established a good relationship with some of the buyers at Her Majesty's Stationery Office and was able to obtain a steady enough stream of tenders and actual work to keep Bill Coffey happy. In addition Jackie Laugenie, at Trader Vies, wanted once again to reprint all his menus, and was quite happy to bear the extra cost involved by taking the job away from my former employers at Donbro.

Amongst the buyers at HMSO was a cheerful cockney-type who did not take his job too seriously: for him it meant the opportunity to have a good time at the expense of his many suppliers. Once I had won his confidence, he gave me every opportunity to win contracts. Like Terry Walker at Benton and Bowles, he too began to give me prices to fill in on certain tender forms so that a printer of his choice would come in with a slightly lower figure and thereby win the contract: in most cases this usually meant the company of which his mistress was a director.

In an attempt to increase my turnover, I hosted a lunch at the Press Club and invited Henry Cooper as the guest of honour. Naturally, buyers were eager to attend and meet the popular boxer. I gave Henry a book on golf by Jack Nicholas; the Press Club made him a Life Member and presented him with the club tie.

A short time after the event, I thought of all the fund-raising for convents and churches that Henry had done over the years, since being received into the Church, and yet up to then had never received any formal recognition for it all. I decided that it was about time something was done to remedy the situation. I therefore wrote a short note to Cardinal Hume, Archbishop of Westminster, pointing out this error on the part of the Church. A year later, Louise and I stood behind the Cooper family in their local Hendon church to witness the cardinal conferring Henry with the Knighthood of St.Gregory.

A few weeks after the new pope, John Paul2 assumed office; I suggested to Bill Coffey that the Hambledon Press ought to publish a calendar with colour photographs of the new Pope. He thought it such a good idea that he and his wife promptly flew to Rome to select photos from the files of Arturo Mori, the Vatican photographer.

When the calendar duly appeared, John Cowling, now working at W. H. Smith, but whom I knew from his days at Benton and Bowles, told me that Bill Coffey was giving everyone at head office the impression that the calendar was his idea. 'But I knew that you were the one behind it,' John told me.

Meanwhile, Louise had obtained a client for beauty treatments: a Riva Gordon, who lived in Belsize Park. She sold pianos, and I recalled seeing her witty adverts in the Sunday Times. Any evening that my wife went to her home, the dear lady would order me a delicious curry from her favourite local restaurant, and send it by taxi all the way down to the Irish Club in Eaton Square.

Riva had a distressing weight problem and had a terrible fear of spiders. Whenever she spotted one in the flat, she would promptly telephone the nearby police station and summon a constable to come to her aid.

When the Irish Club was sold, and we had to seek alternative accommodation, it was Riva who harangued her own landlord into giving us a flat in Hampstead Hill Gardens, opposite the Royal Free Hospital. We were saddened and shocked a few years later to learn from her husband, Alec, that she had taken her own life in the renowned Savoy hotel.

The flat that we now called home was at the top of a big house. Its only furnishings were a couple of beds, basic kitchen equipment a table and a few dilapidated chairs. But despite the lack of the homely comforts that our own furnishings, still stored in Harrods Repository, would have provided, we were very happy during the time we lived there until we found a home of our own.

Later that year of 1979, my entrepreneurial spirit surfaced once more, when it was announced that the Pope was going to visit Ireland in September. Again, I approached, Bill Coffey and suggested that Hambledon Press produce a colour magazine to commemorate what was destined to be a hugely emotional event for the Irish people, at home and abroad. The little man rejected the idea on the grounds that there would be a lot of smart men in Dublin with the same idea. Truly excited by the enormous commercial potential of the forthcoming event, I was determined not to abandon my idea, and immediately began looking around for a 'backer.' Eventually, I stumbled upon Pat Healy from Sligo town, who owned a small pre-print company in Hardwick Street, a mere hundred yards from the church in Amwell Street. When I explained what I intended to do about the Pope's visit to Ireland, his response was immediate: 'Can I get a piece of the action?' He then sent me to a Ken Ward, a 'print-farmer' with an office in St. Cross Street, off Hatton Garden. He was a 'spivy' looking guy. But his enthusiasm for the project dispelled any initial misgivings I had of doing business with him.

But looking back on the events of that time, I regret that I had not the courage to seek a small loan from the Bank of Ireland in Seven Sisters Road where I had my account, and handle the project myself. The fact that the manager and his entire family were travelling over to Dublin for the Papal visit ought to have encouraged me.

Shakespeare's words in Julius Caesar are a chilling reminder of where I went wrong:

"There is a tide in the affairs of men, which, taken at the flood, leads on to fortune. Omitted, all the voyage of their life is bound in shallows and in miseries."

When I left Ken Ward's office, we had agreed that Ken Ward Associates would act as the publisher and financial backer for the publication. My task would be to organise the photography, edit the material and write the captions. My share of any profit was agreed at 40%. To provide the photographs I obtained the services of Anwar Hussein, who specialised in photographing members of the Royal family, and Mike McEwan of the Daily Express. What I didn't realise at the time was that Mike was a fashion photographer and not used to the hurly-burly of life as a photo-journalist. In the end, however, he was to provide me with one of the best photographs of the papal visit: a smiling Pope John Paul pointing to the sun, which had just then broken through the mist over Galway Bay. I had tried to employ award-winning Fleet Street photographer, Tim Graham, as well, but another publisher had already booked him for its weekly magazine. To co-ordinate everything in Ireland, I chose Leo Simmons, a fellow Catenian, who worked for the Daily Express.

Watching the amazing scenes on television of over a million people assembled in Dublin's Phoenix Park, I knew that my instincts had been justified: everyone in that enormous crowd would want a souvenir of the day that they saw their Pope: even if they appeared only as a dot on the extreme edge of the double page photograph I used. When asked by Ken Ward what I thought the initial print-run ought to be, I suggested a figure of 75,000

315

would be a realistic number with which to start. The printer Ward chose was ABC printer of Ditchling Common, Sussex.

I had already approached the head of News Buying at W. H. Smith to ensure that we would have their support when it came to placing our publication in the shops. One of the staff then provided me with the names of three distributors. The first one I approached was Punch. But a well-spoken executive was dismissive of the whole idea. 'How many copies of the Universe and Catholic herald are sold each week? he asked. I gave him the figures. 'Well, there you are then,' was his reply. I approached SM Distribution in Brixton, who's Managing Director, Jim Bums, enthusiastically agreed to handle the magazine in the United Kingdom and Ireland.

To write an introduction to 'Ireland's Historic Visitor,' I approached Patrick O'Donovan of the Observer and Catholic Herald, who readily agreed to do the job for the fee offered him of 200 pounds.

Within a week of 'Ireland's Historic Visitor' going on sale, we printed a further 50,000 copies, such was the demand from the retail trade in Ireland and mainland Britain. W. H. Smith's Kilburn branch for example sold close on 1,000 copies from an allocation of the same number. In addition, each day's post to Ward Associates brought further orders from churches and individuals scattered the length and breadth of the country, and even occasionally from overseas, who were unable to purchase locally because all copies were sold out.

Such was the success of 'Ireland's Historic Visitor' that Ward arranged for me to telephone a prominent Dublin Accountant, John Wood. Standing by Wood's side in Dublin during that call, was a man by the name of Sean Quinlan. He, Wood said, was very experienced in selling into the religious market in Ireland and the USA. It was then arranged that Ken Ward would fly to Dublin two days later to discuss ways of increasing the sales of the magazine, particularly in the USA. I was the one they wanted to travel over to Dublin, but I was reluctant to leave Louise and the children on their own, a grave mistake, as events were to prove. A few days later Quinlan departed for the USA and Pat Healy went missing.

As time went by, I continued to visit Ward's office on a daily basis and noticed that he was becoming more and more distant, uncommunicative and very tense, as he smoked one cigarette after another, like a man waiting for something terrible to happen to him. I asked him casually one day how Quinlan had got on in the U.S.A. 'How would I know, he wouldn't be in touch with me,' he answered brusquely. That was the moment I knew that something underhand was happening in connection with my publication. But finding evidence was going to be the problem. It was then I regretted my decision not to travel to Dublin.

I left W. H. Smith's Hambledon Press under pressure from Bill Coffey and found a job with a small printing company in Hardwick Street, four or five doors away from where Pat Healy had his office. It was a strange feeling to park my car each morning within yards of SS. Peter and Paul's. Interestingly, the van drivers of the delivery company that did work for Ward used the office below mine for their breaks between jobs.

Shortly before Christmas, Ken Ward handed me the sales figures for the publication. They were well below what I expected, and there was no mention of sales in America. I questioned the figures validity, given that we had put well over 130,000 copies into the market, and that all the indications were that 'Ireland's Historic Visitor' had been a publishing triumph. He lit another cigarette and glanced down at his desk. Just then, the telephone rang. As Ward turned slightly away from me to take the call, I happened to glance down at the comer of the desk near me and saw a letter-heading with the name 'Bahamas Patent Tokens' on it. I immediately realised that this could well be an offshore company through which my 'partners' were conducting clandestine sales of their own, or an 'Off-the-Shelf Company,' company they had set up to handle such profits, especially those from the USA. When Ward glanced over his shoulder and saw on what my eyes were focused, he quickly grabbed the letterhead and turned it upside down, then resumed his conversation. Before leaving, Ward gave me a check for £2,000. He urged me to accept the full amount of £8,000 owed to me as my share of the profits, but I politely refused, because I knew that a greater sum of money was owed and more importantly, I sensed that he was trying to get rid of me. I needed an excuse to continue calling at that office.

Visiting Ward again about a week before Christmas, I met Jim Bums, the Managing Director of S.M. Distribution. I quickly made him aware that 'Ireland's Historic Visitor' was my brainchild.

'You must come to our Christmas party. I'll leave two tickets for you with Ken,' the genial Scotsman said. Ken Ward looked glum and lit another cigarette.

When I called to the office on St. Cross Street on the day of the S.M. party to collect the tickets, only young Andrew Cowan, Ward's assistant was there. Ward had gone home early, and there were no tickets for me. Before I left, Andrew told me that his boss had bought 22 presents for his wife.

On a Friday evening early in January of 1980, I got home early and made a telephone call to the Stoke Newington Office of Boldleigh Transport Ltd., the delivery company Ward used, and was immediately put through to Mr Elms, the Managing Director. Using a fictitious name, I said that we were sporting publishers and wished to send a large consignment of magazines to Ireland. Would he be interested in handling the delivery, I wanted to know.

'Yes,' was Elms immediate response. 'No problem. We would take care of all the paper work for you. As a matter of fact, in December we took over to Ireland 100,000 copies of a magazine on the Pope; and they want more, they can't get enough of them,' he added.

I tried to remain calm as I digested this startling piece of information. 'That must have been a big load,' I suggested.

'It was. We had to do it in runs of 25,000 a time. By the way, who gave you our name?'

'Oh, I only work here. My boss gave me your number and told me to contact you,' I told Elms, and quickly hung up. 'Got them!' I exclaimed excitedly to Louise. About an hour later the telephone rang. I picked up the receiver and a well-spoken woman asked if that were a certain number. I told her that she had the wrong number. As I replaced the receiver, my sixth-sense warned me that Ward and Healy knew about my earlier telephone call to Boldleigh Transport. Someone, probably Ken Ward, had been alerted and was listening on an extension line to identify my voice as the same person who had been told about the huge, undisclosed delivery of 'Ireland's Historic Visitor' to Dublin.

The following Monday morning I climbed the stairs to Healy's office and was not surprised to find Ward and Healy having a serious conversation. I challenged them to deny that they were cheating me out of my contractual share of all profits from the sale of 'Ireland's Historic Visitor.'

'You've been playing detective, Martin,' Ward said sneeringly.

'I'll do more than that, I'll bring in the Fraud Squad' I retorted angrily.

With that, Healy leaped to his feet, grabbed his briefcase and sped to the door of his office. In another second he would have disappeared but for the shout from Ward. 'Calm down, Pat. Come back.'

I argued with both men for about another five minutes until Ward said: 'Well, we did initiate it, Martin,' meaning that it was they in concert with, the man Quinlan, who had increased the sales of our publication in Ireland and the U.S.A. Therefore, by their reasoning, I had no right to a share in the substantial profits these sales had generated. Recognising that it would be futile to argue any longer, I left the office with one final comment: 'I'm not finished with you yet.'

I soon realised that I had been too hasty in confronting my 'partners.' I ought to have been more astute and built up a solid base of evidence against them before any confrontation. Within a short space of time I noticed that Ward and Healy had each removed their company's nameplates from outside their street doors.

Shortly afterwards, I had a stroke of luck when one of Boldleigh's drivers walked past me as I sat in a client's reception, close to Smithfield Market. I rose up and quickly and followed him out into the street.

'Excuse me, does your company do deliveries to Ireland?' I said to the driver, as he was about to enter his vehicle. He eyed me suspiciously for a second or two.

'Yes, we do. We took over a 100,000 copies of a picture book on the pope a few weeks ago.'

'Who would I speak to at your company about a delivery to Ireland?' I wanted to know.

The man reached into the van and handed me headed notepaper, pointing to the name, Elms, listed as a director. 'Speak to him.'

Within a few days of that chance meeting, all Boldleigh's drivers ceased using the office on the floor below where I worked. While deciding on my next move, I was sacked.

At that month's Catenian meeting, I met Kevin Skerritt, a big, heavily-built Irishman and a solicitor, with an office in Argyle House, opposite St. Pancras Station. With him was his younger brother, Tony, who preferred to be called Anthony, and who boasted after a few glasses of wine that he banked at Coutts.

As the evening progressed, I unburdened myself to the solicitor of the problem with Ward and Healy. Before we parted company, we had fixed a meeting for the following day at which, not only did Skerritt agree to pursue my 'partners' for my share of the profits, but to my astonishment suggested that we form a publishing company of which I would be the Managing Director, and which he would fund with 30,000 pounds. I would receive a weekly salary and be given a company car.

When I reached home that night and told the exciting news to Louise, she said, 'Well, you won't have to worry now; he's a solicitor' While I was considering what my first publication was going to be, it was announced that the Pope would visit Paris in June. With the experience of having successfully covered his Irish visit, I immediately started preparations to produce something similar to 'Ireland's Historic Visitor' for the French market.

The two Skerritt's also ran a sub-contracting plastering business, taking on work for big construction companies in the London area. From bits of whispered conversations I overhead between them, I deduced that they were having problems with their suppliers because of outstanding debts. The quantity surveyor who worked for them was also owed a substantial amount of back pay.

When we arrived in Paris to await the Pope's arrival, Anwar Hussein was again with us, but this time so also was Tim Graham, who was slowly gaining prominence as specialising in photographs of the Royal Family; Mike Panchaud, a designer with Penthouse Magazine completed the team.

By this time, I began to notice that the Skerritts had a peculiar habit of bestowing nicknames on everyone with whom they came in contact. For example, June, the solicitor's secretary, was 'County.' I was 'Sports Car,' and a banker friend of mine, Michael Woods, was 'Wooden Top.' I learned later from an investigative reporter with the Sunday Times that this habit was a common trait amongst members of the criminal fraternity.

When 'La Visite Memorable' went on sale, the 160,000 copies were quickly sold out. The Polish Pallottine Fathers in Paris snapped up the last remaining 2,000 copies. What a pity I was not able to persuade N.N.M.P, Hachette's distribution subsidiary, to take at least another 100,000 copies.

Apart from a few pages in Paris Match, not one French company, like their counterparts in the UK and Ireland at the time of the Pope's Irish visit, had seen the commercial potential in his visit.

'La Visite Memorable' lived up to my expectations, both in sales and quality. But to my amazement, my name as editor was not listed amongst the credits. Instead, I stared unbelievingly at the name of D. Reichenback, the married name of Skerritt's cousin, Betty Skerritt, who lived at Compiegne. When I challenged Skerritt about this irregularity, his answer was: 'We're all editors.'

He maintained a similar cavalier attitude regarding the profits from France. Eventually he handed me enough francs to pay Anwar Hussein and Tim Graham, and suggested that I change the French currency at my own bank. The two photographers accompanied me to the Bank of Ireland, in Seven Sisters Road, and waited outside in one of their BMWs, I think it was Anwar's, until I came out and paid them in sterling.

Through a London contact I arranged an appointment with a publisher in Lourdes and promptly made arrangements to fly down to the pilgrimage town within a couple of days. I then telephoned Betty Skerritt in Compiegne, to see if she could put me up for the night in order for me to catch an early flight from Paris to Lourdes.

I took Betty Skerritt out to dinner in a Chinese restaurant near her home. During the meal, she informed me that she and her husband were separating. So that was why he was absent, I thought. Afterwards as we walked home, she linked her arm firmly in mine and kissed me.

While I was preparing to undress for bed, Betty walked in unannounced and mumbled something about fixing the pillows, as she leaned over the bed. They looked all right to me. Again, as in so many other instances where I knew that women were looking to have a sexual encounter with me, I failed to meet their expectations.

Two women from the Paris printers arrived in the office looking for their money. Skerritt made certain that he was absent when they came. I, with some embarrassment, explained that the solicitor controlled the company money and assured them that I would do my best to have payment made as soon as possible. I was by then a very worried man. It was obvious that my partner was working to his own agenda, whose outcome I hardly dared to contemplate.

At the first opportunity, I entered the solicitor's office and after a brief search through his files, found the Banner Publishing folder. Words cannot convey the shock I felt when, upon scanning the contract between the Parisian distributor NNMP and Banner Publishing; I saw that the signature on the company's behalf was that of Betty Skerritt. I now knew why the solicitor had left me in the Range Rover outside the office of NNMP, while he went inside with his cousin. Naively, I thought her presence was to continue the fiction that he could not speak French. Without any delay I copied the document and retreated to my own office and began gathering the various papers relating to the business in France and, as an afterthought, my car's logbook.

Going through the files I also learned that Anthony Skerritt owed a substantial sum of money to American Express: which explained why he tended to keep such a low profile. I copied the address of the law firm acting for American Express and immediately wrote to them telling them where they could find Tony Skerritt, especially on a Friday morning, and also giving them the vehicle registration number of the brothers' Range Rover and where it was usually parked.

The day after my discovery of Betty Skerritt's involvement in the affairs of Banner Publishing, the solicitor appeared in the doorway of my office and sternly announced that he wanted the office for someone else, and that I could wind up everything relating to our company from home.

When I left Argyle House that evening for the last time, I had with me every scrap of paper that I thought would be useful with which to 'hang' this most corrupt of men. The next day, I wrote to the Law Society and made a personal call at the office of the Fraud Squad attached to Holborn Police Station. The detective who interviewed me did not appear too interested in what I was telling him about Skerritt, until I mentioned that he was a practising solicitor. He fixed an appointment for me to return the following day for a meeting with an inspector. The Law Society, I soon discovered, had moved swiftly after receiving my letter, and had taken over Skerritt's law practice.

When I met with Inspector Wooding of the Fraud Squad, I had all the papers with me that I had removed from the solicitor's files. Somehow the evil man had learned that I had them, for, despite the pressure he was under, he had the audacity to write to me demanding that I return all the documents that I had taken from his office.

Out of a job, I had no option but to sign on at the Mill Hill unemployment exchange in Bun's Lane, while Louise managed eventually to obtain some part-time work in a local nursing home. Our combined income just about managed to cover the ordinary household bills, but our mortgage repayments became more and more infrequent, even with help from Social Welfare towards the interest. At one stage, I was compelled to seek assistance from the local branch of the St. Vincent de Paul Society, which most kindly gave us a grant of 130 pounds.

One Sunday afternoon in September, as Louise, the children and I were about to return home from the local park, I suddenly suggested that we drive out to Bushey, where Skerritt lived, just to see what, if anything , was happening. As we drove past his home, I saw him loading cases into a car with a French registration.

I drove along to the roundabout at the end of the road and turned back the way I had come, and as I approached Skerritt's house, the French car drove out of the driveway and turned right. I expected the vehicle in front of me to head towards London and one of the channel ports. Instead it veered off to the left in an easterly direction. He must have recognised my car, I thought, and was intent on confusing me as to his ultimate destination. I called out the car's registration to Louise, who wrote it down on the back of her hand.

Immediately upon arriving home, I telephoned Scotland Yard and told a duty sergeant that Skerritt was under investigation for fraud and that I suspected he was fleeing the country and gave him Inspector Wooding's name. A few days later, 1 had a meeting with the Inspector who told me that the solicitor had been spotted boarding a ferry at Harwich, but that there were insufficient grounds at the time to detain him. At the same meeting, he also informed me that he had questioned Tim Graham and Anwar Hussein regarding the payment I made to them after changing the French money Skerritt gave me. To my astonishment, Inspector Wooding said that both photographers had denied any such transaction took place. 'Why do you think they said that?' he wanted to know. I could offer no explanation.

'Perhaps it has something to do with their income tax.' he suggested quietly.

Around this time, the solicitor, who travelled the world on behalf of Mars, and who sold Skerritt my car, telephoned to ask about the car and its logbook. I told him that both were in my possession. He then told me that Skerritt had not paid him the purchase price of 2,500 pounds for the Citroen. 'He would charm the birds off a bush,' were his parting words.

At the next and last meeting with Inspector Wooding, I showed him my bank statement clearly indicating the date and the sum of francs lodged in the account and withdrawn in sterling at the same time and on the same day. I was most disappointed in Tim Graham, whom I had always thought to be a decent young man. Anwar I distrusted ever since he lied to me regarding his expenses for having brought his car over to France.

Confident that I could claim compensation for Skerritt's malpractice in allowing me to sign a contract when the company was not yet incorporated, I approached the Law Society. My case, as I saw it, was clear and simple. But after the initial meeting at the Society's Chancery Lane headquarters and a number of letters between us, the Society refused to consider any compensation on the grounds that Skerritt was acting at the time as a director of Banner Publishing. I knew that this decision was logically wrong. Surely, I reasoned, Skerritt's presence at the signing of a contract was not only as a director but also more importantly, as the legal advisor to the publishing company; even a bank manager agreed with this analysis.

If only the Law Society had lived up to its moral and legal obligation, what heartache and suffering my family would have escaped since then.

In the midst of all this turmoil, I was still continuing with my efforts to build up a case against Ward and Healy. One move I took was to telephone a Jesuit priest based in Galway, a cousin of a fellow

Catenian. The priest, I was told, was a close friend of Monsignor Horan at Knock Shrine, County Mayo, which I knew had to have received a big delivery of 'Ireland's Historic Visitor,' but of which there was no mention in the sales figures Ward provided.

The Jesuit was most friendly and co-operative and told me, he had spent a convivial few hours with the Monsignor the previous evening. He asked for my phone number and promised that I would hear from him within a few days.

When he phoned, it was to tell me that Monsignor Horan denied having any knowledge of 'Ireland's Historic Visitor' being sold at the shrine. 'I don't think he was telling the truth. He didn't want to get involved,' the Jesuit commented.

A few months later, a private detective I employed was able to send me two copies of my magazine she had purchased at Knock Shrine. If that were not enough proof that Monsignor Horan lied to his priest friend, the Monsignor himself was to tell me a couple of years later that nothing was bought for the bookshop at the shrine without his approval, as he ushered me out of the Presbytery in Knock, saying *"God bless you"*, as he door closed behind me. A few years later he died while on a pilgrimage to Lourdes.

Occasionally, as a form of diversion from my troubles, I began paying regular visits to the home of freinds, who now had three children as a result of their having gone on a number of sun-shine holidays.

As it was usually lunchtime when I called, my freind's wife and I would share a few sandwiches and a glass of wine during the hour I spent there. She was very attractive and offered her lips to me upon my arrival and departure. She was good company and even sexually more appealing. On two different occasions when we were alone in the house, she brought me upstairs on the pretext of showing how untidy the au pair kept her room. On the second such visit, she closed the bedroom behind us and stood close to me smiling invitingly.

On one such visit she informed me that one of my Pallottine colleagues was a source of scandal when he attended their parties. The priest in question would stand alongside one of the women present and furtively pull down the zip or undo the fasteners on the back of her dress, then place his hand on her bare flesh. I could not believe what I was hearing. He was also drinking heavily, even before saying mass in the morning.

Another lady friend I visited less frequently was Kay Gannon. Sean and she now lived in Wembley where, on my first visit to the house, I found Kay sunbathing in the garden wearing shorts and a barely adequate top. The size of her breasts surprised me: fully clothed they had never attracted my attention.

After we had a cool drink indoors, she invited me upstairs to see the rest of the house. Upon entering the main bedroom, I was surprised to hear a sharp intake of breath as she closed the door behind us. I stood in the middle of the floor admiring the room and its furnishings and doing my best to avert my eyes from Kay's well-proportioned figure, as she pointed out various items in the room, many of them bought in Harrods, she boasted. Eventually, she sat down on the bed. The colouring in her face was changing to a soft shade of pink and her features were softening so that she began to look ten years younger. I was suddenly startled to hear her say: 'Turn your back, Martin, the hook of my top is broken.' I was even more startled to hear my own voice tell her that I would fix it, as I walked towards the bed.

That same evening when I met a mysterious Irishman at a charity auction at Bonham's, I also came in contact with a wealthy, elderly widow who lived near Sloane Square. I called on her a couple of times, and felt that she was testing me when she kept asking me if I had any knowledge of handling a person's finances. On the occasion of my last visit to her, she hinted that she was willing to pay me to have sex with her. It was a tempting offer, given the seriousness of my financial position; and there was always the chance as well that she would pass me around her circle of rich, lonely, women friends. It was tempting, but once again, the years of indoctrination and priesthood proved too strong a bulwark to overcome; even when, on one occasion, she opened the door to me wearing only a slip through which the outline of her body was clearly visible.

On another occasion, when I visited my freind's wife, she told me how the same Pallottine priest, already mentioned, had tried to rape a young Irish woman who was staying the night in the Provincial House in Golders Green, where her sister, a Pallottine nun, looked after the domestic arrangements for the resident priests.

Sometime during the night, the young visitor woke up to find the priest climbing into her bed. Barely awake, she didn't know what to do as he whispered for her to relax. As he pulled up her nightdress and forced her legs apart the woman could not believe this was happening to her. Fortunately, as he tried to enter her, he was unable to sustain an erection, and breathlessly slid off her and began to cry. The poor woman lay there frightened and simultaneously shocked at the priest's conduct. Eventually, her assailant slid out of the room as silently as he had entered. When his victim had recovered her composure she went immediately to her sister's room and told her what had just taken place.

In the early morning, the two women left the house and went to stay in another part of London. The nun left the Order the same day. The Priest, my informant told me, always tried to persuade her to go upstairs whenever he came to her home.

Our only income by then was still my unemployment benefit and the few pounds Louise earned. We had fallen behind with the payments for the children's education at St. Anthony's; also despite receiving help from Social Security to pay the mortgage where arrears there too were rapidly spiralling out of control.

On a sunny morning in September, I stood with a tearful Louise and our three small bewildered children and watched the locks being changed on our front door. At the moment I had no idea where we were going to sleep that night. The only course of action open to me was to approach the parish priest and ask him if we might stay the night at Damascus House, run by his fellow Vincentians on the Ridgeway.

Seated across the table from the red-haired priest, pouring out my troubles to him, I could see a, look of annoyance appear on his face when I made my request; and it was only with the greatest reluctance that he left the room to make the phone call. When he returned he informed me that we could stay for one night only. I thanked the man and made my way towards the door. As he was closing the door behind me, I heard him repeat: 'Remember, it's for one night only.'

This was a man, the son of the local doctor in Easkey, where my uncle Willie lived and, as you will recall, from where my father fled in 1923. The priest would have known about me when I was at college. I certainly knew of him.

After a three day stay at Damascus House, where the nuns treated us with Christian charity, aunt Nellie's money arrived to enable us to travel to Enniscrone.

As I drove along the M6 towards Liverpool, I reflected on the strangeness of life. Here I was with a wife and three children returning to the very place where my Odyssey began thirty seven years ago, when a young girl pushed me into the waters of Killala Bay. What the future held for us I could not tell, but at least we would have a roof over our heads and be amongst family. *"The world will teach you"*, I recalled again my aunt telling me on many occasions. It certainly had, and with a vengeance, I thought grimly,as we reached the outskirts of Liverpool, minutes away now from the ferry which would take us across the sea to Ireland, away from England and all our troubles.

Now that my story is ended...
I can say with Dickens's David Copperfield:

"Whither I shall turn out to be the hero of my own life,
or whether that station will be held by anybody else,
these pages must show".

THE END

& LIFE CONTINUES

Myaunt had the warmest of welcomes for us upon our arrival; she was especially thrilled to meet the children for the first time. The exciting news she had for me was that Joan too had returned to Ballina after the death of her father, in order to care for her mother, and was now working in the Unemployment office, a hundred yards down Bohernasup, where they now lived.

Over the next few days, I was to learn that many people had been approaching aunt Nellie in an attempt to have her sell a site on her land for a son or daughter to build a house; the purpose being to give them a presence alongside her as she grew older. 'But now that I have you here, that will stop them,' she said.

There was an indoor toilet in the house now, and the thatch had been removed and replaced by a galvanised roof. But there was still no bath or shower; a fact that decided me, three weeks later, to move the family into Ballina, where we rented a house on a small estate at the Quay. I had still the car from London, so the distance of two miles from the town was no obstacle.

I signed on at the Unemployment office, and saw Joan working behind a desk, but it would be a few days later before we met face to face. But prior to that, I had called at her home, only to receive a very frosty welcome from her mother. I believe we were to exchange barely ten words between that moment and her death. I helped carry her coffin to the graveside.

The arrival of an American and Japanese factory in the area had transformed Ballina. There were now a number of housing estates, on the outskirts of the town. New shops had been opened and motor cars filled the streets. However, I thought the heart had gone out of the town with the removal of the bus office from Pearse Street to a site near the railway station.

Another change was the ending of the cattle fairs in the Market Place and outside the cathedral. The selling of cattle now took place in the Mart on the Crossmolina road.

But the changes had extended to the countryside as well, where one saw evidence of the huge sums of money that had come from Brussels in the form of subsidies and grants to farmers. New houses had replaced the thatched cottage; hay barns were very much in evidence, and a car and tractor stood in the concreted farmyard. No horse or donkey was to be seen. Most fields were in grass; so there would be no threshing machine making the rounds of the farms come November. Many small farmers were now working in one of the factories, and therefore had no time for sowing and harvesting crops: most of them, however, did manage to cut and save the turf.

But the most amazing change I found was that in the sexual mores of the women. The wife of a local businessman invited me to spend a weekend with her at a hotel where she was attending a convention; a neighbour told me she was alone for lunch that day, and a woman I had known since my youth entered the bedroom in her home where I was staying overnight,as I was beginning to undress. She came forward and kissed me twice in quick succession,waited a few seconds and then left the room. Her husband was asleep downstairs.

At first, the novelty of living in Ballina hid my growing anxiety of how I was going to support my family, when the little capital I had ran out. Our situation eased, when Louise opened a beauty salon in a room given to her by the landlord, on condition that she supervised his keep-fit classes.

Her first client was the sister-in-law of the future President of Ireland, Mary Robinson. When the business grew too large for the small room, Louise moved to larger premises above an accountancy practice. She soon was being invited by Ladies' Groups around the county to give talks to them on the subject of skincare with the emphasis, naturally, on using Elizabeth Arden creams to achieve the best results.

I was an embarrassment to the local clergy, who mostly barely acknowledged me whenever we met. On one occasion at a social event in the parish centre, I introduced my self to the bishop. Upon hearing my name he snorted and turned his back on me. The only one of the priests who had any time for me was Peter O'Brien. He told me that, as a student at Maynooth, he used to cycle over to Enniscrone from his home in Culleens, to watch me play for Enniscrone United. On one occasion, he called to the house at the Quay and handed me £40 of his own money.

In 1999, I made contact with a Cathal Magee in Dublin with whom I proposed that we publish a pre-visit magazine of the forthcoming visit of Pope John Paul 2 to the U.S.A. We signed an agreement. He was the brother of the now disgraced John Magee, bishop of Cloyne in Co.Cork, and secretary to three popes. *"I'll get you out of that estate"*, he told us on more than one occasion.

From an office belonging to Walter Annenberg, billionaire publisher and former U.S.A. Ambassador to the Court of St.James's, Cahal telephoned me to say that he would have to restrict my share of the profits to £90,000. No problem, I told him.

When he returned to Ireland, he bought his wife a new car and the bishop took delivery of a Ford Scorpio costing £24,000. It was delivered to him at the Silver Spring's Hotel in Cork. There was no money for Martin Gordon and we continued to live on the estate.

When my wife, Louise, challenged the bishop about his purchase of the car, he told her that the priests of the diocese had bought it for him. He lied to Thomas Finnegan, the Bishop of Killala, who had telephoned him on my behalf, that he had no imput into the American magazine.

The years passed quickly, with us just about managing to survive. The old, dilapidated school at the Quay closed and was replaced by a newly-built one on Cregg's road, almost on our doorstep. I produced a small booklet commemorating the event, and got in touch with my friend in the Vatican, Archbishop Jacque Martin, Head of the Papal Household, requesting a Papal blessing for the new school. But I was not invited to the grand lunch at the Downhill Hotel.

I became involved with Ballina Town Football club, eventually becoming its Secretary and P.R.O., and soon had a match report appearing in the Star newspaper on a Tuesday. Louise joined the cathedral choir and the local choral group, The Moy Singers, to both of whom she gave 20 years of devoted service. When she left Ballina for Cork, the cathedral choir presented her with a card signed by all the members and £100.

When the car eventually gave up on me, it was time to move into Ballina, where we found a house on Lord Edward Street, but on the 'wrong side of the tracks' as our lovely neighbour, the late Kevin Loftus said to me jokingly on one occasion. In addition, we had been running into arrears with the rent. The landlord cut off the water, and we had to rely on the goodness of our next door neighbours, the Fahy, family to keep us supplied with sufficient water to wash and cook meals.

The new house was very draughty and the fireplace in the living-room did not work. But it suited us fine, now that the girls were attending secondary school at Gortnor Abbey; taking the special bus each morning for the nine miles journey. They were to spend five happy years there. The Jesus and Mary nuns, of course, knew whose daughters they were.

Approaching each Christmas Eve, the Reverend Mother and another nun would pull up outside the house in their car and deliver a large box of groceries.

January and February became difficult months for us, as the bills for fuel and electricity were very heavy. It was then that I had to take to the road, hitch-hiking to knock on priest's doors seeking help. Some refused, others gave a small sum of money grudgingly. The Guardian of the Franciscan church in Galway spoke very kindly to me and gave me £170. The Dominican Prior, on the other hand, sat stony-faced and silent as I told my sad story. As I reached the door, I turned around and said: 'May God forgive you, father.'

The bishop in Sligo fed me a good meal and I left with a cheque for £200; but only after he had told me that we were not meant to be happy: the "we" being priests. I found that very puzzling. Then I was introduced to a wonderful nun who came to our rescue on two occasions.

One Monday morning, the only food in the house was a half-loaf of bread, and the only money seventy four pence. I climbed the hill to the convent of Mercy and told a nun my sad story, mentioning at the same time, the name of the nun in the same Order. She gave me a ten pound note. Later that evening, a letter was pushed through the letterbox, which, upon reading, I discovered to contain the telephone number of the nun in county Kildare, whose name I had mentioned to the nun that morning. I was to telephone her immediately. I did so from the phone box in the Market square. Two days later, a cheque arrived for £500. Over the years, The Pallottine Fathers gave me just over £500 in two payments. On giving me the second payment, the Provincial Bursar said: *"Haven't we given you £250 already?"*

Aunt Nellie made her will out in my favour. But a few years later she sold the farm to Peter O'Neill. I don't know how much he paid her for the land, but I am certain that it was no more than half its value: given the number of potential building sites that were there. Of course, Mrs.

O'Neill in particular was constantly calling on her. She died last year. We made our last house move to Bohernasup; but by then Joan and her mother had both died, and I began to suffer ill-health. A series of operations starting with circumcision, then a heart attack, double break of an ankle and culminating in my being diagnosed with Myasthenia Gravis. Fortunately, a year later, while on a visit to daughter Katherine and son Martin in Cork, I met Dr.Hugh Harrington, a neurologist at the Mercy Hospital, who saved my life a week later, with just twenty four hours to spare, after a horrendous journey in Katherine's car from Ballina. A few days earlier, a lady Neurologist in Galway had given me a pill and told me to come back in a month. 'But even then' she said, 'I cannot promise you a bed.' All of that decided me that we had to move to Cork; and three months later did just that.

A final word: in my last three years in Ballina I joined the local Masonic Lodge, through being friends with two of its members. I then transferred to one of the eight Cork Lodges, where I met Graphic Designer Graham Clarke. If I had not been a Mason, you would not now be reading this book. *"God writes straight with Crooked Lines."*

Since our arrival in Cork, Louse has joined the Carrigaline Singers and I have my Masonic Lodge to keep me busy. I especially like the Friday coffee mornings in our Tuckey Street headquarters, where the 'craic' is great and one catches up on all the gossip. In Freemasonry, I have met with more companionship and friendliness than I ever met with in the priesthood.

I celebrated my 80th. Birthday in April 2011, with a splendid celebration organised by my family. Author and journalist, John Cooney, and founder of the Humbert Summer School in Ballina, was M.C. on the night. My younger brother William came from Glasgow and sang *"I belong to Glasgow"*; I sang *"A Gordon For Me"*; Louise recited a famous Cork monologue, *"The Monument"* and her cousin Melody McNamara sang *"Summer Time"*. Four weeks later, my brother died suddenly in his home. Fortunately, his grandson Declan was with at the time. Our daughters Victoria and Katherine travelled over for the funeral and met many of their cousins and aunts for the first time.

So, there you are dear reader. I have done my best to convey to you a life which, if not remarkable, has been eventful: at least for this scribe. I do hope you have enjoyed your read, and may God bless you and yours.

ACKNOWLEDGEMENTS

Having read "Govan On The Clyde" by Patrick Donnelly; "Up Oor Close" by Jean Faley; "Whose Turn For The Stairs" by Robert Douglas; "The Young Civilian" by Bob Crampsey, I wish to record my debt of gratitude to these authors for confirming my own memories of life in a Govan tenement. In particular, a special thanks to Patrick Donnelly for the use of the photographs of the Pearce Institute and Govan from the air. I was able to identify 5 Harmony Row where I was born. I would also wish to thank Archie Fisher for the usage of the poem "The Shipyard Apprentice".

I wish also to thank Martin Sixsmith for the information regarding Sean Ross Abbey County Tipperary, and Richard Henchion for some background on Fr.Zimmeraman S.M.A and the picture of Wilton college, both contained in his excellent book " Bishopstown, Wilton and Glasheen", loaned to me by my good friend jack Crowley.

I am also grateful to John Cooney, Patsy McGarry, Eanna O'Loingsigh for their kind words and Bishop Paul Colton, who despite his heavy workload and much travel, still found time to join John and Patsy in their commendation of this volume and Eanna O'Louigsigh for his excellent blurb.

Lastly, no words of mine can fully express the debt of gratitude I owe to Graham Clarke for taking over the project of putting my words into a readable format. Nothing was too much trouble for him. Without his expertise and commitment, my manuscript would be just that: a heap of papers lying in a dark corner.

If I have forgotten anyone, I shall be most happy to remedy this error in any future edition.